LITERATURE, IMMIGRATION, AND DIASPORA IN FIN-DE-SIÈCLE ENGLAND

The 1905 Aliens Act was the first modern law to restrict immigration to British shores. In this book, David Glover asks how it was possible for Britain – a nation that had prided itself on offering asylum to refugees – to pass such legislation. Tracing the ways that the legal notion of the "alien" became a national-racist epithet indistinguishable from the figure of "the Jew," Glover argues that the literary and popular entertainments of fin-de-siècle Britain perpetuated a culture of xenophobia. Reconstructing the complex sociopolitical field known as "the alien question," Glover examines the work of George Eliot, Israel Zangwill, Rudyard Kipling, and Joseph Conrad, together with forgotten writers like Margaret Harkness, Edgar Wallace, and James Blyth. By linking them to the beliefs and ideologies that circulated via newspapers, periodicals, political meetings, Royal Commissions, patriotic melodramas, and social surveys, Glover sheds new light on dilemmas about nationality, borders, and citizenship that remain vital today.

DAVID GLOVER is Professor of English at the University of Southampton, where he teaches courses on cultural theory, Irish literature, and Victorian and Edwardian literature and culture. He is the author of *Vampires, Mummies, and Liberals: Bram Stoker and the Politics of Popular Fiction* (1996) and *Genders* (2000 and 2009), and has recently co-edited *The Cambridge Companion to Popular Fiction* (2012).

LITERATURE, IMMIGRATION, AND DIASPORA IN FIN-DE-SIÈCLE ENGLAND

A Cultural History of the 1905 Aliens Act

DAVID GLOVER

University of Southampton

CAMBRIDGE
UNIVERSITY PRESS

CAMBRIDGE
UNIVERSITY PRESS

32 Avenue of the Americas, New York NY 10013-2473, USA

Cambridge University Press is part of the University of Cambridge.

It furthers the University's mission by disseminating knowledge in the pursuit of
education, learning and research at the highest international levels of excellence.

www.cambridge.org
Information on this title: www.cambridge.org/9781107022812

© David Glover 2012

First published 2012

A catalogue record for this publication is available from the British Library

Library of Congress Cataloguing in Publication data
Glover, David, 1946–
Literature, immigration, and diaspora in fin-de-siècle England :
a cultural history of the 1905 Aliens Act / David Glover.
p. cm.
Includes index.
ISBN 978-1-107-02281-2 (hardback)
1. Literature and society – Great Britain – History – 20th century.
2. National characteristics, British. 3. Emigration and immigration in
literature. 4. Emigration and immigration law – Great Britain. I. Title.
PR478.N37G57 2012
820.9'355–dc23
2012012502

ISBN 978-1-107-02281-2 Hardback

In memory of Paul Harris and Loretta Loach

Contents

Illustrations

Acknowledgements

This book has been part of my life for far longer than I care to remember, and the debts I have incurred are many and various. The research and writing could not have been completed without awards from the Arts and Humanities Research Council, the Leverhulme Trust, and the University of Southampton, all of whom enabled substantial periods of research leave, and I would like to thank them for their generous financial support. I was also extremely fortunate to be awarded a Visiting Fellowship at the American Bar Foundation, Chicago, in 2003, which helped me to think through some of the sociolegal aspects of this project, and I am extremely grateful to Director Bryant Garth and to the other Fellows and staff for all their help and hospitality. My editor at Cambridge University Press, Ray Ryan, has been a pleasure to work with; my thanks to him for his unwavering enthusiasm and exemplary patience throughout.

I owe a great deal to the expertise of librarians and archivists at a number of institutions; my thanks in particular to staff at Birmingham Central Library; British Library; British Library of Political and Economic Science; British Newspaper Library, Colindale; Central Zionist Archives, Jerusalem; Hartley Library, University of Southampton; House of Lords Record Office, London; Library of Trinity College, Dublin; London Library; London Metropolitan Archives; National Archives at Kew; National Maritime Museum at Greenwich; New York Public Library; and Tower Hamlets Local History Library and Archives. I am grateful to Damian Collier and A.P. Watt on behalf of The Literary Executors of the Estate of H.G. Wells for permission to reproduce a sentence from the first chapter of *The War of the Worlds* as an epigraph to my Introduction. I would also like to thank the Central Zionist Archives, Jerusalem, for granting permission to quote from their collection of letters by Israel Zangwill.

Many friends and colleagues have helped to make this book possible. For good counsel, insightful suggestions, information, questions,

encouragement, and invitations to speak, my thanks to Peter Bailey,
John Barrell, Eitan Bar-Yosef, Devorah Baum, Johan Callens, Bryan
Cheyette, Liam Connell, Nicholas Daly, Geoff Eley, David Feldman,
Emma Francis, Ben Gidley, Paul Gilroy, Catherine Hall, Clare Hanson,
Stephanie Jones, Desmond King, Tony Kushner, Jan Marsh, Nicky
Marsh, Keith McClelland, Scott McCracken, Gail McDonald, Peter
Middleton, Stephen Morton, Patrick Parrinder, Marcia Pointon, John
Rignall, Meri-Jane Rochelson, Gemma Romain, Jacqueline Rose, Sonya
Rose, Bill Schwarz, Alan Sinfield, Sujala Singh, Barbara Taylor, Jenny
Bourne Taylor, Nadia Valman, Judith Walkowitz, and Catherine Wynne.
I am especially grateful to David Amigoni, Stuart Hall, and David
Trotter for supporting this project during critical periods. My thanks also
to Peter Lawson, who was a very efficient and tenacious research assistant
at a particularly busy moment.

My greatest debts are to my friend and former colleague, Lucy Hartley,
who scrupulously and constructively read a rather tentative early draft in
a very cold climate and helped me to see the wood for the trees; and to my
partner, Cora Kaplan, who will greet the appearance of this book with
enormous relief, not to say disbelief. Without her remarkable forbearance,
scepticism, creativity, and plain good sense, this book would be much the
poorer; I owe her my deepest thanks for sharing her ideas, doubts, and
much else with me.

Introduction

And we men, the creatures who inhabit this earth, must be to them
at least as alien and lowly as are the monkeys and lemurs to us.

H.G. Wells, *The War of the Worlds* (1898)

On 11 August 1905, King Edward VII gave the Royal assent to a new
statute modestly entitled 'an Act to amend the Law with regard to Aliens.'[1]
Also known under its official short title of 'Aliens Act, 1905', this amendment was more than the slight adjustment to an existing body of legislation that its name implied, for in substance it brought about a radical
overhaul of the state's procedures in dealing with foreign nationals seeking
entry to Britain. There had been a number of earlier Aliens Acts, originally dating back to 1793, during Pitt's first ministry, when Lord Grenville
introduced 'an Act for establishing regulations respecting aliens arriving
in this kingdom' in the wake of the French Revolution.[2] But such laws
had been makeshift expedients aimed at monitoring or excluding those
troublesome outsiders – spies, subversives, agitators, and fanatics – whose
presence was felt to constitute a political danger to the country, and they
had quickly fallen into disuse or had been enforced half-heartedly. The
1905 Aliens Act was something very different. Although it was criticised
for lacking teeth, the Act set the precedent for the ever-tightening web of
immigration control that is in place today; and like almost all of the legislation that came later, its introduction followed a heated policy debate in
which statistics and social investigations played a crucial role. The Act
that forms the centrepiece of this book was therefore the first recognisably
modern law that sought permanently to restrict immigration into Britain
according to systematic bureaucratic criteria that were initially administered and interpreted by a new kind of public functionary: the immigration officer.

Immigration laws create borders – not in the sense of natural fron-
tiers or territorial divisions, to take the two commonest meanings of the

term, but borders as sites of discrimination, zones in which migrants are granted or denied a provisional legal status.[3] So, the 1905 Aliens Act made legitimate entry contingent upon inspection by an immigration officer, limiting the points of arrival to a small number of ports to which these officials would be appointed – a list of fourteen towns and cities itemised in the supplementary 'Rules and Orders' that specified the practical content of the statute in fine detail. In these places, the immigration officer's task was to gather information to determine who should be permitted to land and who should not. His decision was not necessarily final: the immigrant had the right to make an appeal before a specially constituted local body, the port's Immigration Board, as did other interested parties, such as the ship's captain or owner, or an agent of the shipping line, any of whom might have to bear the cost of his passenger's return journey. While it represented an important safeguard, the appeal was quite narrow in scope and could not be pursued further once the Immigration Board had reached its conclusion. By placing permission to land within the discretionary power of a full-time state official, under the oversight of a civic body, the Act aimed to insulate the routine work of this new apparatus of control from the wider legal system, and particularly from scrutiny by the higher courts. Like justices of the peace, on whom they were partly modelled, the Immigration Board members were laymen drawn from the ranks of local worthies deemed by the Act to be 'fit persons having magisterial experience, business, or administrative experience'; nevertheless, their remit was carefully circumscribed in order to diminish their legal standing, effectively establishing the boards as extrajudicial panels.[4] At the national level, it was the task of the Home Secretary to set the rules according to which cases were decided; he was not expected to be drawn into individual day-to-day decisions. To all intents and purposes, these contrasting loci of authority were separated by what was virtually a legal void.

Who were the targets of the 1905 Act? In strictly formal terms, the law was primarily designed to exclude 'undesirable aliens' and undesirability was variously regarded as a function of economic distress, ill-health, or criminality. Immigrants who seemed unlikely to be able to 'decently' support themselves or their dependents were refused entry, as were those whose physical infirmities or mental state indicated that they would probably become a burden on the state. If a migrant had been found guilty of an offence overseas that was covered by an extradition treaty, then he or she would also be turned back. Other clauses dealt with the deportation of aliens who had been allowed to land but whose subsequent conduct demonstrated their inherent unsuitability as residents: by being convicted of a crime in a British court, for example, or through becoming a vagrant, or even having been found 'living under insanitary conditions due to overcrowding' (perhaps the most invidious proviso, because it was so difficult to avoid).[5] Yet the Act was far from comprehensive. According to the precise legal definitions given in its own glossary, the word 'immigrant' meant 'an alien steerage passenger', but not all ships carrying immigrants in this technical sense qualified as 'immigrant ships' because this term referred only to those vessels carrying 'more than twenty alien steerage passengers'.[6]

The quantitative threshold above which 'immigrants' became liable to inspection was deliberately kept low (it was reduced again from twenty to twelve in December 1905, albeit temporarily) in order to maximise the total number of ships that came under the immigration officer's administrative gaze, while ensuring that the costs of control were held firmly in check. And by focussing upon steerage-class ticket holders – migrants who could not afford to pay for a cabin – the framers of the Act had devised a way of sifting through the ranks of the poorest passengers who made up the highest proportion of migrants. From this perspective, the 1905 Aliens Act might be read as a response to the rising curve of global migration, particularly after 1870, when sailing ships were being rapidly eclipsed by steamships. As Walter Nugent has noted, in the period to 1914, 'the size of passenger ships, and their speed increased almost continuously', with the very largest vessels on the Atlantic run to the United States carrying up to 1,000 people in steerage.[7] When Ben Tillett, the Secretary of the Dockers' Union, told the House of Lords Select Committee on the Sweating System in 1890 that he had seen 'a party of 500 emigrants, mostly young men, sail out of Tilbury Docks and at the same time about 700 foreigners come in', his alarmist claim would have sounded plausible to many of his fellow Londoners.[8] But Britain was on the periphery of the main circuits of long-distance migration in the late nineteenth and early twentieth centuries. German ships might dock at Southampton en route to New York, but Britain never received anything like the 35 million migrants who travelled to the United States between 1870 and 1914.

Numbers were therefore only part of the story. Turn to the pages of London's *Evening News and Post*, a newspaper that in the 1890s regularly campaigned against what it saw as Britain's unnecessary isolation in an increasingly restrictionist world, and one will find a plethora of crude allegations voiced in a hectoring rhetoric that brooks no disagreement. Here 'undesirable aliens' are characteristically identified as 'destitute Jewish immigrants' (bluntly condensed into the figure of 'the Jew alien'), and it is 'Russian Jews' in particular who are said to be 'pouring into London at the rate of 500 a week'.[9] Poverty is not simply a key attribute in class-based notions of undesirability that conjure up images of a migrant *lumpenproletariat*, but is taken to be indissolubly linked to ideas about race. From the 1880s onwards, the word 'alien' – formerly a term in feudal law designating certain foreign-born subjects and the political jurisdiction appropriate to them – had become a popular synonym for East European Jews, and everyone was aware of this deadly chain of racialising equivalences. Supporters of immigration control might insist, as they sometimes did, that what made these immigrants a social problem was that they were poor, not that they were Jews. In truth, however, racial and class markers could not be disentangled quite so easily: in everyday parlance, 'aliens' simply *were* indigent Jews. Conversely, to be Jewish was to be an alien or a foreigner. In 1901, a 'shabbily dressed man' in Leeds, piqued at having failed to sell the non-Jewish German anarchist Rudolf Rocker a pair of phylacteries, informed his interlocutor with unshakeable confidence that he must be a Jew, because 'all foreigners are Jews'.[10]

The illiberalism of the Act and the rank prejudices that it articulated stood in sharp contrast to the dominant attitude to migrants in the early Victorian era. In the heyday of free trade, the free movement of labour between nations was generally reckoned to be a force for good, promoting vital competition and the diffusion of new skills; the acceptance of foreign workers, particularly when they had come as refugees, was held up as a sign of how remarkably tolerant British society was, compared to its benighted neighbours. In this argument, the flight into Britain of the persecuted French Huguenots in the sixteenth and seventeenth centuries and their success as silk-weavers, engravers, watchmakers, and merchants acquired an almost mythic status. Indeed, this 'friendly invasion' came to represent a major obstacle to the restrictionist case in the eyes of propagandists like the indefatigable Arnold White.[11] In his 1899 book, *The Modern Jew*, White portrayed Britain as a nation in thrall to its own past, mesmerised by 'the great advantages which our population has derived from previous admixtures of foreign blood', and gulled into a misguided belief in its indebtedness to every kind of immigrant. A protracted history of indiscriminate tolerance had blinded the British people to the dangerous realities of the current situation, preventing them from recognising that the incoming Russian and Polish Jews were anathema to the British way of life, in stark contrast to their Huguenot predecessors. The clannishness of the Jews, their ties with others of their race and faith stretching around the globe, produced a sort of half-hidden empire within an empire, 'a Jewish imperium', or what would later be dubbed 'an international Jewish conspiracy'.[12]

True, the new Act did offer protection to immigrants who were seeking to escape religious or political persecution, always provided they could *prove* their claims to the satisfaction of the immigration officer or Board concerned. But these exemptions were the result of intense parliamentary wrangling and avoided any reference to the controversial notion of a '*right* of asylum', which had been so prominent and so contested a feature of the debates in the Commons. For those liberals whose thinking had been decisively shaped by their encounter with John Stuart Mill's arguments on 'social tyranny' in his essay *On Liberty* (1859), the implications of the bill were nothing short of catastrophic. To the eminent Oxford jurist Albert Venn Dicey, incumbent of the prestigious Vinerian chair of English law, the 1905 Aliens Act symbolised a dangerous breach in the continuities of British social life and inaugurated 'in principle, at least, a revolution in national policy'. In an article written a matter of days before the king was to append his signature to the bill, Dicey argued that, once it had passed into law, religious liberty and religious tolerance would quickly become dead letters, and, by the same token, the protectionist agenda that seemed to inform the new legislation was a sign that the country was beginning to lose sight of the benefits of free trade and no longer understood why 'free immigration' was its necessary complement. Worse still, even to give utterance to these classical liberal ideas was to risk sounding like the echo of 'a bygone age'. In Dicey's view, the law in its current form could not hope to succeed; with remarkable prescience, he noted that its failure would promptly induce calls for 'more stringent measures'. If the Aliens Act showed the sorry plight of public opinion now, he wondered, 'how will civilized nations regard the influx of foreigners at the end of the twenty-first, or of the twenty-second century?'[13]

While he did not overestimate the likely effectiveness of the Act, Dicey was sure that it revealed the emergence of a new social and political consensus that had gradually brought into being a 'period of collectivism' in which sectional, and especially class, interests were placed above 'the natural individualism of common law'.[14] He came to see the Aliens Act as just one among a variety of recent laws through which the state was tearing asunder the fabric of personal freedoms: the Unemployed Workmen Act (1905), the Trades Disputes Act (1906), and the Old Age Pensions Act (1908). In characterising his era as a dramatic struggle between sharply opposed philosophical principles, Dicey was not alone and, though there were many disagreements about how 'Individualism' and 'Collectivism' could best be understood, his own deployment of these sometimes slippery terms was part of a broad shift in political vocabulary that essentially belonged to the 1880s.[15] By the time Dicey met his death from respiratory failure in 1922, much of the force of his overly schematic sociolegal history had been extinguished too, and subsequently generations of historians have continued to blur the contours of his work with innumerable qualifications and rebuttals. Instructively, the Aliens Act was one of the earliest casualties of this process of revision. It goes unmentioned, for example, in R.C.K. Ensor's volume *England 1870–1914* in Sir George Clark's authoritative *Oxford History of England* series from the mid-1930s. There Ensor refers admiringly to the 1906 Merchant Shipping Act which made British standards of food and accommodation mandatory for all foreign vessels using British ports (part of a series of 'measures on a grand scale' introduced by an up-and-coming Lloyd George), but he is completely silent on the new arrangements for inspecting immigrant ships which came into effect that same year.[16]

It was not until after the Second World War that references to the 1905 Aliens Act began to reappear in public debate and, more slowly, in the work of professional historians and social scientists. In each case the reappraisal of the Act was overdetermined by the racial politics of immigration in the long wake left by the arrival of the former troopship *Empire Windrush* at Tilbury Docks in June 1948. Paul Foot's incisive discussion of the Aliens Act in his 1965 "Penguin Special" *Immigration and Race in British Politics* took its impetus from the notorious victory of the Conservative candidate for Smethwick on a racist ticket the previous year.[17] Similarly, John A. Garrard's *The English and Immigration 1880–1910* (1971), the first book-length study of the Act, also took 'as its starting-point' the 'parallels' between these two moments of immigration.[18] Despite marked differences in their political analyses and general tone, both books were influenced by the sociology of race relations in the postwar period which focussed primarily upon the barriers to 'assimilation' of 'minority groups' by the 'host society'.[19] Writing in a 1967 article, Garrard argued that what one sociologist had recently 'called "culture shock" was matched three quarters of a century ago by contemporary accounts which were as much a commentary on the reactions of a homogeneous society shocked by the appearance of a mass of strangers as a description of the ghetto itself'.[20]

Garrard concluded that racial prejudice was a 'disreputable category' in British society during this period and that anti-immigration lobbyists were never able to escape the charge of bigotry, a weakness which only strengthened the hand of their opponents and allowed the principle of religious and political asylum to survive intact.[21] A year later, Bernard Gainer arrived at a similar judgement in *The Alien Invasion: The Origins of the Aliens Act of 1905* (1972), which remains the single most comprehensive treatment of the social and political background to the law. Ultimately Gainer believed the 'turmoil' around Jewish immigration to have been 'momentary'; fortunately for Britain, 'sanity at last prevailed,' at least insofar as the 'hostility stopped short at window breaking', and the Act 'preserved the right of asylum'.[22] Like Garrard before him, Gainer felt that the future of Commonwealth migrants in his own day seemed nowhere near as promising as it had been for East European Jews at the turn of the century, in part because he believed that the racial and cultural differences displayed by new arrivals from the West Indies or the Indian subcontinent would facilitate discrimination (Garrard thought the decisive factor was the relative weakness of 'the Commonwealth ideal' compared to the right of asylum). Yet, with the benefit of considerable hindsight, both writers viewed the long aftermath of the 1905 Aliens Act as a victory for the liberal virtues of tolerance and fair play, because (to quote Gainer) 'the immigrants of past years have found the acceptance in Britain denied them in their former homes'.[23]

Today that history is seen somewhat differently; one might say, it has been replaced by two distinct, but overlapping, histories. On the one hand, there are narratives of particular communities, stories of how peoples like the Jews or the Irish have changed, adapted, and made a home within the modern British nation-state, often in the face of considerable hostility.[24] Each has its own history, but increasingly that history has been cast in a multicultural form for it typically presupposes a claim to parity of consideration and equal representation within Britain as a whole. The logical corollary of these singular narratives has been to rewrite Britain's past as, in Robert Winder's words, 'a story of immigration', to insist that this has always been a country of migrants and settlers and that we should 'look for ways to celebrate the part they have played in our history', not least because ultimately 'we are all immigrants: it simply depends on how far back you go'.[25] However, if Winder's story aspires to be a catalogue of triumphs, the successes are unintelligible without an inventory of setbacks, obstacles, and prejudices, a 'list of shameful episodes' that have plagued the immigrant experience and made it the site of 'a constant tussle between kind and cruel impulses' (5). The 1905 Aliens Act figures prominently on this list, less for the restrictions it imposed than for being a key example of how the state could tacitly endorse 'xenophobic reflexes which might, with the proper discouragement, have remained dormant' (200).

An alternative history has sought to situate Britain within a series of transnational currents, noting the convergences between attempts to restrict immigration across Western Europe, North America, and Australasia. As the numbers of 'people on the move world-wide' and 'the distances they covered' increased at the close of the nineteenth century, 'a global network of barriers that successfully confined most of the world's population in their countries of birth' was created, with 1894–1897 and 1905–1908 constituting the peak years of anti-alien initiatives.[26] This age of mass migration gave new urgency to the plight of the refugee and, as Dallal Stevens has argued, what gave the 1905 Aliens Act its enduring significance was not just the apparatus of immigration control that it set in place; the new Act also 'established an administrative and legal framework for deciding refugee cases, and it linked the issue of immigration with that of asylum'.[27] How far this framework represented an improvement on the status quo ante remains a moot point, because the statute made no reference to the concept of the 'refugee' in its provisions. Those immigrants who could prove that they were the victims of religious or political persecution could not be refused entry, but they were still "aliens" in law, and there was no guarantee that the intention behind this clause would be honoured in practice. According to Tony Kushner and Katharine Knox in their major study of the refugee experience in twentieth-century Britain, the 1905 Act 'undermined' any idea of 'free entry for refugees' and marked the beginning of a long history of social struggles to make the right of asylum a reality.[28] Despite palpable victories, the historical balance sheet points towards an uncertain future. Immigration may have become one of Britain's definitive, even inspirational, island stories; in the interim, however, to cite Jeremy Harding's bleak assessment in his polemic *The Uninvited: Refugees at the Rich Man's Gate*, the British state has become 'a master of asylum degradation'.[29]

A victory for liberal principles, or the onset of an insidious tradition of state-enforced exclusion – these strikingly different assessments suggest that the 1905 Aliens Act has lost none of its political pertinence and that the legal precedents which it handed down continue to haunt our troubled present. In a sense, the Act's significance as a political *event* has been heightened in recent years by the increasing salience of liberal ideas in Western democracies, particularly where appeals to universal human rights, equality of treatment, and the rule of law are at issue. Desmond King, for example, has claimed that not only did the Aliens Bill contain 'clear liberal elements' in its final form (as in the provisions on asylum), but that the arguments mobilised against the new legislation ultimately contributed to the development of what he calls 'a liberal political culture' in Britain.[30] At the same time, King's thesis has a disturbing corollary, for he also sees liberalism as prey to irrational 'impulses' or 'pressures' that have the potential to undermine its own commitment to individual rights and equality before the law. He notes, for instance, that the democratic process can serve as a conduit for xenophobic or racist sentiments which threaten to subvert or sideline any resort to liberal principles in law. However, King is careful to emphasise that popular bigotry among the electorate is far from being the only source of illiberal policies, for in 1905, both sides in the parliamentary debate accepted an 'essentially illiberal criterion of relative racial worth' believing that such views could be justified scientifically. What restrictionists and anti-restrictionists fundamentally disagreed upon was whether or not East European Jews should be grouped with 'other white Europeans' in an assumed hierarchy of racial types.[31] Yet it was also a sign of the strength of liberal values that pauperism and criminality had to be substituted for race when the legislation was drafted.

Despite his highly generalised and rather presentist account of liberalism, King's stress upon the deep *cultural* divisions and continuities that underpinned the Aliens Act is surely correct. Liberal *and* illiberal ideas about who had a valid claim to which legal rights and who should be allowed to settle in Britain were closely intertwined and could be found at every level of society. Indeed, the legislation resembled a kind of Freudian 'symptom formation' in which 'two more or less equally strong opposing impulses … find satisfactory expression singly, first one and then the other, though of course not without an attempt being made to produce some sort of logical connection between the two hostile elements'.[32] Such a precarious and unstable assemblage was unlikely to work well in practice, and it is hardly surprising that the history of the Act displays a veritable tangle of contradictions, befitting a Conservative initiative that had to be implemented by an incoming Liberal government, many of whose MPs had challenged it while in opposition.

How was it possible for a law restricting immigration to be passed in a country that had prided itself on offering asylum to refugees and had virtually made the right to freedom of movement across national boundaries an article of faith? This book seeks an answer to this question by returning to the wider historical context within which the law was conceived and looking in detail at the specific cultural milieux from which antagonistic views about the place of the 'alien' in late-nineteenth-century Britain emerged, for it is precisely these particular cultural settings and cultural idioms that King neglects. In spite of the civic and political gains that had been achieved by English Jews in the 1850s and 1860s, the cross-national reach of a militant anti-Semitism – the word started to appear in English usage around 1881 – once again put the security of Jewish communities at risk. To trace the origins of anti-immigrant legislation at the fin-de-siècle, it is necessary to show how the figure of 'the Jew' came to occupy the role of quintessential foreigner in the popular imagination, a process in which the word 'alien' lost its old meanings derived from common law and became a national-racist epithet. Newspapers and periodicals; novels, short stories, songs, and verse; libraries and music halls; debates, social surveys, and public speeches – all played their part. But the fulcrum for the transformation of 'alien' and 'Jew' into equivalent terms lay primarily within Victorian print culture.

This book follows a broadly chronological approach that takes the reader from the beginnings of modern anti-alien agitation to the political legacy of the 1905 Act in the years leading up to the outbreak of the Great War in 1914, when it was punctually replaced by much harsher legislation. But the complexity of this historical material tells against any simple unilinear narrative, and the discussion is also organised around a series of topics, each implying a distinctive political temporality of its own. So, at those moments when the controversies surrounding immigration come up against new forms of diasporic consciousness, the themes of this study overlap with those found in the historiography of Zionism, while standing at some distance from that tradition. By juxtaposing a variety of attempts to give narrative shape and meaning to the question of alien migration in nineteenth- and early-twentieth-century Britain, I hope to illuminate the political and ideological presuppositions that underpinned competing views on the possible futures available to Jews at a time when the meaning of liberalism was itself increasingly under question.

The book begins with an exploration of some of the many lives of George Eliot's *Daniel Deronda* (1876), the single most influential English work of fiction about Jews, Judaism, and modernity in the decade immediately before large-scale Jewish immigration and agitation against it began. Notable for its sympathetic evocation of the Jewish people, Eliot's novel is no less remarkable for the range of responses and identifications it elicited – from Judeophobic parody, to assimilationist self-justification, to proto-Zionism – reactions that mirror and anticipate the twists and turns of Semitic discourse in the latter half of the nineteenth century. In following the contrasting ways in which *Daniel Deronda* has been read, particularly during the period from 1876 to 1914, I argue that much of its power derives from the tensions within the text resulting from the translation of a Messianic theology into liberal, secular forms, a vision that is further tempered by appeals to the cultural status of the English gentleman. Painstakingly set in 1866–1868, *Daniel Deronda* reflects an increasingly mobile world with few legal barriers to entry, while at the same time raising many of the questions posed by new arguments about the relationship between national allegiance, citizenship, and birthright in a post-revolutionary era, questions that Britain sought to resolve in the 1870 Naturalisation Act. These problems were intensified as mass migration began to get under way in the following decade.

Chapter 2 looks at representations of London's East End, the primary site for locating accounts of alien immigration. Although a number of different types of sources are discussed, I concentrate largely upon the novel, because the main thread running through this chapter is the story of how the People's Palace, a new kind of leisure centre, came to be constructed in the Mile End Road, a building that was first imagined in Walter Besant's 1882 bestseller, *All Sorts and Conditions of Men*. Despite having written a romance, part of which involves a philanthropic experiment centred upon the foundation of a female dressmakers' cooperative, Besant always diagnosed the social problems associated with East London as being rooted in the hardships suffered by male labour. This assumption carried over into arguments about alien immigration, a phenomenon that received little attention in Besant's writing as a whole. Tellingly, the Royal Commission on Alien Immigration whose mission was to gather systematic evidence on this question called only 2 female witnesses out of a total of more than 180 people brought in to testify. Moreover, the British Brothers' League, the most powerful East End grass-roots organisation to campaign against foreign migrants in the early years of the new century, also characterised itself in similar terms. When the League wanted to make its presence felt as dramatically as possible, it chose the highly respectable People's Palace as the venue for a mass rally. Ranged against Besant's reformist aesthetic were two East End writers who each offered a sharp corrective to the rosy vision in *All Sorts and Conditions of Men*. The chapter therefore concludes with a reading of the slum fiction of the socialist Margaret Harkness, with its focus on female labour, and the Jewish novelist and dramatist Israel Zangwill's *Children of the Ghetto*. Here Harkness's ambiguous invocation

of a leftist anti-Semitism is juxtaposed against Zangwill's portrayal of
the relationship between Jewish family life, patterns of employment, and
scenes of industrial action.

The rise of 'anti-Semitism' is the central theme of Chapter 3 which
begins with an examination of the European origins of this pseudoscien-
tific concept in the late 1870s and goes on to trace its impact upon open
and coded forms of hostility to Jews in Britain. As the term emerges into
English social and political debate in the 1880s and 1890s, there is a controversy as to its acceptability, particularly during the Dreyfus Affair, and
this controversy continues into the early years of the twentieth century.
The career of Arnold White, a major anti-alien polemicist and organiser
and a writer who argued for what he called 'legitimate anti-Semitism', is
discussed as a key exemplar in the attempt to develop a sustained intellectual rationale for the exclusion of Jews from the state and civil society.
I argue that anti-Semitism was a significant element in the ideology of
Britain's Radical Right, those members of the political class who were
disillusioned with the policies and leadership of the Conservatives and
Unionists. This grouping can best be understood as a counterpublic or set
of counterpublics – that is to say, as a loose oppositional network aiming
to bring about a decisive shift in the climate of opinion, working through
a variety of campaigns and forums – yet one whose project is incomplete
or only partially successful. The chapter examines the cultural resources
available in the wider society focusing on the figure of the Jew in a number of popular fictional and theatrical contexts, especially in relation
to the increasing appeal of melodrama at the fin-de-siècle, from Dion
Boucicault's *After Dark* to the actor Beerbohm Tree's version of *Trilby* via
militaristic spectacles like *The Absent-Minded Beggar* and *Soldiers of the
Queen*. Discussion of these texts feeds into an account of the evolution
of the Radical Right, centred on Leo Maxse's periodical, the *National
Review*, which served as a clearing house for new Conservative political
initiatives, linking tariff reform to racial and national themes. The role
of Kipling in relation to this counterpublic serves as a case study of the
Radical Right's structure of feeling and the chapter closes with an account
of how figures like Major Evans-Gordon and Arnold White mediated
between the well-heeled circles of the *National Review* and the East End
working-class activism of the British Brothers' League.

The two final chapters deal with the passage of the Aliens Bill into law
and the dilemmas faced by the new Liberal government in administering
Conservative restrictionist legislation that they had no hope of repealing.
Chapter 4 begins with an analysis of the role played by accounts of the

immigrant journey by journalists and others in making the case for and against restriction. Travel narratives were an important source of evidence to the Royal Commission on Alien Immigration (1902–1903), but they were also a staple of popular newspaper reports on the alien question. Among the texts examined here are Major William Evans-Gordon's book *The Alien Immigrant* (1903), drafts of which were vainly pressed on the Commission, and the novelist Robert Sherard's bitterly contested articles for the *Standard* in January 1905, both of them interpreting conditions at sea as signs of moral degradation. Their accounts are contrasted with Joseph Conrad's anguished story of migration and exile in 'Amy Foster' (1901), in which the alien castaway is reduced to the degree zero of existence. I then turn to the debates on immigration during the progress of the 1904 and 1905 Aliens Bills through Parliament, with particular reference to the relationship between racial discourse and competing notions of political rights – themes that are also taken up in two novels which staunchly refused to countenance the very possibility of anti-alien legislation: Violet Guttenberg's quasi-*Deronda* romance, *A Modern Exodus* (1904), and Edgar Wallace's thriller, *The Four Just Men* (1905).

In Chapter 5, I look at the fallout from the Aliens Act after it came into force in January 1906. On the one hand, the prospect of controls on immigration intensified divisions within the Zionist movement around the alternatives to settlement in Britain or what, in his opening statement to the Royal Commission, the Zionist leader Theodor Herzl had referred to as 'diverting of the stream of emigration'.[33] Following Herzl's death in July 1904, Israel Zangwill put aside the goal of returning to Palestine in favour of securing a 'free colony' for the Jewish people in East Africa under the auspices of the British Empire, but without success. I argue that the imaginative roots of Zangwill's project can be found in his Edwardian fiction and that his vision of an imperial Zion has a distinctively English coloration. On the other hand, influential members of the Anglo-Jewish community in Britain attempted to open up the regulation of entry by mounting legal challenges to the immigration bureaucracies, and even though these resulted in some melioration, their mixed fortunes encouraged more vocal resistance from recent immigrants who were not afraid to identify themselves polemically as 'aliens'.

However, from 1908 onwards, the political climate became noticeably more hostile with the reappearance of the stock figure of 'the alien anarchist' in fiction and the press. Two exceptionally violent incidents dubbed 'the Tottenham Outrage' (1909) and 'the Houndsditch Outrage', better known as 'the Siege of Sidney Street' (1910–1911), though having little to do with anarchism, set the seal on a negative appraisal of the 1905 Act – long mooted by the Radical Right – and brought strident calls for tougher controls on immigration, together with state blueprints for a tighter bureaucratically-controlled migration regime. As the country drifted towards the Great War, the idea of an 'alien invasion' gained new momentum as part of a political myth of national betrayal in which the Jew represented the conspirator par excellence: clandestine, devious, and utterly rapacious. According to this increasingly paranoid fantasy structure, 'the Jew is everywhere, but you have to go far down the backstairs to find him'.[34] Uttered by a secret agent in John Buchan's *The Thirty-Nine Steps* (1915) – and received with some irony by other characters in that text – this is a remark that can be seen in retrospect to point in two directions simultaneously: forward into the interwar era of Sir Oswald Mosley's British Union of Fascists and also back towards the anti-alien agitation for a new Aliens Act, the time of Arnold White, the British Brothers' League, and the resistance they aroused, which together form the subject of this book.

CHAPTER I

Messianic neutrality: George Eliot and the politics of national identity

In November 1895, Theodor Herzl, the founder of the modern Zionist movement, visited England for the first time, with high hopes of gaining support for his plan to obtain a land in which his people could at last live in freedom and security. 'The campaign's centre of gravity is shifted to London', he wrote excitedly in his diary; and, on arrival, his contacts gave him access to a remarkable cross-section of Anglo-Jewish society.[1] In a little more than a week he had met the novelist and playwright Israel Zangwill, spoken to the artists and professional men who made up the influential Maccabean Club ('the ideal instrument for my needs'), and had been introduced to a variety of rabbis, writers, businessmen and political figures, including the financier and Liberal MP for Whitechapel Sir Samuel Montagu (276). After a fine Sunday lunch at Montagu's 'house of English elegance, in grand style', Herzl fired his host's imagination with an outline of his project and by the time he had left, Montagu had declared that 'he would settle in Palestine with his whole family' (280).

But Herzl's overall reception was decidedly mixed and he faced many questions. Having listened to Herzl outline his scheme, Britain's Chief Rabbi Hermann Adler told him that the plan recapitulated 'the idea of *Daniel Deronda*', as if to imply that there was nothing new in what was little more than a work of fiction. Herzl quickly brushed the comparison aside, insisting that the dream of a Jewish homeland was in fact thousands of years old and that he only wished to set the Zionist project in motion again. The two men disagreed sharply, Adler firmly maintaining that support for Herzl's scheme would have to be contingent upon approval from one of the major Anglo-Jewish philanthropic bodies, while Herzl held fast to his demand for complete independence and refused any suggestion of assistance from 'stupid charity' which would only emasculate his movement (279). However, a few days later, the reference to Eliot's novel occurred again in an altogether more favourable context. On November 25, on Zangwill's personal recommendation, Herzl travelled to Cardiff to meet with Colonel Albert Edward Goldsmid, formerly of the Royal Munster Fusiliers, an officer who had recently interrupted his army career to run the settlements for poor Jewish migrants that had been set up in Argentina by the late Baron de Hirsch's Jewish Colonization Association. On hearing the details of Herzl's plan, the Colonel told him "*That is the idea of my life*"; to explain himself more fully, he later gave an account of his past prefaced by the words "I am Daniel Deronda" (282, italics in the original).

Goldsmid's story began in India where he had been 'born a Christian,' his father serving as Chief Secretary to the Governor of Bombay. But at the age of twenty-one, shortly after starting his first commission in the army, Goldsmid learned that both his parents were of Jewish descent and, to their considerable distress, he resolved to return to his great-grandparents' faith. So too with Goldsmid's wife Ida, who similarly turned out to have been born into a family of Christian converts. The couple's original civil marriage was superseded by a traditional ceremony in a synagogue, since Ida now 'had to become a Jewess' and the Goldsmids' two daughters were also given 'a strict religious upbringing and learned Hebrew at an early age'. To Herzl's ears this story and Goldsmid's 'tales of South America' did indeed sound 'like a novel', but even though he found himself captivated by this man who seemed to him 'like a brother', he found Goldsmid's vision to be very different from his own. 'With Goldsmid,' Herzl recorded, 'I suddenly find myself in another world', vividly evoking an unsecular past that yielded glimpses of an unexpected future, a more thoroughly religious world than Herzl was prepared to countenance. Herzl thought of himself as 'a freethinker', under whose 'national-social flag' each of his followers might 'seek salvation in his own way' (282–283).

What did it mean to identify oneself with the figure of Daniel Deronda in 1895, nearly twenty years after George Eliot's novel was first published? How was it that this book elicited such an intense political and emotional response among its Jewish readers and what did the persistence of these feelings say about what it meant to be a Jew in Britain at the turn of the century? As the entries from Herzl's diaries show, these questions have no single answer, for several distinct versions of the novel were clearly in play in the encounters he describes. The figure with whom Colonel Goldsmid identified, for instance, was not precisely George Eliot's Daniel Deronda – even on the most generous interpretation, the details of the officer's life do not exactly correspond to those of the book's hero. Indeed, the project that Eliot invites her readers to imagine is arguably closer to that of Herzl than to the religious vision of the devoutly orthodox Goldsmid. Unlike the latter, Daniel's discovery of his Jewish origins comes with a crucial caveat: Daniel is adamant that he cannot promise 'to believe exactly as his fathers have believed'.[2]

The incidents from Herzl's first visit to England can be cast as episodes in the long and unusually complicated afterlife of Eliot's novel, a book that gave contemporary narrative form to the prospect of founding a modern independent Jewish polity. In this chapter I explore the political uses that have been made of *Daniel Deronda* – particularly as the problems facing European Jews became more acute – and why this fable of origins has proved to be such an exemplary, yet divisive, text. Writing in the wake of Jewish emancipation, Eliot had hoped that *Daniel Deronda* would help undermine the racial and religious prejudices that continued to disfigure Britain's civil society. But, more than this, her humanitarian critique of the unfinished business of Jewish emancipation had a world-historical dimension. For Eliot sought to demonstrate that there was a deep but little-recognised kinship between Englishness at its finest and an embryonic Jewish national consciousness, based ultimately upon an ethical complementarity between Christianity and Judaism. Within this broad humanist context her aim was, in Michael Ragussis's words, nothing less than 'the reeducation of the English nation in its shared heritage with the Jews', with 'English' also serving as a synecdoche for Western Europe as a whole.[3]

This was a bold, yet risky, enterprise, one whose intractability was exacerbated by the very speculative note on which Eliot chose to end her novel. In speaking directly to the self-understandings that defined the very nature of these two communities, including how they imagined their relationship to each other, Eliot ensured that her text would be inherently controversial since it challenged the unexamined moral assumptions that informed her readers' religious and national sense of belonging. The impassioned responses that Eliot's novel provoked were at their most intense in the period from 1876, when the book began to appear in monthly instalments, to the troubled years around the fin-de-siècle, as moves to bring in a law that would regulate the steady flow of newly uprooted Jewish migrants into Britain intensified. Indeed, if the 1905 Act seemed to repudiate the aims and beliefs expressed in *Daniel Deronda*, the prospect of immigration control lent greater urgency to the notion of a return, the recovery of a Jewish homeland that would bring their diasporic journeys to a tenable end. So, on the one hand, it was a story of mutual recognition, an accommodation between faiths and cultures; on the other, it was a prophecy regained. To some, Eliot seemed to possess near-clairvoyant powers: she was, wrote Zangwill in 1901, 'the great Seer', the woman who looked into the heart of the Jewish Question 'with keener vision than any Jew'.[4] Tell me how you read *Daniel Deronda*, one might almost say, and I will tell you who and what you are.

MESSIANIC TIMES

Despite Eliot's best intentions, many readers, particularly those who were familiar with Eliot's previous fiction, were disturbed by what her husband and her publisher called the 'Jewish element' in *Daniel Deronda*, their phrase for the sympathetic depiction of the Jews in the novel, which they feared would alienate her from her public.[5] Up to a point, their fears proved to be justified. As the story of the financial ruin of Gwendolen Harlech's family and the question of her marriage began to be displaced by Daniel's growing involvement with Mirah Lapidoth, the young Jewess whose attempted suicide he prevents, reaction to successive instalments of the book became increasingly critical, buoyant sales notwithstanding. Beginning with Henry James's 'conversation' on *Daniel Deronda* in the *Atlantic Monthly* (1876) in which 'the Jewish burden of the story' was described as wearisome by one of the imaginary discussants, the notion that this element of the plot could be ignored or excised started to gain ground.[6] Around the same time, the English humorous magazine *Punch* issued a parodic sequel to *Daniel Deronda* (numbered 'Book IX' and illustrated by John Tenniel). In this satirical addition to the novel, Mirah abandons Daniel for his old friend Hans Meyrick and the two lovers are drowned in a shipping accident, leaving the way free for Gwendolen and Daniel to be reunited. No sooner has Daniel developed a romantic interest in Gwendolen that his face perceptibly loses its Jewish features.[7] One answer to the novel's question as to where the Jews truly belonged was: not in this text.

Several early reviewers were also dubious about the credibility of Daniel's intention of establishing a Jewish centre in the East, sometimes conjuring up a Book IX of their own in which his plans came to nothing. Writing in the *Nation*, A.V. Dicey suggested that readers were left feeling certain that Daniel 'will travel about year after year doing deeds of kindness and cherishing noble aspirations', but will fall far short of 'working out any deliverance either for his people or mankind'.[8] The English Jewish critic James Picciotto put the point more bluntly in his essay 'Deronda the Jew' a month later when he argued that the 'dreams' of Daniel and his mentor Mordecai were 'likely to remain dreams for the present', the chief reason being that Eliot had seriously underestimated the pull of assimilation. 'The Israelites have become too firmly attached to the countries of Western Europe, which have given them shelter', Picciotto stressed.[9] From this standpoint, Eliot's desire to reveal the affinities between Jewishness and Englishness only succeeded in making her proto-Zionist gestures redundant.

But this was not the end of the story so far as Eliot herself was concerned. As Catherine Gallagher has emphasised, Eliot's response to those readers and critics who bridled at the notion of Daniel leading a Jewish return to Palestine was to insist that her novel could only be brought to a fitting conclusion by others – that is to say, by real historical agents rather than fictional characters.[10] And, in a sense, Eliot was correct. Precisely because her text lacked a clear and unequivocal ending, offering instead a kind of hypothetical space in which to imagine a newly refurbished Jewish future based on ancient precedent, readers were able to complete her narrative in quite different ways and, as we will see, in the Russian Pale of Settlement, significant numbers of them did so against the background of rising levels of violence directed against Jews. The historical circumstances in which East European Jews encountered *Daniel Deronda* in translation and part-translation in the early 1880s contrasted sharply with those of their immediate predecessors. For, as the position of their communities grew increasingly precarious in the wake of the mass urban pogroms that began in southwest Russia in 1881, Eliot's Russo-Jewish readership came to regard the messianic themes in *Daniel Deronda* as the novel's most precious legacy.

But before turning to the complex origins of these diasporic traditions of reading, I want to look more closely at the contradictory resonances that haunt Eliot's attempt to float the possibility of an independent Jewish state, resonances that interrupt the novel's careful dialogic construction. In particular, I focus on one of the most blatantly dialogical episodes in the book, the debate at the *Hand and Banner*, which was also, not coincidentally, the first chapter to be translated into Hebrew. While Daniel's mission takes Mordecai's dreams as its point of departure, those dreams already condense concepts and ideas drawn from two systems of belief that sit uncomfortably together: Jewish messianic thought as it manifests itself in the heyday of nineteenth-century political liberalism. Whereas the former promises the fulfilment of a collective destiny long foretold, the latter relies upon a far more secular and individualistic model of what the Promised Land might look like.

The tension between these ideas operates at many levels in the novel. As an initial example, consider the two deeply symbolic moments which mark the novel's close: Daniel's marriage to Mirah Lapidoth and the death of her brother Mordecai who has been Daniel's mentor. Occurring in close proximity, these events finally bring to an end the uncertainty and unknowing which was formerly Daniel's personal lot in life, and instead underwrite a firm declaration of identity. Thus Mirah's marriage to Daniel is conditional upon his Jewishness; for, if he had been the Gentile he had once thought himself to be, she would not have felt free to accept him. Taking the form of a distinctively 'Jewish rite', the couple's nuptials are notable for the exclusion of many of the novel's central characters (779). Neither Daniel's mother who had wished to release him from his Jewish heritage, nor his very English guardians who had imagined a more traditionally professional future for him, nor Daniel's closest male friend, nor the book's heroine Gwendolen who has long believed her life to be indissolubly tied to his, can be in attendance, so that the marriage represents and consolidates a break in Daniel's personal history. In contrast to the upper-class world in which Daniel was groomed, the wedding is a markedly plebeian affair, its most prominent guests including a family of 'common Jews' and Daniel's impecunious friends the Meyricks. Though the finest wedding gifts have come from high society, the sons and daughters whose presence enlivens the ceremony by embodying the hopes of new generations are figures from humble, albeit plainly respectable, backgrounds. The marriage party signifies an alliance across class lines, uniting 'common Jews' and Gentiles under Daniel's well-heeled gaze.

Love, marriage and the rediscovery of the Jewish homeland are inseparable here. Although Mirah loses the newly recovered brother that Daniel has found for her, Daniel is of course the one man for whom Mordecai (or Ezra) has long been searching. It is Mordecai's faith in the appearance of a successor that keeps alive the implicit promise, trailed throughout the novel, that Daniel is in reality a Jew; and in accepting this truth, Daniel will take the first step in realising Mordecai's messianic vision of a return by the Jewish people to Palestine. In short, it is Mordecai who immediately recognises Daniel for what he is and what he will be: a fateful identification since it is clear from the outset that this feverish, 'enigmatic Jew' is racked by tuberculosis and is within sight of his own death (380). Although Mordecai will live to see his sister's wedding, his disease is too far advanced to allow him to travel to the Holy Land; indeed, the onset of consumption has come about through his exposure to 'cold and snow' after having turned back from an earlier voyage to the near East ('Beyrout') in order to answer his mother's cry for help after her husband has taken Mirah, her sole remaining child, away from her (522). Unable to reconcile the ties of kith and kin with the fulfilment of what he regards as the racial destiny of his people, Mordecai depends upon a 'marriage of our souls' between Daniel and himself to bring his dreams to fruition (724). Daniel's marriage to Mirah and his intention of making a long trip to 'the East' are then two sides of a single coin, and Daniel's open admission that he is a Jewish man will finally close off all Gwendolen's hopes of a sustained intimacy between them. Nevertheless, Mordecai can be no more than an absent exemplar, a distant ideal, one that Daniel must interpret for himself. But if Daniel's ethical and political vocation cannot be identical with Mordecai's, it is hard to see what his expedition will accomplish. Daniel's anticipated 'Eastern travel' is high-minded and purposeful, yet ultimately seems quite obscure, as though deliberately underdetermined (780). This is a journey that remains in the reader's mind as a few hints and suggestions, but nothing more.

Palestine as the central locus of the East is also a peculiarly ill-defined site – the name occurs just twice in the text and the land is usually referred to as 'Judaea', rhetorically as 'Israel', or, more loosely, as 'the East', a referent that is clouded by allusions to other place names, such as North America, Italy or Persia. The fullest exposition of the meaning of the 'new Judaea', couched in a language of political theology, is to be found at the meeting of "The Philosophers" at the tavern called the *Hand and Banner*, and particularly in Mordecai's inspired contribution to the discussion. Predictably, critical reaction to this scene has come to epitomise the divide that the novel has consistently provoked. Sometimes dismissed as 'perhaps the worst chapter' in *Daniel Deronda* and said to pale beside 'the marvellous descriptions of Gwendolen' in a book that mistakenly sought to transcend the confines of realism, this section had in fact been enthusiastically translated for Jewish readers almost as soon as the novel appeared.[11] Amongst its defenders, 'Mordecai's orations' were 'perhaps the greatest *tour de force*' of Eliot's career, as the Jewish critic and scholar Joseph Jacobs had argued in 1879.[12]

Mordecai's oratory is surely meant to convince. But – well *before* he learns of his own suppressed ethnic back story – these speeches are a vital moment in Daniel's growing awareness of the contribution that a specifically Jewish national self-understanding might make to the course of world events, a realisation that transforms and fulfils 'his boyish love of universal history' (173). At the same time, Mordecai's ideas set the terms of what will become Daniel's mission by enabling him to grasp how deeply contested that self-understanding must be in a time when the Jewish people are, as Mordecai repeatedly stresses, 'dispersed' and 'degraded' (173, 510). The pride in their own rhetorical mastery displayed by the club members invests the disputatious elaboration of arguments and positions with a force and energy that tends to brush aside the intricately meditative general consciousness that normally envelops the words, thoughts and actions of the novel's protagonists, giving them their point and pathos.[13] The debate is, needless to say, rigged: while the members of this 'company select of the select among poor men' are hard-headed and quick, the floor soon becomes a forum for Mordecai's visionary, almost sermon-like, utterances which finally reduce his fellow 'philosophers' to silence (504). As the narrator's voice intercedes once more, we learn that, despite his having advanced these views in the past, Mordecai never spoke with such insistence and resolution or sense of 'crisis' before. He has reached 'a new phase' that will be the beginning of the end (519).

The topic for discussion is 'the law of progress' (505), and no sooner has it been announced than a clamour of contentious ideas is heard: traces of Comtian positivism, materialism, and Darwinian or Spencerian evolutionary theory. And from these broad, loosely articulated positions, the conversation turns to the question of agency, to the role of passion in historical change, and comes to fix upon the plight of nationalism and 'the idea of nationalities' (506). But there is really only one 'nationality' at issue here, and everyone is aware that Mordecai's speech is motivated, that he has 'a particular meaning' in mind (508). So, with mixed feelings ('Not one member of the club shared his point of view or his emotion'), this circle of largely un-English autodidacts is led, once again, to confront the future of Judaism in the course of what Miller, the second-hand bookseller who acts as 'moderator', designates 'a Jewish night' (510). Indeed, such is the power of Mordecai's eloquence, with its Biblical cadences and prophetic intensity, that, for all the group's devotion to secular rationalism, it is difficult to imagine a debate among 'The Philosophers' that did not devolve into 'a Jewish night' – though Daniel is mistaken in his estimate of the likely number of men of 'Jewish descent' in the room (504). If, for Mordecai, always conscious of the presence of Jewish interlocutors, the Jewish Question is always the ultimate topic on the agenda, his most cogent adversaries are located somewhere within the liberal camp. Each of the other members of the group is set at an angle to Mordecai's overtly Jewish background; each wittingly or unwittingly disregards or downplays his own national affiliations; and each, as in the 'incongruity' that Daniel discerns between Pash the watchmaker's scepticism about 'nationality' and 'the strong stamp of race on his features', resists too easy an equation between his racialised self and his civic identity (506). For where 'liberal ideas' are taken as the measure of man, the Jews are found wanting: too wedded to the past, too 'obstinate' in their 'adherence to the superannuated', they are, in Lilly the English clerk's crushing phrase, an underdeveloped, 'stand-still people' (512).

Mordecai's riposte to what he sees as the bloodless liberalism enshrined in this appeal to the inevitability of 'the law of progress' – and to the accusation that the Jews' greatest failing lies in an inability to advance into modernity – is to bring it face to face with the disruptive powers of 'Messianic time' (519). Against the gradualism, the steady meliorism, and even the modulated utopianism of his interlocutors, Mordecai counters with a philosophical caesura, the interruption of the smooth discourse of history by a perfectly realised and therefore spiritualised will. 'Messianic time' is, however, no simple construct. The two distinct registers employed by Mordecai when using this term suggest rather different, and perhaps not entirely reconcilable, emphases. In the debate at the *Hand and Banner*, Mordecai's messianism is triumphalist, even militaristic, in its overtones, foregrounding not the act of founding the state, but the 'will' to act, to 'will the planting of the national ensign', which is 'to will our own better future and the better future of the world'. Here the future that is subsumed under the rubric of 'Messianic time' seems curiously secular in form, gesturing towards a parity of recognition with other nation-states, described as 'a new brotherhood with the nations of the Gentiles'; and, only a moment before, Mordecai has prepared the ground for this image by making reference to the founding of the North American colonies (518–519). But when he returns to this phrase, after the other philosophers have left, Mordecai's language has turned inwards and has taken on a more densely spiritual colouration. Entry into 'Messianic time' is now the destiny of purified souls, those whose engagement with the discipline of kabbalistic doctrine has finally brought them their freedom from this 'mortal region', creating a space for 'the birth of new souls' who will follow in their wake (520). This is the point at which discipline invites discipleship, with only the presumption of Daniel's 'race' standing as a barrier between them. It is a vindication of Mordecai's commitment to the teachings of 'the Cabbala' that Daniel finally learns to see himself in truth, to overcome his own self-estrangement, and to discover a people to whom he belongs.

Daniel's discovery and his partial identification with Mordecai together represent an induction into a temporality that is at once historical and cosmic. For much of the novel, Daniel's sense of stasis, of incompleteness, is presented as a solitary condition, an inner deficiency that drives his half-knowing search for a larger vocation that can heal his alienated self. Until then, he will move through the world 'like a yearning disembodied spirit, stirred with a vague social passion, but without fixed local habitation to render fellowship real'. Like Mordecai, Daniel is 'enigmatic to his friends' and serious to a fault (348–349). But Daniel is also enigmatic to himself. The paradox of Mordecai's life is that, while he too seems set upon a solitary course – so awkward and obsessive that Ezra Cohen, the pawnbroker with whom he lodges, thinks of him as slightly unhinged – the racial consciousness which feeds his desire for kindred souls is necessarily a wish to realise a collective endeavour. The Jewish notion of a messianic future involves a public or communal aspiration: as Gershom Scholem has observed in an important essay on messianism, in Judaism, redemption must be an 'event' in the life of a people, not that of an individual soul, and as such, it will take place 'on the stage of history'.[14] But in *Daniel Deronda*, the hiatus between the lives of particular characters, emblems of the fate of a people, and the capacity for historical change is a constant source of difficulty for the novel.

If taking *his* place 'on the stage of history' represents a key transition for Daniel, it is a step that is hedged about with qualifications. Faced with the tradition of his forefathers, a tradition that he has never really experienced, that was denied him by his mother, Daniel immediately disavows it, at least in part. He will live as a Jew, but differently. What then of Mordecai, his mentor, the man who would seem to be the obvious collaborator in such a venture? Amanda Anderson has argued that Daniel 'actively resists Mordecai's vision' of a complete identity of thought between them. Put more strongly, she claims that the two men 'occupy radically different philosophical universes' and that their positions are incompatible.[15] On this reading, Daniel's recovery of his Jewishness has the advantage over what is presumed to be Mordecai's romantic quasi-racial nationalism by virtue of being more self-conscious, more reserved, more thoughtful, as though he were still imbued with the 'scepticism' that had long been 'his particular lot', yet now possessed the resources enabling him to escape its 'oppressive' force and to temper it with his gift for sympathy (601).

Anderson is surely right to stress the dialogical construction of the novel, but as the colloquy in the *Hand and Banner* indicates, we are sometimes being drawn into a dialogue of the deaf. In her analysis, the journey towards a civically oriented form of cultural nationalism that Daniel comes to embody is guided by two demanding but vital encounters: first, Daniel's intense friendship with Mordecai; and second, the two meetings with his 'unknown mother', the celebrated actress Alcharisi – now the Princess Leonora Halm-Eberstein (595). Out of these unlikely relationships will come a movement with the capaciousness and generosity to accommodate and appreciate rival, and arguably hostile, traditions – very much a tribute to the liberal spirit, not least because it would never allow itself to dispense with these interlocutors and so relegate them to the role of vanishing mediators of a better modernity. For, in Anderson's account, what she sees as 'the modern project of nation-building' in *Daniel Deronda* is implicitly a placeholder for a social world based upon a more humane moral and social philosophy than hitherto, a 'universalism' whose 'terms are set by the excluded particular' of the Jewish experience, an ethical stance that can learn from both Mordecai *and* Alcharisi. This 'project' is said to represent Eliot's best authorial self, an alternative future glimpsed between 'the fault lines' of her narrative and later in the worries that beset the conflicted figure of Theophrastus Such in Eliot's final book.[16]

But do Daniel and Mordecai inhabit quite such 'radically different' mental worlds? And how much does Mordecai owe to his fellow 'philosophers'? By the nineteenth century, the messianic belief system that Mordecai so commandingly represents was shot through with contradictions, pulled in contrary directions by several distinct ideological currents. Mordecai is at pains to distance himself from the kinds of concepts that preoccupy his fellow-philosophers – 'growth, completion, development' – and he does this by placing them in apposition to the Jewish tradition that he is seeking to animate and by attempting to redefine their meaning (515). So 'the strongest principle of growth lies in human choice,' which is then identified as a 'divine principle' for the Jewish people: 'to choose that God may again choose them' – what he has earlier called 'a dependent growth' (509, 519). Taxed with his critics' claim that he remains wedded to superstition, Mordecai counters with an appeal to 'the living fountains of enlarging belief'; challenged that he is not 'a rational Jew' like his fellows, he argues that 'to be rational' is 'to feel the light of divine reason growing stronger within and without' (509).

Still, his insistence upon a national solution to the Jewish Question shows his continuing indebtedness to Enlightenment ideas and at the same time reveals a source of strain within messianism between the desire for a restoration of the kingdom of Israel and a generalised utopian vision of a new beginning. Here again the language of Mordecai's exhortations is instructive. Consider his plea for the necessity of 'a new Jewish polity, grand, simple, just, like the old – a republic where there is equality of protection, an equality that shone like a star on the forehead of our ancient community' (516); or contrast his devotion to kabbalistic thought with his insistence that his beliefs entail 'no superstition' (515). In what is an uneasy amalgam of the mystical and the secular, the past and the future, Mordecai seems to conceive of time as a series of repetitions in which the new is conditioned by the old while the new resuscitates the old. However, hovering in the background of his appeal to 'Messianic time' is the intimation of a world shaken by the catastrophic and shocking appearance of something unprecedented, an event that will end history as it has hitherto been understood ('a sense of a crisis which must be seized'), when the 'reason of Israel' at last becomes 'the seed of fire' (517, 519). But that possibility is never made explicit. Instead, the old and the new are presented as mutually supportive moments, and where the terms of his argument are being stretched to the utmost, they become indistinguishable.

Mordecai's defence of Judaism as a politico-religious creed therefore places the messianic element in his thought under maximum pressure, raising questions as to its compatibility with his more secular phrasing. When he insists that 'the angel of progress' speaks directly to the Jewish people, it is easy to forget that, in making his vision intelligible to himself and others, Mordecai has been obliged to borrow from the liberal idiom of equality, citizenship and republican government, well understood by his fellow philosophers (518). This rapprochement between messianism and contemporary liberalism does have positive effects insofar as it opens up a space that Daniel, as a young man brought up in a liberal household, can begin to occupy emotionally and intellectually. What seems to emerge is a common task, a *modus vivendi* that both men can come to share. Yet the basis of this syncretism in which two different systems of thought undergo a process of cultural translation remains unexamined, leaving the political substance of Mordecai's views altogether vague and lacking in detail.

Historians of messianic thought have drawn attention to the contradictory strands within this body of ideas, and the case outlined by Mordecai very much reflects the dilemmas of the period, though these are never really acknowledged in Eliot's novel. In the profoundly otherworldly emphasis of much messianic Judaism, it is by no means clear that redemption can form part of, or be an event within, mundane existence.

As Anson Rabinbach has observed, 'the chasm … is too wide to be bridged by determined action or profane events'.[17] Thus from within the stricter confines of the Jewish mystical tradition, such a position would be unthinkable and a sign of the penetration of messianism by nineteenth-century liberal philosophy. In Gershom Scholem's history of the vicissitudes suffered by messianic thought, for example, belief in 'man's unassisted and continuous progress, leading to the ultimate liberation of all the goodness and nobility hidden within him' is nothing but a perversion stemming from 'the combined dominance of religious and political liberalism' in the modern era.[18] What this corrupted messianism omits, in Scholem's view, is 'the theory of catastrophe' that gives the prospect of a redemptive ending, an ending in which revelation and 'dread and ruin' are indivisible.[19] Indeed, Scholem's historical critique casts doubt on whether a proper Jewish community can truly be said to exist under diasporic conditions: it is precisely that community which needs to be created anew.

But the references to liberalism in *Daniel Deronda* are no less problematic, and this is especially so when Mordecai attempts to outline in relatively concrete terms what the 'new Jewish polity' might look like. Take what is, at first glance, one of Mordecai's oddest, yet ultimately most revealing, formulations: his description of a fully restored Israel as a solution to conflict, 'a halting-place of enmities' or 'a neutral ground for the East' (516). These two phrases imply somewhat different possibilities, both of which came to play an important role in the codification of Zionist thought and also in making the argument, – by no means the exclusive property of Jewish social critics at the fin-de-siècle – that the creation of a Palestinian enclave for the Jews would undermine the rationale for laws controlling immigration by destroying the need to seek entry into Britain. Theodor Herzl made precisely this point in his evidence to the Royal Commission on Alien Immigration in July 1902, a restatement of the case advanced in his 1896 pamphlet *Der Judenstaat* in which he argued that, if the Jews were to gain a home of their own (Argentina and Palestine are the two sites he mentions by name), then the inter-communal basis of anti-Semitism would be removed at a stroke. All that was needed, Herzl insisted, was 'a neutral piece of land' – in other words, a territory that had no other pressing claims upon it; and this notion slid seamlessly into a definition of how such a homeland would be constituted, that is, as 'a neutral State' – by which Herzl presumably meant a non-aligned state, although he was also clearly aware that it 'would remain in contact with all Europe, which would have to guarantee our existence'.[20]

FREEDOM AND THE NEUTRAL STATE

Although it is questionable whether Herzl ever read *Daniel Deronda*, there is a noticeable similarity between some of the political flourishes in Mordecai's speech and the ideas advanced in *Der Judenstaat*; consequently, one finds a comparable slippage around the use of the word 'neutral'. Largely ignored in studies of Eliot's work, the deployment of this important political concept forms a link between the moment of *Daniel Deronda's* inception and diasporic readings from the fin-de-siècle. What then is its derivation in Eliot's text? When Mordecai conjures up the prospect a Jewish nation-state, his specific politico-historical reference point is, perhaps surprisingly, the newly formed parliamentary democracy in Belgium. While acknowledging the 'difficulties' that the Jewish people are likely to face, Mordecai asserts that the new Israel will function in the East as Belgium does 'for the West', without ever spelling out what this might mean in practice (516); later in the debate he gives the claim greater generality when he speaks of 'a new Judaea, poised between East and West' (518). Eliot had visited Belgium en route to Weimar in July 1854 and would have been well aware of the country's turbulent history. But Mordecai's pointed allusion to Belgium as a political template is silent about the country's recent past. So it is important to pause and ask what it meant to describe Belgium as 'neutral' in the mid-nineteenth century and how far this description might be applied to other possible state formations.

In fact, the creation of the modern Belgian state was quite fortuitous and owed much of its political character to the place it occupied in relation to the major power blocs that held sway in Europe at the end of the Napoleonic wars. Originally part of the Netherlands, the Belgian *départements* had been annexed by the new Republic during the French Revolution, but after Napoleon's defeat, the Great Powers incorporated these territories into a United Kingdom of the Netherlands under the Dutch Protestant king William I. William's autocratic rule was deeply unpopular among the largely liberal and Catholic Belgian population who felt that their interests were being blatantly ignored, and in September 1830, the protests of the working classes and bourgeoisie escalated into what rapidly became a successful, full-scale revolution. On 4 October, Belgium was proclaimed an independent nation by the new provisional government.

With much stronger states at each of its borders, this unilateral declaration was never likely to be sufficient to guarantee the country's future.

Once the new Belgian National Congress announced that it wished to become a parliamentary democracy with a constitutional monarch, there was considerable manoeuvring among the Great Powers around the question of which European royal family could supply the most suitable candidate. But official recognition by Britain, Prussia, Austria and Russia and their public affirmation in January 1831 'that Belgium should be permanently neutral' were not enough to prevent an unsuccessful Dutch invasion attempt a mere six months later.[21] The paradox of Belgian independence was that it only survived because, and so long as, it was backed militarily by the major European nations – and it foundered the instant that this concord began to weaken, as the First World War horrifically demonstrated. And, *mutatis mutandis*, the question of international relations necessarily forms the half-buried subtext of Mordecai's peroration.

Belgium was widely admired as a modern liberal state throughout the Victorian era – certainly in contrast to markedly less democratic regimes like those of Napoleon III or Bismarck – and *'Freedom as in Belgium'* was the rallying cry and 'ultimate goal' for many European progressives.[22] To that extent the analogy between Belgium and 'Judaea' adds an aura of plausibility to the latter. But the ideal to which Mordecai alludes was belied by Belgium's increasingly conflicted domestic politics. The state-form adopted in the Belgian constitution was far from problem-free. The constitutional protection of free speech, freedom of assembly, and a free press (combined with strict limits on the role of the monarch) also included freedom of religion. Under the provisions of the latter, state subsidies were permitted for all denominations and, while this partly defused the Catholic demand that their church should become the established state religion, disagreement over this issue meant that the early political alliance between Catholics and liberals was potentially fragile. Moreover, the protection given to freedom of speech was severely qualified by another article in the constitution, which made French mandatory for 'all civil and military functions', leading to agitation in support of Flemish cultural and language rights in the 1840s.[23]

These divisions were already apparent by the mid-1860s, when *Daniel Deronda* is set, and they represent the hither side of the liberal vocabulary which Mordecai employs in giving shape to his vision of Israel's future. To acknowledge the problematic relationship between language, state power, and religious authority would necessitate confronting the heterodox and unstable nature of Mordecai's messianic discourse and clarifying what was religious and what was secular in his claims. Herzl's far less ambiguous attempt to formulate a 'State of the Jews' in largely

secular terms provides an instructive comparison, with its priests positioned firmly 'within the confines of their temples' and an army kept
'within the confines of their barracks'.[24] His critics, such as the cultural
Zionists Ahad Ha'am or Martin Buber, saw this blueprint for a pluralis-
tic, even multi-faith society as altogether too idealistic to form the basis
for a genuinely Zionist future – particularly as later reimagined in Herzl's
1902 novel *Altneuland* with its 'principles' of 'Liberalism, Tolerance, Love
of Mankind!'[25] How far Mordecai's stirring rhetoric in *Daniel Deronda*
would have been open to similar objections remains a matter of specula-
tion, but the contentious history of the Zionist movement casts a retrospective shadow over Daniel's project.

DIASPORIC READINGS

In the late nineteenth and early twentieth centuries, reactions to the
Hand and Banner debate within the wider Jewish community split and
hardened. While the serialization of the novel was still in progress, there
were already signs that polarization was beginning to occur between
those who praised Eliot's book for its sensitive treatment of Judaism and
those who took it to be the portent of a transcendent future. In July 1876,
Haim Guedalla, a member of the influential Montefiore family, argued
in the *Jewish Chronicle* that Eliot's notion of 'a new Judaea' was not as
far-fetched as some readers supposed, and he also wrote directly to Eliot
two months later with details of his land purchase scheme and tried to
enlist her support in encouraging Jewish settlements in Palestine.[26] In a
move that set the agenda for a raft of selective translations of the novel,
Guedalla sought to further his cause by rendering the *Hand and Banner*
chapter into Hebrew, which was then published in the East Prussian
weekly *Ha-Magid* in autumn 1876. Others were more guarded in their
enthusiasm. In a lecture on *Daniel Deronda* to the Jewish Working Men's
Club and Institute in London's East End in December 1876, Hermann
Adler (then Deputy Chief Rabbi) drew attention to the scene in the *Hand
and Banner*, but was careful to depict Daniel as a typical example of 'the
Jewish philanthropist', a man who acts for the good not just of 'his own
people, but extends his sympathies to the whole of mankind'. Adler never
specifically mentioned Daniel's proposed journey to the East and spoke
somewhat vaguely of Mordecai's 'ardent love for the Land of Promise'
and his desire to 'restore it to its pristine greatness, its freedom and political importance'.[27] What Adler took pains to avoid was any implication
that Deronda was a political leader in the making, for the possibility of

such a leader, even in a novelist's imagination, would have unsettled the modes and structures of authority within the Anglo-Jewish community as Adler then understood them.

In the same issue, the *Jewish Chronicle* published the first instalment of a two-part article on *Daniel Deronda* that echoed Adler's interpretation of the novel. According to this anonymous reviewer, Eliot's book could be read as a fable of the gains, but also the limits, of Jewish emancipation, showing 'the Jew dwelling in safety, freed from the ghetto, come into contact with modern civilisation and culture', a condition that was vitiated solely by 'social ostracism' now that 'legal persecution' had been consigned to the past. Today the relatively small numbers of Jews in Western Europe rarely looked towards a 'Jewish polity' to provide hope for a better future, the reviewer noted, adding, with true metropolitan hauteur, that it was 'the multitudes swarming in the northern and eastern Jewish beehives, who cling to the personality of the Redeemer ... and whose most fervent yearnings are towards the land of their forefathers'.[28] This despised audience was precisely the one that Guedalla had aspired to reach in the pages of *Ha-Magid* and that was to prove decisive for the growth of the Zionist movement, particularly from the mid-1880s.[29] Gradually a readership came into being in Austro-Hungary, Poland and Russia that absorbed *Daniel Deronda* through summaries, extracts and political commentaries, whose disconnection from the original novel seriously reduced its literary nuance and moral complexity. A prominent example was David Frischmann's Hebrew translation of *Daniel Deronda*, a section of which initially appeared in St. Petersburg in 1887, followed by a fuller version in 1893. Yet when the latter was published, it quickly became clear that Eliot's text had been heavily abridged in order to speak more directly to the interests of East European Jewish readers. Of Eliot's original seventy chapters, only fifty remained. Nevertheless, not only was the book a huge success, but, more significantly, shorter adaptations of Frischmann's text were marketed as children's books – an indication of the high regard for the novel among this community and its potential as a medium of instruction.

Frischmann's *Deronda* remained the only version of the novel available to readers of Hebrew until 1935, when a still more severely abridged text began to replace it. In fact, there was no complete Hebrew translation until 1991.[30] Still, for all its shortcomings, the popularity of Frischmann's work marked an important shift in the reception of the novel. In the late 1870s, when a German translation had made Eliot's book accessible to a wider circle of Jewish readers, critics like Philippson and Lehmann

commended the author for the thoughtfulness with which she had portrayed the Jewish community, but – like Adler in England – they had
played down Daniel's professed aim of giving his people 'a national centre, such as the English have' and avoided the political questions it raised
(774). But with the emergence of a network of locally based Zionist societies in the 1880s, as the situation of Jews in Poland and Russia was rapidly deteriorating, Frischmann's *Deronda* flourished and gave a new lease
of life to a single-mindedly restorationist reading of Eliot's book. At the
turn of the century, in an article in Ahad Ha'am's new monthly journal
Ha-Shiloah, the Russian Zionist Mordecai Ben Hillel Hacohen invoked
Frischmann's translation as a peerless ideological resource for Jewish
nationalists. From a Zionist standpoint, he insisted, 'there is no better
book than this wonderful story'.[31] This was, in Hermann Adler's view,
precisely the sort of misguided interpretation that ought to be discour-
aged, which he did from his first reading of the novel. To the end of his
days, Adler believed that any attempt to bring a Jewish state into being
went against Jewish teaching, and he openly preached against Herzl's
cause. Whereas Hacohen was a delegate to the First Zionist Congress
in 1897, Adler had condemned it. Moreover, Adler 'was the only western
European rabbi to contribute to a collection of anti-Zionist articles' that
appeared in Warsaw in 1900, a last-ditch attempt to stem the Zionist tide
in Eastern Europe.[32]

Hacohen's title, 'Israel and its Land in Fiction', was a misnomer insofar as it foreclosed the very questions that George Eliot was concerned to
leave open. In 1876, Eliot had declined to endorse Guedalla's Palestinian
scheme – a venture similar to those in which Hacohen was later involved –
because she believed that to do so would have constituted an abuse of her
position as a writer. Nevertheless, the path from Guedalla to Hacohen,
epitomised by the educational value ascribed to Eliot's book, is an indication of how far interpretative emphases had changed by the end of the
late Victorian period. Guedalla's championing of *Daniel Deronda* obviously differed from Adler's more conservative approach, but in Hacohen's
eulogy the novel has passed beyond the confines of Anglo-Jewish philan-
thropy to become recommended reading within East European Zionist
circles. Aamir Mufti has argued that *Daniel Deronda* marks the close of
an 'era of emancipation' for the Jews in which 'the ideal of liberal citizenship and assimilation into individual European societies' is not so
much abandoned as displaced on to the 'global stage'. According to this
view, assimilation is reconfigured, transferred from the nation-state to the
international arena: the Jews are to be inducted into the community of

(civilized) nations *as a nation*.[33] However, the cultural mediations involved in the dissemination of Eliot's novel discussed earlier show how fraught this project of nation-building was in theory and in practice, as contradictory as Mordecai's vision of 'a new Judaea' or the friction between Herzl's plans for a secular *Judenstaat* and Goldsmid's religious dream of a Greater Palestine. Mufti is right to identify a moment *after* emancipation, but he fails to credit the role ceded to *Daniel Deronda* in East European Jewish *self-organisation* by the 1890s, or what was called 'autoemancipation' by the early Zionist thinker Leo Pinsker: the belief that in the last analysis the Jews can only help themselves.[34]

NATIONALITY AND THE MOVEMENT OF SUBJECTS

Eliot's open-ended depiction of the aspiration to create 'a political existence' for the Jews in 'Judea' is the novel's greatest strength and yet its greatest weakness. Part of the book's transnational appeal was due to the way in which the lack of specificity surrounding Daniel's journey to the East provided a screen onto which a variety of readers could project their hopes and concerns. However, its vagueness also led less sympathetic critics to dismiss the whole idea out of hand or licensed purely figurative readings of the kind encouraged by Hermann Adler's 1876 lecture – readings that only further muddied the possible meanings of the novel. But the question of a return to Palestine does not stand alone, since it necessarily returns the reader to the question of agency and to the much-contested credibility of Daniel's role in this venture. In this section I turn to some of the problems associated with Daniel's identity, focussing particularly on its political underpinnings in order to shed more light on why *Daniel Deronda* is such a watershed text in the period prior to 1905.

For readers who have been favourably impressed by Daniel's gathering maturity in the novel, extricating himself from uncertainty and advancing into an independent-minded sense of purpose, his character is, as Adler argued, that of a doer, an active presence in the lives of those he touches. This view contrasts sharply with that of other contemporary critics, like Leslie Stephen, who saw in Daniel little more than the idealised personification of a 'principle', while A.V. Dicey regarded him as 'incurably weak' and 'a slave to circumstances', suggesting that even Daniel's decision 'to devote himself to the service of his countrymen' was a response to 'a question from a stranger'.[35] In each case Daniel is said to fall short of the standards of literary realism, a persistent worry in a book that often deliberately works at the limits of representation; and both criticisms imply that, insofar as he fails to display a capacity for self-reflection and moral autonomy, Daniel could be said to lack character. A version of this point has been pressed further, suggesting a fatal circularity in the novel that effectively undermines Daniel's fateful decision to 'call myself a Jew' (698). In Peter Brooks's stark antithesis, 'Daniel chooses to be a Jew, but that choice seems to be predetermined because he is a Jew'.[36]

In fact, Daniel's assumption of his Jewishness inhabits a much more complex temporality than Brooks's formula allows. On learning the truth of his origins from his mother, Daniel accepts his 'birthright' swiftly and unhesitatingly, but this acceptance is followed by a slower and rather more hesitant working through of its implications. Astounded by his mother's revelations, Daniel responds with an incredulous question – 'Then I *am* a Jew?' – a question whose emphasis comes close to making a constative utterance, announcing the selfsame condition that it ostensibly queries (605). Yet, by the time he sees her again at their second and final meeting, the concern with Jewish suffering is already beginning to shape a new conception of his life's work and he now considers it his 'duty ... to identify myself, as far as possible, with my hereditary people' (637). The crucial qualification 'as far as possible' suggests that his Jewishness is a matter of moral identification, rather than simply of heredity, a personal endeavour that can never be completely fulfilled. Despite the close collaboration between Daniel and Mordecai, for example, the two men remain separated by a time-lag that delays Daniel's full understanding of the religious tradition into which he is now being drawn – an understanding that is always mediated by his Christian upbringing. If this is the case, however, then who or what is Daniel? It is as though neither his Jewishness nor his Englishness is quite enough to 'secure' – the word that is deliberately used by his dying mother – a sense of where he rightfully belongs. In Alcharisi's eyes, to be Jewish is to endure a form of 'bondage', a denial of the personal liberty she associates with England, the place of her birth, while to be 'an English gentleman' – which she conceives as her greatest gift to her unwanted son – is to cauterize the self against the wounds of Jewishness, freeing Daniel of its claims and the opprobrium he would otherwise encounter (605). By contrast, Daniel is shocked that someone should try to "choose" his birthright for him. But biology is not quite destiny in this novel, and by carefully probing Daniel's sense of himself and the mysteries of his genealogy, Eliot explores a variety of answers to the conundrum of his identity.

When Daniel considers whether he might be the Jew for whom Mordecai is searching, he is inclined to think that 'uncertainty' is 'a condition to be cherished for the present' because he is at first unwilling to believe that his real father could be anything other than English, even though he has no clear idea as to who that man might be (497). However, when Daniel learns from his mother that he is indeed a Jew, this clarification does nothing to remedy the uncertainty of his legal status and remains as nebulous and underdetermined as his journey to the East. On his mother's side, Daniel's family is English, albeit 'of Portuguese descent', and later he tells Mirah and Mordecai that he comes from 'a line of Spanish Jews'; nevertheless, of his mother's father we are told only that he 'had been in various countries' (610, 721). Daniel knows that he was born in wedlock, but as to his place of birth, or the nationality of his father, no definite information is given in the text. Indeed, as he enters the room to meet his mother for the first time Daniel finds himself unable to 'conjecture in what language she would speak to him', though he is sure that 'it would not be English' (602). He subsequently learns from her that the question of his upbringing was decided in Naples and, although his family seem to have been domiciled in Italy, the itinerant lives of his mother and his physician grandfather tell against any settled bourgeois existence. And although Sir Hugo had happily (and devotedly) acceded to Alcharisi's request that he should bring up her son as 'an English gentleman', it was he who insisted that Daniel continues to bear 'a foreign name'. The surname 'Deronda' is meant as a sign of dissociation, partially disguising who he is, but also offering a clue, for it turns out to be the name of a distant, half-forgotten branch of the Charisi family. In a wider sense, the very act of renaming has a more pointed significance because it is revealed as a quintessentially Jewish gesture and so reconnects Daniel to his people. Despite her show of indifference, Daniel's mother knows this perfectly well; as she observes, 'The Jews have always been changing their names' (615).

Daniel's Englishness appears in the novel as a cultural code rather than a token of his legally sanctioned national identity. Because the story of his past lacks certain key facts, it is entirely possible that Daniel would have been unable to prove himself a British subject. We are not told whether he was born on British soil, nor is it clear whether he had an English father – crucial factors in deciding to which state a person owed allegiance, according to the patchwork of precedents that were in play during the 1860s. These legal questions are touched on only very lightly in *Daniel Deronda*, because Eliot is primarily concerned with contrasting national and cultural traditions. Revealingly, Mordecai is without question a British subject: 'England is the native land of this body', he tells Daniel, adding that 'my true life was nourished in Holland', which in turn led him to pursue his religious studies in Germany (370, 380). Mordecai's Britishness is thus a secondary and largely inessential attribute, subordinated to the 'larger outlook on my people, and on the Gentile world' that his search for knowledge has brought him – a phrase later echoed in Sir Hugo Mallinger's reference to Daniel's 'large notions about Judaism' (478, 765). If Mordecai can feel himself to be a modern incarnation of those medieval souls that 'had absorbed the philosophy of the Gentile into the faith of the Jew', Daniel's destiny recapitulates that of a more formidable ancestor (479). Well before the expedition to the East has been announced, Mordecai links Daniel to the Biblical Moses by referring to him as 'an accomplished Egyptian', someone whose real identity is at first hidden by another and whose future must lie elsewhere (634). Yet Daniel does not try to disavow his Gentile past, and it is what he has learned from the past, however painful his experiences have been, that has given him the personal qualities that Mordecai recognises and admires.

Daniel's bitter exchange with his mother in their first meeting – both of them 'shaken by a mixed anger' – turns upon the clash, already noted, between choice and birthright. In choosing for him 'what I would have chosen for myself', Alcharisi has denied Daniel the opportunity to inhabit what he is, condemning him to a kind of false self (605). But it is the transposition of a private internal struggle into the arena of public affairs that intensifies the dilemma that Daniel faces. On the one hand, there is an acute sense of the givenness of one's lot in life and of the need to be reconciled to what Daniel describes as 'an inherited yearning – the effect of brooding, passionate thoughts in many ancestors' that demands understanding and fidelity. But on the other hand, there is a complex language of volition and discrimination which can never be entirely folded back into these quiddities. Had he not met Mordecai before he had discovered the fact of his Jewishness, Daniel is sure that he 'would have rebelled against it'; now, however, his 'consent' is whole-hearted (723). Nonetheless, in response to Mordecai's eager call for 'the marriage of our souls', Daniel is more cautious, urging that 'what we can't hinder must not make our rule for what we ought to choose' (724).

The language that struggles to articulate such difficult decisions is very different from that which signifies the rights and responsibilities of 'citizenship', Mordecai's word for those political ties that lack the deeper resonances of 'the Hebrew blood' (515). Citizenship is likened to 'a fresh-made garment', an outer covering or adornment that cannot touch the inner substance of a people's historical being. In cleaving to such a superficial identity, one denies one's fellows and becomes 'an alien in spirit', and hence one is forced into what can only be a parasitic relationship to a genuine, living community (509). This troubled attempt to portray a condition of spiritual estrangement collapses the legal distinctions used to identify an outsider or foreigner and configures modern citizenship as a form of alienation. In British law, the term 'alien' traditionally designates a person who fails to qualify as a British subject – in other words, someone whose relationship to the Crown is ephemeral and adventitious. Lacking the subject's 'indelible' attachment to the monarch, a bond that would endure throughout the whole of a subject's life, the alien instead owed only 'temporary' or 'local allegiance', as the influential eighteenth-century jurist William Blackstone famously put it.[37] Aliens came under the protection of the king for the duration of their residence in England, but their rights were strictly limited. However, Mordecai's trope makes the alien's plight far worse than it would have been under English law. The alien is now irredeemably cast as an interloper and a pariah in virtue of having lost that vital 'sense of brotherhood with his own race'; he can never truly belong among those who are his rightful kin (509).

One reason why legal matters remain in the background of Eliot's novel, and perhaps why the question of Daniel's Englishness can remain unresolved, is that this was a period in which the laws relating to nationality and the movement of peoples were in flux. In Western Europe, the early 1860s saw an easing of restrictions on travel, and freedom of mobility became a much more acceptable idea than hitherto. In the case of Belgium, for instance, passport regulations were abolished, which 'meant that aliens did not have to ask for permission to immigrate', and illegal immigration ceased to be an offence (although vagrancy and destitution could result in expulsion).[38] But the 1860s was also a period in which problems of what political allegiance meant and the forms that it could take were coming to a head, most crucially in Britain where the feudally-derived model of sovereignty was directly challenged by changes in the nature of the modern state.

The period between 1866–1868, when *Daniel Deronda* is set, and 1876, when the novel was published, represents a watershed in British nationality legislation. By the 1860s, the traditional notion of allegiance that had defined the relationship of British subjects to the Crown had come under unprecedented strain because of the massive impact of the American War of Independence and the French Revolution. With the rise of new republican forms of government, Britain found itself obliged to consider some kind of practical accommodation with states that were founded upon a substantially different principle of political inclusion. As we saw in the earlier discussion, under English law stretching back to the Middle Ages, to be an English subject was to occupy a permanent and lifelong status, determined by whether or not one had been born within the royal dominion and could therefore be said to owe obedience to the reigning monarch. Although there were rights and responsibilities on both sides – and despite the fact that under some conditions, such as conquest or a process of naturalisation, non-subjects could be turned into subjects – identifying oneself as a British subject was never a matter of choice so far as the vast majority of the population was concerned.

In revolutionary France or the United States, by contrast, the concept of citizenship had come to be based upon popular consent, and sovereignty was theoretically a product of the people's will – a doctrine that was regarded with deep-seated hostility by most British politicians. By introducing the criterion of consent in the 1790s, the French republic was able to call into question the legitimacy of a political order founded on a preordained loyalty to a king or queen, making that bond appear forced and arbitrary; and it offered dissident nationalists, republicans and socialists a rational model of government that depicted royalism as a relic of a superstitious age. To take one prominent mid-nineteenth-century example: the threat posed to the British political class by the Irish Republican Brotherhood or 'Fenians' did not derive solely from their uncompromising desire for an independent Ireland and their willingness to resort to violence. It also stemmed from the Fenian demand for a state-form that was explicitly opposed to the idea of a constitutional monarchy. The threat was far from negligible. By 1865, just seven years after its inception, the Fenians were said to have recruited some 80,000 members across the United Kingdom.[39]

Moreover, this was also a period in which large-scale patterns of labour migration were becoming visible. Throughout Europe, traditional rural economies were experiencing severe disruption as the development of capitalist enterprises changed the nature of employment, forcing wage labourers to make much longer journeys to find work, either within short-term work gangs in distant parts of the countryside or by being pitched into the rapidly expanding cities. Migration had long been a key factor in Irish social life, for instance, but after 1800, what was once a 'stream became a flood'.[40] At a conservative estimate, between 1815 and 1870, some 4 million people left Ireland, many of them crossing the Atlantic to America, where American citizenship carried obvious practical advantages while also providing a way of repudiating what was perceived as a coerced allegiance to the British Crown. If Irish labour and Irish patriotism were regarded as particularly troublesome problems by the British authorities, this was never more the case than when the Irish insisted that they stood outside the jurisdiction of the British courts, particularly when they claimed that they had become American citizens. The initial response of British jurists was unyielding: the relation of a British subject to the king was 'indelible'. As Chief Justice Baron Piggott put it when delivering judgment in the case of the Irish-American John Warren: 'according to the law of England … which has been administered without variation or doubt from the earliest times – he who once is under the allegiance of the English sovereign remains so forever'.[41] Characteristically, Piggott cited Blackstone as his legal authority.

The 1870 Naturalisation Act was an attempt to legislate a way through the anomalies, challenges, and hard cases that had been accumulating at least since the jurisdictional dispute enshrined in *Calvin's Case* (1608). But in so doing, the Act also showed the impact that the theory and practice of liberalism was having upon the conduct of business and government by redefining the role of the state. Where subjects had once been knitted into a complex web of feudal duties, obligations and protection, the liberal argument did not merely seek to unpick such closely woven threads in the name of freedom or the market. Its formula was more nuanced, but devastating in its implications. In Michel Foucault's forceful paraphrase, the liberal system of governance effectively promised a new, more autonomous type of subject: 'I shall produce for you that which allows you to be free. I shall do it in such a way that you are free to be free'.[42] Liberal modernity therefore assumed a form of life in which the state was constantly engaged in determining the limits and the risks that free and active subjects must face. It is the state that acts as 'the local guardian of the world republic of commerce', encouraging and permitting 'individuals to trade and to travel freely across its borders,' and granting 'this right both to foreigners and citizens'.[43]

In marked contrast to its ideological competitors, liberalism articulated a coherent vision of an international order that was underwritten by nation-states without being reducible to what nation-states do. This aspiration towards a worldwide political and economic system reached its closest approximation to reality in the second half of the nineteenth century. And, precisely because liberalism was conceived as virtually global in its reach, the principle of freedom of movement weakened the distinction between citizen and non-citizen. However, such broad cosmopolitan principles could never abolish this distinction entirely; in the messy business of daily government, modern liberal polities have always had to concern themselves with the management of large aggregate populations, even when their byword has continued to be the promotion of individual liberty.[44] Against this background, the 1870 Naturalisation Act represented at least a partial liberalisation of sovereignty by bringing in an element of choice in those instances where subjects wished to assume or abrogate their British national identity. In redefining the conditions of naturalisation, the law now recognised its reverse side: where they could demonstrate allegiance to another country, subjects could divest themselves of their status as Britons by making 'a declaration of alienage'.[45]

Taken at face value, Daniel's assertion that henceforth he will call himself a Jew and take the welfare of his 'own people' as his 'first duty' implies a philanthropic vocation, a watchful engagement with those 'many indifferent faces and vulgar figures' that would come naturally to someone who 'was fervidly democratic in his feeling for the multitude, and yet, through his affections and imagination, intensely conservative' (348, 352, 698). Like all philanthropists, Daniel's stance entails a certain distance from the subjects of his concern. He cannot aspire to be the kind of Jew his grandfather was because he knows that '[t]he effect of my education can never be done away with' and so part of him will always respond with 'Christian sympathies' (637). However, his journeys overseas and the fact that some of the most decisive revelations about his family and its history occur and, more importantly, place him outside England suggests that his loyalties are now split, as though learning how to be a Jew must necessarily take him away from the country he had thought was his home. To become a Jew in Daniel's case is not just a matter of embracing what his mother terms 'the bondage of having been born a Jew' (605). It also means consciously seeking to loosen the social and personal ties that formerly held him, a situation that foreshadows the 'capacity … to renounce' one's allegiances that the 1870 Naturalisation Act began to envisage for the first time.[46] What kind of subject may yet be fashioned by Daniel is deliberately left open by Eliot, as is the character of the 'national centre' he hopes to initiate, if not complete – and the two are, of course, closely intertwined (774). The signs are ambiguous and do not divide neatly between Mordecai and Daniel. Is it to be an imperial metropolis like London (as Daniel has sometimes been thought to imply) or an independent state capital like Brussels (as Mordecai's otherwise romantic vision would seem to suggest)? What sort of settlement is it that 'the condition of [Daniel's] race' ultimately requires? (773).

Daniel Deronda has been read as a novel that, uniquely in Eliot's work, is steeped in the culture of modernity – technologically, epistemologically, and politically. As Josephine McDonagh has pointedly observed, this is 'a much bigger, busier, more uncertain and complicated world' than that of Eliot's previous fiction, a world in which people are constantly on the move and, once they have arrived, typically find themselves among a heterogeneous throng of strangers, whether flocking around the gaming tables or collecting along the strand to witness the end-game of a tragedy at sea.[47] The novel depends heavily upon a sense of inescapable, but frequently bewildering, differences – of class, language, nationality, and race – differences that strain and finally overwhelm the protocols of Eliot's habitual 'domestic realism', transforming the novel into, in McDonagh's words, 'an allegorical tale of political rejuvenation'.[48] The exact nature of that 'political rejuvenation' remains a matter for conjecture, then and now, and critics have drawn upon nineteenth-century Jewish thinkers from Moses Hess to Leopold Zunz in order to assist them in interpreting how this 'rejuvenation' is to be construed. But because *Daniel Deronda* is a text written in the mid-1870s and set in the mid-1860s, one should be careful not to project Eliot's novel into a future for which it is scarcely prepared. In legal and ideological terms, *Daniel Deronda* belongs to a phase of European modernity when bureaucratic restrictions on travel in the form of visas and passports were generally being relaxed or removed altogether, and when the position of subjects and citizens was starting to become somewhat more flexible, as Britain's rather cautious 1870 Naturalisation Act indicates.[49] At the same time, the novel stands at the cusp of a step change in the scale of migration during the final decades of the century that was to call many of these measures into question. As the size and speed of passenger steamships rapidly improved, the combination of transoceanic maritime travel with transcontinental rail networks created a highly efficient 'web of mass transportation', resulting in a huge increase in global migration.[50] The flow of migrants to the Americas rose from 2.6 million between 1871 and 1880 to more than 17.9 million between 1901 and 1910, matched by comparable increases to the two other major destinations, Southeast Asia and Northern Asia.[51]

These crude figures mask the different kinds of migrants, mingling the refugee and the homesteader, the indentured labourer and the itinerant railway hand. The contrast with *Daniel Deronda* could not be more striking. There the *mass* movement of peoples is assigned either to cultural memory, as when Daniel finds himself haunted by the image of 'the multitudinous Spanish Jews centuries ago driven destitute from their Spanish homes' only to meet their death on 'crowded ships', or to the futuristic rhetoric of a return, as in Mordecai's call for 'another great migration, another choosing of Israel to be a nationality whose members may still stretch to the ends of the earth' (517, 598). Set against the pathos of such urgent imaginings – tellingly dubbed by Eliot 'the wide travel of imagination' – much of the mobility in the novel is on a relatively mundane, small-scale, and sometimes banal footing: the downward slide into less genteel accommodation by Gwendolen's family, the Mallinger household's shuttling between Diplow Hall and London, or Grandcourt and Gwendolen's sailing holiday around the Mediterranean (694). While it is integral to the plot that the individual adjustments involved in these moves are often occasions for anxiety, it is debatable whether they are part of what Edward Said once diagnosed as 'a generalized condition of homelessness' in the nineteenth century, a predicament that Daniel's pro-jected journey to 'the East' can presumably be expected to overcome. The character that comes closest to embodying 'the spiritual and psychological rootlessness' that Said discerned in the novel is that of Joseph Kalonymos, a man of 'restless travel' and 'punctilious observation' who has *chosen* to be 'a wanderer' (696–697).[52] Yet spiritually Kalonymos is perfectly secure in his Jewish faith and lacks the religious curiosity that drove his bosom friend, Daniel's grandfather. For a devout nomad like Kalonymos, to travel is better than to arrive. He seeks no homeland.

If Kalonymos is hardly a spiritual exile, then neither is he the prototype of the late-nineteenth-century refugee or economic migrant whose num-bers began to swell the traffic up and down the shipping lanes and across the railway networks. Unlike the major characters in *Daniel Deronda*, none of these figures was exactly a free agent, and in any case as the cen-tury wore on it became increasingly apparent that "free" migration always occurs under definite legal conditions, whether through oversight of how labourers are recruited or via the blunter instruments of travel documents and border controls. By the late nineteenth century, who could travel and to which destinations were determined as much by government regula-tion as by the availability of transport, obliging migrants to move through social and political terrain that was not of their own choosing. Although a scattering of piecemeal initiatives can be traced as far back as the 1850s, the late 1870s and early 1880s saw the beginnings of systematic immi-gration control in parts of Australia and in the United States, specifi-cally directed against workers of Chinese origin. These laws may sound like a very far cry from the Jewish Question that Eliot was addressing in her final novel, but they provided both the template and the precedent for attempts to bring to a halt the immigration of East European Jews into Britain at the fin-de-siècle. Laws like the 1882 Chinese Exclusion Act in the United States signalled the end of the liberal state ideal upon which the plot of *Daniel Deronda* depends and which, in a tantalisingly oblique manner, it seeks to promote. After 1876, any notion of preserving what Deronda's grandfather had extolled as 'the balance of separateness and communication' between Jews and their others began to sound suspect (697).

Between 1876 and 1880, the widespread outrage at Disraeli's pro-Turkish *realpolitik* in the East and at what was seen as his moral indifference to the massacre of thousands of Christian Bulgarians at the hands of the Turkish armed forces brought about a reopening and reframing of the Jewish Question. In a remarkable reversal of opinion, this attack was led by the same alliance of radical liberals, high churchmen, and provincial nonconformists who had hitherto been the most vocal supporters of Jewish civil and political rights. Even Gladstone's usually high-minded rhetoric sometimes lapsed into anti-Jewish sentiment, and by April 1878, the invective against English Jews had reached such a pitch that Rabbi Hermann Adler, once the optimistic champion of *Daniel Deronda*, now felt obliged to defend his community against the charge – promulgated by the Liberal historian Goldwin Smith – that the Jews were unpatriotic. Of course 'we Jews feel ourselves bound by the ties of religion with our brethren in foreign lands,' Adler wrote. But then, in a phrase that seems to hark back to his earlier stress upon Daniel's 'intense overflowing sympathy', Adler insisted that it was precisely because 'we are Englishmen' that 'it behoves us to sympathise with the oppressed throughout the globe'.[53]

Eliot's own take on these 'anti-Judaic advocates' was revealed through the medium of her quirky persona, Theophrastus Such, in the most famous of her final essays, 'The Modern Hep! Hep! Hep!' (1879).[54] According to Eliot's narrator in *Impressions of Theophrastus Such*, the 'confidence [of these former friends of Anglo-Jewry] has been succeeded by a sense of mistake', 'a regret that no limiting clauses were insisted on, such as would have hindered the Jews from coming too far and in too large proportion along those opened pathways' (155). Yet even though her text belongs to the same fraught political moment as Adler's essay 'Can Jews be Patriots?' the positions advanced there deliberately eschew the kind of closure that Adler was at pains to establish. Eliot's dialogism, pushed to further extremes than in *Daniel Deronda*, once again permits no comforting resolution. In

Theophrastus's exploratory discourse, 'separateness' and 'communication' are terms that cannot immediately be reconciled, and it is only through the optic of a universal history that the self-development of nations can be seen as the source of a new and higher synthesis to come, the 'inevitable movement' towards 'the growing federation of the world', 'the education of mankind', and, more problematically, 'the quicker or slower fusion of races' (156, 160). It is only from within this grand, yet unfulfilled, narrative that 'the notion of a renovated national dignity for the Jews' can be assigned its true value (163).

These ideas are only very tentatively and somewhat hesitantly sketched out, and one mark of the instability underlying them is the fluctuating, and at times relativizing, meanings of the word 'alien' in Theophrastus's meditation. If the addressees of the essay can only be 'we English', this 'colonising people' are unquestionably 'an alien race' in the eyes of the subjugated 'Hindoos', and throughout the text the term 'alien' designates the outsider, the oppressor, the recalcitrant other, including one's own otherness to oneself, as when converts make 'an outward renunciation' of their Jewishness but 'with the lack of real love towards the society and creed which exacted this galling tribute', or when Christians fail to recognize that 'cross, creed, and baptism' have rendered their proselytizing zeal 'cruel, rapacious, and debauched' (146, 153–154). To hold oneself apart from those with whom one shares historic and religious common ground, as some Christians have done in their relations with the Jews, is to risk falling into a state of 'moral alienation', and represents as great a danger as succumbing, in Theophrastus's notorious phrase, to 'a premature fusion with immigrants of alien blood' (154, 158). The work of individual nations remains to be completed before the barriers between the peoples of the world can be cast aside. The 'not yet enough', the insipidity and lack of substance that Theophrastus finds in the ideal of 'a common humanity' at the present stage of world history, deflates the 'highly virtuous' dream of an imminent 'cosmopolitanism', just as a similar flaw undermines the conviction that 'communism' can muster the 'social energy' necessary to turn its political ambitions into a reality (147). These too are 'premature' imaginaries: neither is able to generate the emotional resources upon which human action crucially depends, 'the satisfaction of a great feeling that animates the collective body as with one soul' – an identical spiritual formula to that which is canvassed in *Daniel Deronda* (146).

'Alien' as used here carries the widest possible signification, running from ethical critique to racial biology and moving across nations and cultures; and yet Eliot seems almost deliberately to skirt around the term's specifically legal connotations. What makes this evasion particularly curious is the way in which 'The Modern Hep! Hep! Hep!' takes the issue of immigration to be integral to the Jewish Question, stressing the diasporic condition of the Jews – 'the seven millions scattered from east to west' – as a key factor in creating a remarkably gifted people who are 'proud of their origin' and ready to go to any lengths for the good of their community (162). It is entirely characteristic of Eliot's philosemitic turn of mind that she justifies her praise for the nobility of the Jews by comparing their 'superlative peculiarity' to 'that sense of special belonging' (our 'peculiar destiny as a Protestant people') which she believes to have preserved 'migratory Englishmen from the worst consequences of their *voluntary* dispersion' (148, 150, 156 my emphasis). There can be no valid reason to deny asylum to the persecuted and suffering alien, 'to tear the glorious flag of hospitality which has made our freedom the world-wide blessing of the oppressed,' not least because the English themselves are so patently willing 'to settle wherever money is to be made and cheaply idle living to be found' (159–160).

From 1865 to 1881 – the decade and a half before the mass migration of East European Jews into Britain began – approximately 19,000 Jews settled in England, with slightly more than 60 per cent of these coming from Russia and Poland in order to escape famine, political turmoil, or military service, and to find a better life.[55] Yet, as early as 1877, *The Times* noted that the previous two years had seen an excess of emigrants over immigrants and that 'English emigration has assumed larger proportions year after year' – a statistic that seemed to point towards a different estimate of the migratory Englishman's import than that rhetorically invoked by Eliot in her appeal to the notion of an English diaspora.[56] *The Times* was especially concerned that the bulk of Irish emigration might be coming to England and Scotland rather than the United States, but the excesses and deficits of demographic change were soon to become the indispensable background to debates about restrictionist legislation once the period of mass migration was underway. George Eliot necessarily wrote in innocence of this troubled future. But the twin solutions to the Jewish Question that she put into the mouth of Theophrastus Such – that is to say, as much immigration as can be humanely countenanced, coupled with as generous support as possible for the establishment of a Jewish nation *elsewhere* – together defined the limits to the liberal decencies available within the late Victorian British state. In the hands of ardent supporters of immigration control like Major William Evans-Gordon or Arnold White, its options could be adjusted to form a policy of a very different stamp, one calculated to forestall any possibility of 'a premature fusion with immigrants of alien blood'.

The world evoked by *Daniel Deronda* stands in opposition to that ushered in by the 1905 Act because it remains a world of mobile subjects who can move across Europe and beyond without let or hindrance, a world in which national allegiances might still retain a certain fluidity, notwithstanding the division between those who could only conceive of Britain as a temporary home or foothold and those for whom it was a real, if precarious, domicile that must be maintained at all costs. As Herzl's diaries indicate, by the mid-1890s, the question of where the Jew rightfully belonged was taking on a new salience as the Jewish community in Britain steadily began to increase in size, following the destabilisation of Russia and Eastern Europe. Although Eliot's novel preceded the surge in Jewish immigration that began in the 1880s, its invocation of a Palestinian horizon was a salutary reminder of the strains within the Jewish diaspora, a reminder that was to figure strongly in the formation of the novel's reading publics. From the outset, the obstacles to the messianic dream were formidable and the realisation of a Jewish homeland truly was, as the *Jewish Chronicle*'s earliest reviewer noted, 'a task worthy of Deronda's powers'.[57] The local brutalities that would intensify these aspirations among East European Jews were revealed barely a week later when, in late December 1876, new reports of what the *Chronicle* called 'the Roumanian Atrocities' began to surface, in which hundreds of Jewish families had been driven from their homes in a burst of nationalist fervour.[58] One might have been forgiven for thinking that perhaps Daniel's mother had been right after all.

CHAPTER 2

Palaces and sweatshops: East End fictions and East End politics

I followed the people that came over in the same boat that I came by into the East End of London, and there I went into a place. They could see I had just come over, and there was a boot-finisher living in the same house, and he said it would be very wise for me to start learning the finishing trade. ... What hours were you made to work? – From 6 till 12 as a rule, barring Thursday night. Then it was a rule we always worked all night.[1]

Here, in the East End ... there are no strollers. All day long the place is full of passengers hasting to and fro, pushing each other aside, with set and anxious faces, each driven by the invisible scourge of necessity which makes slaves of all mankind. Do you know that famous picture of the Israelites in Egypt? Upon the great block of stone, which the poor wretches are painfully dragging, while the cruel lash goads the weak and terrifies the strong, there sits one in authority. He regards the herd of slaves with eyes terrible from their stony gaze. What is it to him whether the feeble suffer and perish, so that the Pharaoh's will be done? ... If the Israelites desisted, they were flogged back to work with cats of many tails; if our workmen desist, they are flogged back by starvation.[2]

That road is the most cosmopolitan place in London; and on a Saturday night its interest reaches a climax. There one sees all nationalities. A grinning Hottentot elbows his way through a crowd of long-eyed Jewesses. An Algerian merchant walks arm-in-arm with a native of Calcutta. A little Italian plays pitch-and-toss with a German Gentile. And among the foreigners lounges the East End loafer, monarch of all he surveys, lord of the premises. It is amusing to see his British air of superiority.[3]

London's East End has a long history as an immigrant destination; between 1650 and 1800, it had been variously settled by the Irish, Sephardic Jews from Spain and Portugal, Huguenot refugees from France, and Lascar seamen. By the mid-nineteenth century, there were approximately 20,000 Jews in London, the majority in the East End, and when Daniel Deronda goes in search of Mirah's lost brother, he begins by 'rambling in those parts of London which are most inhabited by common Jews', named as St Mary Axe and Whitechapel, before walking west towards Holborn (364). The area included some of the worst slums in London, an inexhaustible topic of discussion in pulpits and periodicals, and from the late 1880s onwards, the East End became the epicentre of anti-immigration agitation in Britain. The cluster of quotations at the head of this chapter offers a composite depiction of everyday life in East London in this latter period. Each moves beyond social observation towards social diagnosis, shaping mundane details into a moral economy and highlighting phenomena that readers could only ignore at their peril.

The selection commences with the recollection of an arrival, the only avowed statement of fact in the three examples cited. In evidence given on 29 May 1902, an anonymous Polish Jewish witness tells the members of the Royal Commission on Alien Immigration of his entry into England some two decades previously and his subsequent journey to Spitalfields where he lodged in 'a seven-roomed house' while learning his trade as a boot-finisher. Having informed the Commission that if his political views were to become known to his employers he would risk losing his livelihood, "Mr B" agreed to testify only on condition that his name was withheld from the public record. Although written in a very different register, the second passage provides some insight into the sorts of factors that might have fuelled his apprehension. Intensifying the visual power of the busy scene before him, its author consciously mythologizes the harshness of the East End labour market by likening it to a brutally archaic system of slavery in which the manager's indifference to his employees' hardship replaces the slave-driver's whip, but draws a Biblical parallel that carries a promise of deliverance. In the last of the three extracts, however, the fictional description of Whitechapel Road is diametrically opposed to the previous image and overturns every one of its assumptions. Here is the East End at rest, a thronging, demotic panorama of interracial and inter-religious fraternisation, in which London appears as a world city. It is not a comfortable tableau, for the figure of the British 'loafer' strikes a jarringly ironic note, a self-deluding 'monarch' whose 'air of superiority' encourages the knowing observer to smile with a certain 'superiority' of her own. This is a street scene that turns out, perhaps unsurprisingly, to be edged by violence, for the Englishman – 'looked upon as scum by his own nation' – is ready to forcibly eject the foreigners that pass before his supercilious gaze (13).

The Biblical comparison is taken from Walter Besant's *All Sorts and Conditions of Men* (1882), an enormously popular novel in its day which had a major impact upon urban policy in the East End, whereas the third passage is from a lesser-known work of fiction originally published under the pseudonym "John Law" as *Captain Lobe: A Story of the Salvation*

Army (1889), and republished in 1891 with the more topical title *In Darkest London*. Its author was Margaret Harkness. These two novels were closely connected; indeed, I argue that Harkness was deliberately attempting to write both a riposte and a supplement to *All Sorts and Conditions of Men* that would bring to the fore all of those aspects of the East End that Besant sentimentally repressed. Though deeply flawed, Harkness's work helps us to see that the racial homogeneity so characteristic of Besant's representation of the East End was a key condition for the idealized reconciliation between social classes that underpinned the novel's reformist ending. More than this, Besant's imaginary ending prefigured the construction of a real People's Palace for East Londoners which many hoped would permanently transform the cultural ethos of the entire area. These struggles over the meaning of the East End, and especially of East End *labour*, fed into and helped to define the racial politics in the 1890s as concern over immigration became increasingly vocal. Beginning with Walter Besant's writings and closing with Israel Zangwill's novel *Children of the Ghetto* (1892), this chapter explores competing accounts of the role of Jews and other migrants in the slum fiction and related literature of the period, examining the ways in which these texts interacted with and participated in the political arguments around alien immigration that came to a head with the appointment of a Royal Commission to look into this question in 1902.

If the East End was widely regarded as the most troublesome zone of the capital throughout the Victorian period, the final report of the Royal Commission on Alien Immigration can be read as an attempt to fix upon one particular narrative of the causes of cultural and economic impoverishment in which race and degeneration went hand in hand. Or at least this was the aim of those who had hitched their political reputations to the demand for immigration control. The path that led to the Royal Commission was prepared by exposés like Arnold White's collection of essays, *The Destitute Alien in Great Britain*, which appeared in January 1892, followed by its summer sequel, W.H. Wilkins's *The Alien Invasion*, six months later. Detecting a growing tendency across the civilized world 'towards the crystallization of national life from native elements only', White and his contributors sought to show why it was necessary to expel 'those alien constituents' whose increasing numbers were lowering wages, eroding working conditions, driving down living standards, destroying the vigour of the general population, and spreading disease.[4] Because the nation's economy was a delicate but ordinarily self-regulating balance between capital accumulation and population growth, what the presence

of the alien set in play was not the virtuous cycle assuring the survival of
the fittest, but rather an acceleration of those pathologies of industrial
society glimpsed through the negative contra-Darwinian prism of degeneration theory. The East End served as a touchstone for these fears and,
although there was no real uniformity as to the nature of the threat it
posed, anti-alien polemicists constantly returned to this area of the city as
a source of loaded examples of the damage that the alien caused, couched
in the most lurid language. 'There is need to go and see for oneself what life
is behind Aldgate, in Bethnal Green, and where the Semitic face pushes
out the "flat-nosed" Saxon', wrote the East End clergyman, the Rev. G.S.
Reaney, in his essay on 'The Moral Aspect' of 'the Alien Question.' There,
what one would find was a kind of multifaceted Gresham's Law, according to which 'the language of the pavement' was no longer 'the English
oath or the brutal Cockney jest', for example, but a foreign tongue that
'comes from over the sea' spreading 'street by street in Whitechapel', spoken by a community that was only ever able to learn the vices of the host
society. 'As they come, so they remain', Reaney concluded grimly: 'aliens,
children of another race, amongst us, yet not of us'.[5]

'AN UTTERLY UNKNOWN TOWN'

Arnold White was one of the most energetic of the anti-alien lobbyists in
the 1890s and his particular forte lay in presenting problems of poverty,
race and immigration in the idiom of Victorian social medicine, especially that of eugenics. In focusing upon the metropolis – White's first
book in 1886 was *The Problems of a Great City* – he was able to join the
style of urban social research pioneered by Henry Mayhew and Charles
Booth with contemporary racial ideology. While trying to carve out a
new career for himself in the early 1880s, White had become fascinated by
the East End and developed numerous contacts among philanthropists,
reformers and leaders of the trade union movement, with the result that
he was invited to stand as the Liberal candidate for Mile End in 1886,
albeit without success. As in the case of Margaret Harkness's fiction, one
way of reading the agenda advanced by White and his collaborators is
as a robust and realistic counterweight to the phenomenally successful
mawkishness of *All Sorts and Conditions of Men*, whose sales had reached
a quarter of a million by 1905.[6] For many middle-class readers, Besant's
novel *was* the East End, or at least an East End with which they felt comfortable, and he was frequently credited as the first writer to have put this
name for the district into general circulation. In fact, the phrase was at

least a century older. At the beginning of the 1780s, for example, the term was used to describe the 'narrow, dark and ill-paved' zone from Ratcliff Highway to Limehouse 'inhabited by sailors and other workmen … and by a great part of the Jews'.[7] But it was Besant who popularised the idea of the East End as a city in its own right, 'immense, neglected, [and] forgotten' for too long.[8]

Besant's writings were part of a wider revival of interest in the area. Around the time that *All Sorts and Conditions of Men* was being serialised in the upmarket fiction magazine *Belgravia*, George R. Sims anatomized the plight of London's urban underclass with remarkable journalistic flair in a series of newspaper articles subsequently collected in *How the Poor Live* (1883). These articles seem to have inspired the Rev. Andrew Mearns's equally sensational pamphlet, *The Bitter Cry of Outcast London* (1883). With its call for state intervention to alleviate the condition of 'the abject poor' that Mearns had observed in Ratcliff, Shadwell and also across the river in Bermondsey, it was one of the most influential publications of its kind. Much of the impact of Sims and Mearns's work stemmed from the fact that they saw the East End as part of a pattern of distressed communities across the capital, reflecting the economic downturn and the growing housing crisis after 1880. Both writers saw urban destitution as a breeding ground for socialism and communism, and were determined to bring home to their readers the harsh realities of grinding poverty. In their unsparingly bleak prognoses, moral degradation shaded into political chaos, and Sims, mindful of the example of the Paris Commune of 1871, raised the spectre of a Parisian-style revolutionary mob taking to the streets and threatening the entire social fabric if nothing was done.

Besant's perspective was far more benign. Unlike Mearns and Sims, he turned his inquiring gaze discreetly away from the very worst sights afforded by East London and located its social problems not in the insecurities of the casual labour market and the difficulties of finding steady employment, but in the remorseless rhythms of labour imposed upon those already in work. This was the message of the Biblical tableau cited at the head of this chapter. Besant believed that moral degradation in the East End was due, not to the unbreakable link between economic hardship and criminality identified in *How the Poor Live*, but to the absence of suitably edifying forms of leisure to compensate for the harshness of their working lives. In Ruskinian vein, Besant claimed that what was needed was the creation of a new cultural base that would bridge the divide between his middle-class readers and ordinary East Londoners, a gulf that arose from spiritual, not material, impoverishment.

Besant never really changed his mind about the East End, despite having good reason to do so. In 1901, after having been involved with the
area for more than twenty years, he again described it as 'an aggregate of
nearly two millions of people, living all together in what ought to be a
single city under one rule', with a population size that placed it well ahead
of 'Berlin or Vienna, or St. Petersburg, or Philadelphia' – phrases that
might have been taken directly from his 1882 novel. Notwithstanding
the distinguished company his comparisons invoked, the refrain running
throughout Besant's guidebook-cum-survey – that 'no other city in the
world is like East London' – was predicated upon the continuing failings
of this bleak urban tract of land: its miserable architecture, the lack of
restaurants and hotels, an absence of major newspapers or weekly mag-
azines, the loss of any sense of patriotism or civic pride, matched by a
reluctance to move towards an integrated system of local government that
might bring order out of the jumble of wards and parishes, where everything was 'stamped with the unmistakeable seal of the working class.'
Most saddening of all to a man who had been instrumental in founding
the Society of Authors must have been the realisation that there was 'not a
single bookseller's shop' in this urban centre, 'not a single place in which
the new books of the day, the better literature, the books of which the
world is talking, are displayed and offered for sale'. What distinguished
East London was its drabness, 'the unparalleled magnitude of its mean-
ness and its monotony'.[9] It was a cultural desert wholly lacking in purpose
and imagination.

Although *East London* was the last in a series of books on the capital to
appear before Besant's death in June of that year, it was not quite his final
word on the subject. In 1902, his posthumously published *Autobiography*
looked back over his long association with the East End to see what he
had learned. Once more we see a proletarian metropolis, a 'huge hive of
working bees' functioning entirely at the behest of a utilitarian present
and therefore bereft of any useable past.[10] Besant regarded this deracinated spectacle of ceaseless effort with profound ambivalence. On the one
hand, industriousness and energy were extremely attractive qualities to a
writer who had led a remarkably industrious professional life, combining
a literary career with regular ventures into social and educational reform,
and supporting himself for eighteen years as the chief administrator of
the Palestine Exploration Fund, an organisation that he transformed into
a highly remunerative network of local societies running the length and
breadth of the country. In Besant's eyes, 'monotony' was not the whole
truth about the East End; on closer acquaintance, its mean streets were

full of life, providing an endless source of vitality and passion and hope for the future. On the other hand, no unprejudiced observer could fail to be aware that the inordinate demands made upon these poor unfortunates by their work were completely stultifying, as though all their energy were being compressed into an ill-fitting mould that left little room for more fully human forms of activity. As in *All Sorts and Conditions of Men*, the soullessness of wage slavery means that it *is* slavery.

Besant's own solution to what he regarded as a breakdown in the relationship between social classes took the form of a thought experiment in which two young people who come from opposite ends of society are able to meet and fall in love. Harry Goslett, the orphaned son of a sergeant who died in the Indian Mutiny, has been adopted by a Liberal peer Lord Jocelyn Le Breton and kept in ignorance of his humble East End origins until his twenty-third year. It is Lord Le Breton's 'humorous' fancy that, upon reaching maturity, Harry could return to East London as a cultural emissary, encouraging 'the lowest classes' to better themselves (21). Taking up residence in a boarding house in Stepney Green, Harry meets and falls in love with a dressmaker named Angela Kennedy, a young woman whose poor but respectable exterior also conceals an unexpected personal history. For not only is she one of the first Cambridge woman graduates – appropriately her subject is Political Economy – but she is in reality Angela Messenger, heir to an East End brewing fortune. As she tells a close Cambridge friend early in the novel, this makes her 'a native almost of Whitechapel', and her ambition is to introduce a different political economy into Stepney and Whitechapel and so improve the lot of her fellow East Enders (13). She sets up a dressmakers' cooperative in which the employees work shorter hours, belong to a profit-sharing scheme, and have ample leisure opportunities for lawn tennis, reading, singing and dancing. Angela believes, rather like Lord Le Breton, that once having tasted the fruits of culture, her workers will find that there is no going back, and from these small beginnings the East End will gradually be humanised. The 'Stepney Dressmakers' Association' is the antidote to the East End sweatshop, a spectre barely registered in *All Sorts and Conditions of Men* (but given greater, albeit still somewhat sanitised, substance in Besant's 1886 novel, *Children of Gibeon*).

Although Harry is as ignorant of Angela's true identity as his own, he has a vision of how the East End could be transfigured. What if a family fortune like that of the Messenger family was used to fund a recreational centre devoted to the arts, 'a Palace of Delight' for 'converting this dismal suburb into a home for refined and cultivated people!' (71). Angela secretly takes Harry at his word and at the end of the novel she leads him to a splendid building 'hidden away ... in a corner of vast Stepney' where she reveals to him that his dreams have come true (405). In addition to a fine concert hall, a theatre, a gymnasium, and a reception room in which 'a thousand couples may dance ... without crowding', the Palace boasts a multitude of other rooms – 'billiard rooms, card-rooms, rooms with chess, dominoes, and backgammon tables laid out, smoking-rooms for men alone, tea and coffee rooms, rooms where women could sit by themselves if they pleased, and a room where all kinds of refreshments were to be procured' – while on a second floor were still more, rather smaller rooms, where those patrons of the Palace 'who know already will teach the rest' (411). The novel closes with the marriage of Angela and Harry, their false selves publicly cast aside, and the grand opening of the Palace of Delight to all the people of the East End. In a brief final paragraph we are told that the building 'is in working order now' and that 'Stepney is already transformed' (435). Predictably, the real East End story that was about to begin, only partially anticipated by *All Sorts and Conditions of Men*, proved to be far more complex than Besant had ever envisaged.

THE PALACE OF DELIGHT VERSUS THE PEOPLE'S PALACE

On 14 May 1887, Queen Victoria formally opened the Queen's Hall of the People's Palace in the Mile End Road and, just five years after the publication of his novel, Besant's fiction ceased to be the 'impossible story' announced in the book's subtitle. Of course it would be misleading to lay all the credit for this development at Besant's door. The origins of the People's Palace can be traced back as far as 1841, when insurance industry magnate and Mile End property-owner John Barber Beaumont left a legacy dedicated to promoting the 'Intellectual Improvement and Rational Recreation and Amusement' of people living in East London. Although this scheme had fallen into abeyance by the late 1870s because of administrative problems, new plans were drawn up by the Charity Commissioners in 1882 and, seeking to capitalise on the success of *All Sorts and Conditions of Men*, Sir Edmund Hay Currie (then Chairman of the Beaumont Trustees) sought Besant's support in constructing a real 'Palace of Delight' within the purlieus of Mile End.

Currie was able to orchestrate an impressive roster of backers for the project by securing the patronage of the Royal Family and important sponsors like Lord Rosebery and the Duke of Westminster. The Prince of Wales himself was present at an inaugural fundraising soirée at Bethnal

Green Museum in 1884 where large donations were pledged and, together with Princess Alexandra, laid the foundation stone for the new building in June 1886, with Besant in attendance. However, despite royal involvement, financial difficulties continued to dog the venture and, after a further drive to secure adequate investment, a 'Queen's Fund' was set up in April 1887. In contrast to the imaginary 'Palace of Delights', persuading the West End to put money into the East End was never easy.

At first, the new institution went from strength to strength. In May 1888, a swimming baths was opened, then a technical school the following October, and shortly afterwards a long-awaited gymnasium was finally added. A Winter Garden was built in 1892, stocked with palm trees and exotic plants, and by the turn of the century the Palace's range of activities was quite phenomenal, including oratorios, choral and orchestral performances, organ recitals, chamber concerts, baby shows, dog shows, a variety of annual flower shows, music festivals, Shakespearian plays, and 'humorous entertainments and animated pictures, the latter being about the largest shown in London (the screen 30 feet square) and absolutely up-to-date', according to an official Palace guide, not to mention the Annual Costermongers' Donkey Show held in the gardens.[11] Even this list was by no means exhaustive. In 1891, for example, *The Palace Journal* advertised minstrel shows, Gilbert and Sullivan, a People's Palace Military Band, and popular lectures on such topics as the French Revolution.[12] However, this rich portfolio of attractions failed to satisfy Besant who became deeply disappointed by what he saw. What had gone wrong?

Earlier in this chapter I noted the continuities in Besant's writings on the East End, the repetition of tropes and sentiments indicating that his understanding of the area was relatively fixed. Yet as the fictional 'Palace of Delight' with its vast array of recreational rooms began to be displaced by the story of an actual People's Palace, its dreams and its disasters, a note of disenchantment started to colour Besant's cherished narrative outline. In 1891, looking back over his work as editor of *The People's Palace Journal*, Besant insisted that there was no one among 'the thousands' of young people he encountered who showed 'the least rudimentary indication of any literary power whatever'.[13] It was, he later wrote in his *Autobiography*, 'a dead failure'.[14] Nevertheless, in *East London*, Besant had just about been able to hold that sense of defeat at bay. While there was always 'a lurid picture' of the East End to be painted, he observed, the possibility remained that 'wherever the better things are offered' they would be taken up gladly, 'not by a few here and a few there, but by thousands'.[15] Hope and disappointment are precariously balanced: not one amongst 'thousands' shows any sign of literary talent; 'thousands' are ready and eager to benefit from social improvement. Perhaps all was not quite lost.

Besant's growing disillusionment was symptomatic of a fundamental dilemma. In his *Autobiography*, Besant bemoaned a growing enthusiasm for technical education that was turning the People's Palace into 'a polytechnic and nothing else' and, exaggeration aside, his claim did reflect a real division within the Palace's budget as well as its raison d'être.[16] The showcase exhibitions and entertainments centred upon the Queen's Hall were constantly running up substantial deficits, particularly under Currie's chairmanship, whereas the laboratories and workshops had been funded by the Drapers' Company, whose far more secure sources of income gradually increased its control over the Palace's day-to-day administration. Ultimately this de facto transfer of power only exacerbated the internal split within the institution and did nothing to resolve the issue of how to safeguard the long-term financial viability of the Palace's cultural mission. By the late 1940s, the Palace had finally run out of makeshift solutions and the last traces of Besant's 'impossible story' disappeared under a mountain of debt.

Nevertheless, as Besant's reflections suggest, the Palace's economic worries were also problems of cultural capital. In *East London*, he listed its many successes: 'the thousands of lads who attend the classes at the palace', the 'working-men' that came to the various lecture series – 'the most intelligent and the best educated of the whole population' – who 'crowd round' the speaker 'and beg him to come again', 'the balls given in the Queen's Hall [that] were crowded, and the people … as orderly as could be desired.' But, against this rosy picture, Besant stressed the difficulty of instilling a love of books and reading. The East End 'craftsman … has not yet begun to read books; at present he only reads the paper; [while] his children read the penny dreadfuls' and are only just starting to read books'.[17] Behind these observations lay a fear that moments of cultural consumption might become occasions for collective disorderliness – a misgiving that was commonplace in Palace's early years. In 1887, five months after the building had opened, the *Echo* reported that the Library and Reading Room were 'for the third Sunday opened free to the public' from two in the afternoon until ten at night, with staff volunteering to work without pay. Reassuringly, the several hundred people who came along were entirely well behaved, 'a pleasant relief' after 'the rioting and disturbances which have taken place in the West-end during the last few days'.[18]

The reading public at the People's Palace was evidently smaller than that for other cultural activities – hundreds rather than the thousands that the Queen's Hall could accommodate. According to the *Echo*'s correspondent, the most sought-after books were by popular novelists like Frederick Marryat, Edward Bulwer Lytton, and Charles Lever, whereas Dickens, Scott, Thackeray, and George Eliot followed at some distance behind them, with Carlyle as the leading author of non-fiction. In the early 1890s, the chief librarian noted a buoyant demand for sensation fiction – *Lady Audley's Secret* and *East Lynne* were particular favourites – and there was a keen interest in weekly publications with a strong visual appeal like the *Illustrated London News*, *Punch*, and the *Graphic*.[19] This was a relatively brief episode in the Palace's history – its book-lending services were eclipsed by and absorbed into the Mile End Public Library in 1902 – but it points to a greater appetite for reading than Besant was prepared to credit. Some of the choices of texts and authors reveal the gendering of popular taste – the vogue for Tennyson's poetry among women was specifically mentioned – and it is likely that subtle class fractional distinctions of skill, craft, and experience also shaped East End reading habits. However, as in other parts of Britain, the broad split between popular fiction and "classic" novels suggests that many readers wanted more immediate forms of narrative pleasure than those apparently offered by Scott or Eliot.[20]

Patterns of discrimination in popular reading can also be compared to preferences for other forms of recreation at the People's Palace: on the one hand, there were choral and orchestral societies or chamber concerts, drawing in a middle-class clientele, some from outside the East End proper; at the other extreme, and featured far less prominently, was the demotic carnivalesque world associated with the music hall in which one might find – to quote from a 1903 concert handbill – 'funny facial expressions, comic stand-up, comedienne, dancers and singers, female impersonator, ventriloquist'.[21] When Angela reveals 'the Palace of Delight' to Harry in *All Sorts and Conditions of Men*, she announces that 'this is our own Palace, the club of the working people', as though these attributions were one and the same (411). Besant's deft sleight of hand neatly and unselfconsciously removes any hint of a gulf between middle-class philanthropists and the untutored masses, silently endowing the latter with the same high-minded sense of purpose as their presumed betters. And in so doing, Besant's novel deflected attention from the covert role of a 'Palace of Delight' in providing an antidote to indigenous working-class institutions. Yet, as with their choice of reading matter, 'the working people' did try to make the Palace their own, exploiting the few opportunities that were open to them. Amongst the advertisements for concerts in 1903 was one publicising a benefit on 11 May for an unemployed workman with failing eyesight – a small exercise in mutual aid.

It is therefore revealing that the music hall is conspicuous by its absence in Besant's novel. Early in his friendship with Angela in *All Sorts and Conditions of Men*, Harry mentions in passing a 'theatre and a music hall in Whitechapel Road', only to make it clear that the idea of 'a Palace of Delight' would offer an alternative to these dubious plebeian pleasures (70). In his other writings, Besant was more openly hostile to popular theatres, though he was sometimes prepared to concede that the music hall was a fairly harmless pastime. In *East London*, he alleged that the theatre was 'an institution capable of ruining a whole generation', but regarded the music hall as 'vulgar enough, but not otherwise mischievous'.[22] Attitudes to popular entertainment, and to the music hall in particular, were important markers of divergences in outlook among the Palace's various publics, engaged in a struggle over what the social meaning of a 'club of the working people' might be. Strong opinions were in play from the start, but consistent argument was not. Well before the new building opened, the *Saturday Review* published an unusually forthright column, entitled "How to Spoil the People's Palace", which attacked the trustees for failing to apply for a liquor license and also for planning to allow entry on Sundays.[23]

The contest for symbolic ownership of the People's Palace took many forms and would never be definitively settled, but these cultural wrangles did matter and the stakes were very high. This was especially true when politics entered the very building which Besant had hoped would make it an irrelevancy – a case in point being a packed and well-publicised rally in the Queen's Hall arranged by the British Brothers' League, the largest and best-organised of all the anti-alien groups, on 14 January 1902. As we will see in the next chapter, the BBL was primarily a working-class organisation whose leadership was co-opted by zealous parliamentary lobbyists like the MP for Stepney Major William Evans-Gordon. By associating themselves with the People's Palace the BBL were making a bid for respectability, moving out of the public house and into the concert hall, and it was significant that they were able to claim support for their cause from popular writers like Marie Corelli and Arthur Conan Doyle. Almost two years later, on 10 November 1903, anti-alien campaigners again turned out in force at the Queen's Hall calling for the full implementation of the

Royal Commission's recommendations on immigration.[24] *All Sorts and Conditions of Men* has been described as 'that rare thing, a work of fiction that made something happen', but Besant had little, if any, control over what happened next.[25]

The phrase 'all sorts and conditions of men' was a deliberately loaded title, misleadingly implying a more inclusive view of London's inhabitants than Besant's novel was able to articulate. Besant's urban temple of culture too conveniently dissolves class antagonisms from opposite ends of the socio-economic spectrum by filling the void he believed to lie at the heart of the East End. This model of class harmony and reconciliation is proof of Harry Goslett's assertion that there is a 'brotherhood of humanity' – against Lord Jocelyn's insistence that only 'one sort and one condition' has any lasting importance and that is his own (23). For the novel's social alchemy to succeed, any internal divisions *within* these two major class blocs had to be, not so much denied, as discounted. Although Besant was keen to make his readers aware of the distance between respectable churchgoers and 'the more numerous class of those who cannot call themselves respectable', he tries to show that the most refractory problems can be solved if only they are tackled with spirit and determination. 'Put down the roughs yourselves with a strong hand', Angela tells the radical Dick Coppin firmly. 'Clear out the thieves' dens and the drinking shops' (319). Indeed, in a rhetorical move designed to out-radicalise the radical tradition, a kind of popular sovereignty is presupposed, an age of the common people in which they 'shall reign as never yet king was known to reign' (264).

The image of a working-class community that emerges in *All Sorts and Conditions of Men* has none of the insularity or recalcitrance which was to be a pronounced feature of the London slum fiction that began to displace Besant's vision of class cooperation later in the decade. Despite the novel's title, his portrayal lacks any feel for the cultural heterogeneity of these communities – an attribute that, along with the literary transcoding of working-class dialect, became one of the key signifiers of the otherness of "slumdom" (intriguingly, a word that also seems to date from 1882, the year of the book's publication). In peripheral figures like those of 'Lascar Loo, living on one lung and the memory of past excesses' in Rudyard Kipling's hugely influential short story 'The Record of Bedalia Herodsfoot' (1890), or the 'little dark woman, who looked like a Jewess' seen summoning

Figure 1. 'Israel in Egypt' by Sir Edward Poynter. By permission of the Guildhall Art Gallery, City of London.

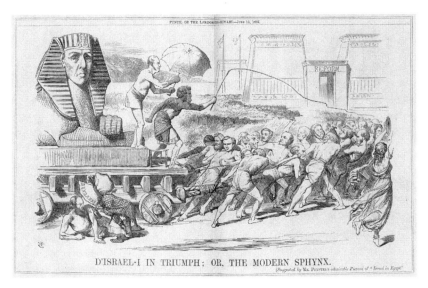

Figure 2. 'D'Israel-i in Triumph; or, The Modern Sphynx' by Sir John Tenniel.
By permission of Cambridge University Library.

up rough justice for the eponymous adulteress in Somerset Maugham's
Liza of Lambeth (1897), we catch glimpses of a complex and diverse street
culture ('Gunnison Street' or 'Vere Street') that defies any crude classifi-
cation into the respectable and the rough.[26] Perhaps the most vibrant, but
also the most troubled, of these street scenes is the description of Saturday
night in the Whitechapel Road in Margaret Harkness's renamed novel *In
Darkest London*, with which this chapter began. A moment's comparison
with the passage from *All Sorts and Conditions of Men* with which it has
been paired shows it to be precisely the type of 'lurid picture' that Besant
sought to avoid. However, the contrast is more than merely suggestive; I
argue that *In Darkest London* should be read in part as a critique of the
politics enshrined in Besant's celebrated bestseller.

When Besant elevates the proletarian rat race by aligning it with Biblical
suffering, the 'famous picture' to which he refers is undoubtedly Sir Edward
Poynter's vast 'Israel in Egypt', an oil painting that made the artist's reputation when it was first exhibited at the Royal Academy in 1867 (see Figure 1).[27]
The verses from the first chapter of *Exodus* that inspired Poynter's canvas also supply an intertext for Besant's own cautionary narrative – 'And
the Egyptians made the children of Israel to serve with rigour. And they
made their lives bitter with hard bondage'. The painting showed scores

of naked and half-naked slaves pulling a massive red granite lion while being lashed by overseers, and, although hugely successful, Poynter's work sparked considerable controversy among critics and visitors to the gallery.[28] The *Art Journal*, for example, thought it portrayed 'a disagreeable, not to say revolting subject', and this frisson of distaste was picked up in allusions to Poynter's work in other cultural sites, allusions that subverted the painting's disquieting overtones for narrowly political ends.[29] In the cartoonist John Tenniel's hands, the Biblical symbols were transposed, with 'D'Israel-i in Triumph; or, The Modern Sphinx' replacing 'Israel in Egypt' (see Figure 2). Here, instead of a granite lion, we find a Judaised sphinx bearing the impassive face of the leading Tory Benjamin Disraeli being pulled by a body of enslaved, half-clad Members of Parliament towards an archway labelled 'Reform' (i.e. the 1867 Reform Act).[30]

In Tenniel's allegory of hauteur and power, the position of the Jew, emphasised by the archaic spelling of Disraeli's name in the caption, has been radically revised: it is now muscular Englishmen who take the place of the captive Israelites, in thrall to a figure who was often caricatured as an alien interloper (or, at best, an 'alien patriot').[31] The qualities of remoteness and unfathomability embodied in the Egyptian statue were commonly ascribed to Disraeli, but here they stand in stark contrast to the feverish and strenuous movement of the other figures in the drawing. The Tory statesman – later dubbed 'the Primrose Sphinx' by Israel Zangwill in his book *Dreamers of the Ghetto* (1898) – sits above the fray, staring into the middle distance, as if these minions (including a clearly unsettled Gladstone) were beneath him, as they quite literally are in this sketch.[32] Blank and unconcerned, Tenniel's representation of Disraeli plays into the conspiratorial stereotype of the Jew as parasite, living off the labour of others. And curiously enough, the description of Poynter's painting given by Besant arguably fits Tenniel's *Punch* cartoon better than the original canvas, because there is no figure in that tableau which corresponds quite so precisely to the 'one in authority ... with eyes terrible from their stony gaze,' the one who cares little 'whether the feeble suffer and perish' as Tenniel's Disraeli (85). It is as though Besant's memory had commingled caricature and Biblical narrative, erasing the differences between them.

Tenniel's foregrounding of contemporary anti-Semitic tropes in his ideological reversal of 'Israel in Egypt' in 1867 brings out what Besant's allusion to Poynter's narrative painting somehow manages to omit: the increasingly prominent role played by the Jewish Question in British politics and society. Besant seems to have been slow to register the changing social character of the Palace's locale, mentioning only the presence of 'honest Germans' amongst the shopkeepers of St George's-in-the-East, the numbers of 'foreign sailors' in the streets of Shadwell, and a small Swedish church congregation (131–133). The Seventh Day Adventists are said to be 'as much separated from their fellows as the Jews', but, oddly, no Jews are identified with the East End (332). Yet, as Todd Endelman has argued, by the middle of the nineteenth century, 'the small but steady trickle of Jews from Eastern Europe' was already putting pressure on community resources in London, where two-thirds of the capital's Jewish population lived in its eastern districts, and similar difficulties were also becoming apparent in Manchester and Birmingham.[33] It might be said in Besant's defence that his novel was composed at the tipping point of the rise in Jewish immigration that began in the pogrom years of 1881–1882, and that this explains why Margaret Harkness's fiction from later in the decade was so preoccupied with migrant Jewish labour. However, in the thirty years or so between 1850 and 1882, the numbers of Jews in London had risen from around 12,000–13,000 to more than 30,000. This figure had doubled by the time the House of Commons Select Committee on Emigration and Immigration reported in 1889.[34]

In fact, Besant failed to find a place for the history of immigration until he wrote *East London* and, unlike his earlier work, that book included a generally optimistic chapter devoted to 'the alien' which gave pride of place to the new Jewish communities. For Besant, Britain's record of tolerance and the advantages of assimilation boded well for the future. And he described the quiet pleasure he had experienced sitting in a synagogue, meditatively listening to the hymns which were said to have been 'sung when Israel went out of Egypt'.[35] Yet by the time *East London* was published, the terms of the debate had shifted. 'Apparently Sir Walter does not see in the invasion of aliens the dangers that others do', a columnist for the *Illustrated London News* told its readers in April 1901, incredulous that Besant did not take immigration to be *the* major issue facing East Londoners.[36] 'That sleepless watch-dog, Mr. Arnold White' was therefore an altogether more reliable guide to the problems facing the nation, according to the *ILN*.[37] An anonymous reviewer of White's *Efficiency and Empire* in May 1901 raised a sceptical eyebrow at its overly polemical style, but thought the argument for 'the increasing degeneracy of our city-bred populations' was well-made. This was a book 'every Englishman should read'.[38]

However, contrary to the impression created by the *ILN*, there were definite limits to Besant's philosemitism. Although he followed Charles Booth in believing that Judaic teaching stimulated the intellect, giving poor Jewish workers a market advantage over 'the dull mind, untrained and simple, of the English craftsman', Besant thought that this competitive edge was confined to the lower rungs of the class structure and that it would be risky if it were not. If Jews were to show signs of achieving greater power and success in the professions than they already had, then their advancement might cause the kinds of fears and resentment that lead to anti-Semitism. 'So long as we can hold our own in the higher fields', Besant argued (the use of the words 'we' and 'our' are again symptomatic), 'there will be no Judenhetze in this country'.[39] In short, it was in everyone's interests that Jews should know their place.

Besant has long been read as an incurable optimist whose sentimentality was closely linked to his notion of social reform. For reform to be feasible, the working classes in the East End had to be culturally impoverished, but not so bereft that cultural uplift was out of the question. The exaggerated premises underpinning Besant's novel are there to ensure that nothing needs to change fundamentally to guarantee that the 'impossible story' was indeed possible. In the final decade of Besant's life, these assumptions were becoming much harder to sustain, as a reading of Margaret Harkness's 1889 novel *In Darkest London* makes plain.

'THE SCUM OF LONDON'

In Harkness's narrative, Besant's imaginary consensus is brutally and summarily dispatched by an unnamed parish doctor ('a modern Prometheus') the loss of whose family and also his lover has driven him to devote his entire professional life to helping the East End poor. Quoting verbatim from Engels's *Condition of the Working Class in England*, he insists that the complacent residents of the West End are too 'bad' or 'mad' to recognise that 'the whole of the East End is starving', pointedly redirecting the charge of degeneracy usually levelled at the poor. The world of letters is complicit in this collective myopia, for 'people prefer to read the pretty stories about the East End made up by Walter Besant'. Not only do these cosy fictions hide the truth; they also generate a false sense of security. The doctor is sure that 'if things go on like this we must have a revolution', a day when the hungry East Enders will march on the West End, killing and destroying whoever and whatever stands in their path. Lest the obvious historical parallel be missed, his prediction is deliberately voiced at the opening of a chapter that takes its title from a visit to 'The Bastile' [sic], the name given to a Whitechapel workhouse (154–155).[40]

Margaret Harkness was an unlikely chronicler of East End misery. The daughter of an Anglican country clergyman, she had initially trained as a nurse at London's Westminster Hospital and later worked at Guy's. But while in London, her horizons widened and, supported by her second cousin, the social reformer Beatrice Potter, she began writing essays and fiction, moving briefly into radical socialist politics in her late twenties and early thirties as she did so. Her new friends included Eleanor Marx, Olive Schreiner, and Friedrich Engels, whose criticism of her first novel, *A City Girl* (1887), guaranteed her a permanent place in the history of Marxist aesthetics. Certainly she knew the East End well. In a letter to her sister Laura in November 1887, Eleanor Marx refers to Harkness as someone who has 'lived there for years' and 'had *never* known anything approaching the distress this year'.[41] The late 1880s saw Harkness at her most politically active: she helped Eleanor Marx to explore the East End in 1888, was for a short time a member of the Social Democratic Federation, and became a strong supporter of the Dock Strike in 1889. This intensely busy period was also notable for a remarkable outburst of creativity during which she published her three best-known London novels, together with a fourth set in the sweatshops of the Manchester garment industry. But in the early 1890s, her political views moved toward the right. She fell out with many of her former friends, including members of the Engels circle, who now saw her as politically suspect. Abandoning the East End for New Zealand and Australia later in the decade, she lived in India during the Edwardian era, writing and publishing intermittently until her death in Italy in 1923.

Engels's celebrated caveat regarding the political limitations of Harkness's realism in *A City Girl* has tended to obscure the specificity of the intervention that she was attempting to make in the late 1880s. But realism was a much debated concept in this period, and other critics read Harkness's work quite differently to Engels. In an odd comparison, the *Whitehall Review* declared the 'pictures' in Harkness's second novel *Out of Work* (1888) to be 'as minute and faithful as are Frith's "Derby Day", "Ramsgate Sands", and "Railway Station"', invoking a widely admired set of paintings in which members of a variety of social classes harmoniously inhabited the same communal space in an unheroic anthropological counterpart to Besant's dreams of cultural reconciliation.[42] The parish doctor's speeches from *In Darkest London* clearly show that this was not the effect that Harkness sought to achieve, but even her choice of subtitles was meant to signal a corrective to rosier views of contemporary society like that of Besant. In sharp contradistinction to the 'impossible story' that was *All Sorts and Conditions of Men*, Harkness deliberately labelled *A City Girl* 'A Realistic Story'. Similarly, in an attempt to demonstrate that there was nothing exceptional about the East End, *A Manchester Shirtmaker* (1890) was tellingly identified as 'A Realistic Story of To-day'. There was never any flirtation with the picturesque, nor any slide into populist wish fulfilment, in her early fiction. Moreover, as Sally Ledger has noted, Harkness's work shows some obvious affinities with Zola's naturalism – an author mentioned by name in *Out of Work* and *In Darkest London* – though her view of the aetiology of urban degeneration tended to focus on the impact of the social environment upon the casual poor, in contrast to the role played by heredity in Zola and his British disciples.[43]

This latter point was picked up by Engels who argued that *A City Girl* was 'not quite realistic enough'. Defining realism not merely as 'truth of detail', but as 'the truth in reproduction of typical characters under typical circumstances', Engels argued that what was missing from Harkness's narrative was any sense of how the 'circumstances which surround them and make them act' enable them to resist their oppressors. The working-class figures in her novel appeared to lack any capacity for self-organisation, relying instead upon forces outside or 'above' their own social milieu to raise them out of their 'torpid misery'. Yet Engels ended his letter with an important qualification, seldom mentioned in accounts of this correspondence. Strictly speaking, he conceded, Harkness was right: 'nowhere in the civilized world are the working people less actively resistant, more passively submitting to fate, more *hébétés* than in the East End of London'.[44] So perhaps the stirring of proletarian militancy belonged to a more revolutionary future and to novels that were still to be written. A year later, Engels described the 1889 Dock Strike as proof that his conjecture had been correct. By being drawn into the modern trade union movement, the 'mass of broken-down humanity' that had been 'drifting towards total ruination' was transformed into a disciplined body that struck terror 'into the hearts of the mighty dock companies'.[45] But what of Harkness? Was her radical fiction waiting for just such a catalyst?

The answer is far from certain, particularly when one remembers the subsequent loss of her socialist beliefs. But there is little in her writing that offers hope of a better future. The fleeting experience of happiness is likely to be interrupted by grim reminders of life's remorseless realities for those at the bottom: by the death of the heroine's illegitimate child and desertion by her lover in *A City Girl*, or the involuntary separation between sweethearts that occurs in *In Darkest London*. And when Harkness focuses upon the downward spiral of trapped individuals, as in *Out of Work* or *A Manchester Shirtmaker*, her heroes and heroines finally succumb to death, suicide, or madness. Politically, Harkness's writing often acts as an irritant or a warning as much as an insider's perspective on slumdom, and already at this stage in her work the despair in her fiction sometimes seems to evoke scepticism about socialist politics rather than commitment. At their most vivid and dramatic, her novels echo with clashing voices, contending positions, urgent pleas, and denunciations that the narrative can barely contain. In these moments, Harkness's work is unrestrainedly dialogic, in perhaps the strongest sense of this term, deliberately flouting realist conventions and, when necessary, introducing anomalous characters who 'do not exist in East London', as a didactic footnote insists in *In Darkest London* (82). Engels commended Harkness for avoiding the trap of the *Tendenzroman*, for choosing not to write what he called 'a point-blank socialist novel'. But the noisy heteroglossia of her fiction raises many more questions than it can answer.

Not that Harkness's novels lack conviction. In the opening to *Out of Work*, for example, the Queen's Golden Jubilee visit to the East End is described by an authoritative narrative voice that is unwavering in its concern to state the truth that the official version of events tries to cover over. The reporters at the celebrations are depicted as busily 'concocting stories of the royal progress' that will make no mention of 'the hisses which the denizens of the slums had mingled with faint applause as Her Majesty neared her destination'. There will be no 'hint that the crowd about the Palace of Delight had had a sullen, ugly look which may a year or so hence prove dangerous'.[46] The hisses from the crowd in fact prefigure the hisses directed against the police and soldiers in the Trafalgar Square unemployment riots of 1887, which form the brutal climax of the novel and are likened to 'a nightmare, after reading a chapter of Carlyle's "French Revolution"' (favourite reading at the People's Palace Library).[47] Nevertheless, in Harkness's writing the bloody intransigence of class politics is always haunted by other needs, different struggles, alternative narratives that agitate to make themselves heard and sometimes occur only in distorted form.

Thus her portrayal of the undifferentiated proto- (or, perhaps, sub-) revolutionary East End crowd in *Out of Work* needs to be juxtaposed with the representation of Whitechapel Road on Saturday night in her next novel, *In Darkest London*, which in turn offers a further comment on Besant's fictional world. In *All Sorts and Conditions of Men*, it is only in the West End that the inhabitants are able to lounge or stroll 'as if they had nothing to do' and 'forced labour is pushed into the background'; in East London, the careless figure of the *flâneur* is quite absent (85). In its apparently relaxed familiarity, Harkness's set piece brings something of the ease of the West End to Besant's frenetic East End streets – indeed, it is tempting to read its vernacular cosmopolitanism as an inventory of everything and everyone that Besant omits. But there is more going on here than such a reading would recognise.

Consider the genealogy of the topical allusions in Harkness's titles. In the original 1889 version, *Captain Lobe* was taken from the name of a Salvation Army officer carried over from *A City Girl*. His movements back and forth across the East End unify the disparate scenes in what would otherwise be a largely episodic novel: hence the subtitle 'A Story of the Salvation Army'. However, when *Captain Lobe* was republished in 1891 in 'a new and popular edition', as *In Darkest London*, the aim was to capitalise on the Salvation Army device by invoking General William Booth's evangelising tract from the previous year *In Darkest England and the Way Out* and clinching the connection by commissioning Booth to write a short introduction to the novel. Booth's title was itself a play upon another success story from 1890, Sir Henry M. Stanley's *In Darkest Africa*, which had been a follow-up to Stanley's bestselling travelogue *Through the Dark Continent* from 1878. In a question from *In Darkest England*, General Booth laid bare the rhetoric of equivalences that had emerged and hardened during the 1880s: 'May we not find a parallel at our own doors, and discover within a stone's throw of our cathedrals and palaces similar horrors to those which Stanley had found existing in the great Equatorial forest?[48] No answer was necessary, and Booth's formula soon became ubiquitous. So, in the same year that Harkness's novel was repackaged, the Rev. A. Osborne Jay, vicar of Holy Trinity in Shoreditch and a powerful advocate of slum clearance, published his *Life in Darkest London*, amalgamating the cultural idioms of General Booth and George Sims.

As John Marriott has shown, the rediscovery of the metropolitan poor in this period took a variety of forms, without any unitary rationale or overarching interpretation.[49] But the idea that the East End represented an urban 'dark continent' circulated widely in the early 1890s. At one point in her novel, Harkness maps this idea onto the contrast between day and night. In the daytime, 'the worst London districts ... put on a veneer of civilization; but at night the slummers show themselves to be worse than savages' – an observation supported by reference to Professor Huxley's dictum 'that it is better to be born a savage in some heathen land than a slummer in Christian England' (196).[50] Yet her description of Saturday night in Whitechapel complicates this judgement by installing a different set of oppositions. The efflorescence of 'nationalities' withers very quickly as Hottentot, Algerian, Indian, and Polish Jew are resolved into the composite term 'foreigners', and the perspective inscribed in the passage, though heavily ironised, becomes that of the imperious East End layabout – 'monarch of all he surveys, lord of the premises', yet 'looked upon as scum by his own nation'. This self-aggrandising figure in 'a tattered cap' regards himself as British to the core and is ready 'to kick the foreigner back to "his own dear native land" if only Government would believe in "English for the English" and give all foreigners "notice"' (13).

The omniscient narrator is careful to generalise the type of the 'loafer' into that of 'the parasite', noting that this is a social individual who can be found in West End clubs as much as in East End pubs. However, like the later suggestion that 'the worst part of this slum belongs to the Prime Minister', this passing observation remains unexplored (196). Of far greater significance is the treatment of xenophobia as a peculiarly working-class phenomenon, a theme that also appears in the novel's pred-ecessor, *Out of Work*, where hatred of the 'foreigner' is a constant refrain, doubling as invective and explanation. '"Why should they come here, I'd like to know?"' demands one 'rosy-cheeked little woman'. '"Why should all them foreigners come here to take food out of our mouths, and live on victuals we wouldn't give to pigs?"' she continues, indignant that London is now 'just like a foreign city'. Her outburst is no isolated cry: we are told that the 'chiefly political' songs at the music hall like "England for the English, and Heaven for us All" take up the same chorus, orches-trating the desire 'to "chuck" the foreigner back to "his own dear native land"' while the audience 'wave their handkerchiefs' and call for encore upon encore. And when *Out of Work*'s central character, the unemployed carpenter Jos Coney, returns to his village having failed to find work in London, he overhears the same complaint in his local pub: '"The country's going to the dogs along of these foreigners. I'd like to weed 'em out."'[51]

In *Out of Work*, xenophobia has no single target and can as readily embrace the royal family as the foreign worker. The prime candidate for such bigotry, the figure of the Jew, is presented as a peripheral figure, divided into the all but assimilated and the *outré*: on the one side, the mild and always sympathetic barber and dentist Uncle Cohen who lives in a local boarding house and is so unassuming that he is imagined to be a potential convert; and on the other, the 'little Jewess' in the adjacent gin-shop, 'holding a fowl in her arm, which would by-and-by be killed in Hebrew fashion'. At only one point do these stereotypes begin to coalesce with the discourse of the foreigner to produce a focussed anti-Semitism, when Jos Coney's sweetheart casually informs her Methodist class-leader that the unwanted carpenter 'thinks Jews and foreigners do jobs so cheap he hasn't a chance'.[52]

But within *In Darkest London* the Jew has become the archetypal foreigner and any real distinction in usage has collapsed. Among the most class-conscious and directly political characters in the novel is the 'labour-mistress' or forewoman of a sweet factory named Jane Hardy who 'belong[s] to a circulating-library' and believes in 'combination, fighting the upper classes, and justice' (92). Yet she is adamant that she would 'never take on a Jewess. The East End is just overrun with foreign people, and that makes matters worse for us English' (95). Moreover, her prejudices are given the stamp of authenticity by being presented as the observations of a knowledgeable eyewitness. Jane attests that she has travelled 'to Hamburg in a sailing vessel', returning in a ship that 'was full of Polish Jews and Russian beggars, with bundles of rags for luggage and enough babies to fill a cabin', utterly 'miserable', 'hungry and sea-sick' (95). No one wants these unfortunate men and women, 'the scum of Europe', as Jane later calls them (219). At first their destitute condition prevents them from landing; then, once they are off the ship, the captain refuses to have them back on board and they are taken away by a policeman. After a night in the cells, '"The Jewish Board of Guardians will fetch'em," says he, "and some sweater will take 'em into his shop to undersell us English"' (96). The policeman's words and Jane's vituperative commentary are seamlessly fused together in the telling of her story.

Jane Hardy's anti-Semitism is particularly disturbing because it is always knitted into her insight into social conditions, a symptom of the frustration she expresses that is articulated as a set of facts. Her voice is that of a compromised socialist who believes that 'the social revolution' is 'no nearer than when I first began to study these questions', and at the end of the novel she is contemplating leaving England and becoming a migrant (220). A blunt Northern autodidact, she is presented as an admirable woman and also as a social type that 'one comes across' regularly (one of a number of signs that Harkness is trying to heed Engels' earlier criticisms), 'full of energy, pioneers of their sex in questions connected with female labour', and unwilling to be treated differently from men (221). But, like 'the modern Prometheus', her tough-mindedness comes at a price. She asserts on more than one occasion that it would be better for the 'girl babies' of the poor to be strangled at birth, as she insists they are in China, including her infant self in this Swiftian programme of eugenics. At the same time she is a pragmatist, a spinster who puts her 'principles in [her] pocket' in order to support her aged mother, and a disciplinarian who has the tight lips of a repressed hysteric: while the sight of a mouse would bring on a fit, she is 'the sort of woman ... that buries her dead tearless' (92–94). If the Promethean doctor can describe himself as a victim of 'the disease of caring', Jane Hardy also stands for a socialism that carries the stigmata of its pathological origins. And, like the Salvation Army, its closest competitor for the hearts and minds of the East End slummers, socialism tends to appear as a limited and noticeably deformed doctrine striving for something better. What makes *In Darkest London* so bleak, however, is the constantly nagging doubt that the East End could ever produce the human resources needed to create a just and decent society. Every scenario – the workhouse, the 'penny gaff', the sweet factory, the police court – reveals that its people have adapted themselves to the very conditions that are destroying them, conditions they are powerless to surmount or improve. Socialism is often little more than a distressed cry of pain.

In Darkest London ends with a scene at Tilbury Docks where hundreds of young women are emigrating to Australia, much to the anger of Jane Hardy who remonstrates with them for letting in 'the scum of Europe' (219). The word 'anti-Semitism' does not explicitly appear in the text and had in fact had only come into the English language in the early 1880s, but the figure of the Jew goes to the heart of *In Darkest London*'s radical scepticism about the future. The open sense of hostility towards Jews takes two forms in Harkness's novel. Initially, it is a cultural reflex, belonging to the history of jingoistic sentiments that are paraded in the music hall and the public house. But later, from the lips of Jane Hardy, anti-Semitic prejudice becomes more self-conscious and is aligned with an educated discourse, or at least with a subject who has been diligently pursuing an education: hatred of Jews is linked to discipline and self-denial, as though it were somehow earned, the fruit of bitter experience. This sense of a hard-won anti-Semitism is exceptionally pernicious, in part because it legitimises itself in terms of a movement across the line that divides the respectable from the rough, a line that plays a central role, as we saw in the work of Walter Besant, in sustaining the project of cultural uplift. Here is an anti-Semitism that is ready to leave the street corner for the political platform, to make its stand as something other than vulgar prejudice.

If there is a curious indeterminacy about *In Darkest London*'s anti-Semitic prejudices, it is not because their warped judgements resist correction or defy interrogation. Rather, the problem lies in the uncertain positioning of the reader. In the case of 'the East End loafer', it is made abundantly clear that his bigotry is inseparable from his self-delusion and that his beliefs are unworthy of serious consideration. With Jane Hardy, the question becomes: how serious can she be? When she talks of infanticide, of unsentimentally slaughtering 'the girl babies' at birth, she makes out that such a fate would be 'so good for 'em and so bad for the capitalist', 'shaking her fist' in conclusion, so that this tirade involves her in deliberately striking a pose (93). Is her anti-Semitism a pose of a similar kind, a method of psychically distancing herself from what she regards as the useless kind-heartedness of the young factory girls whom she supervises, a way of suppressing emotions that she cannot allow herself to feel? We cannot be sure. And because Jane's socialism is set off against the dedication of the Salvation Army, men and women whose work she respects despite having no religious sympathies of her own, it is possible that Christian self-sacrifice is intended as the necessary practical supplement to a heartless politics. Crude and underdeveloped, the depiction of Judaeophobia in Harkness's *In Darkest London* fails to provide the seeds of a critical microhistory of what Hannah Arendt once called 'leftist anti-Semitism'; instead, it remains a side narrative of emotional exhaustion that inconclusively flickers in and out of focus.[53]

THE ALIEN SWEATER

Harkness's later writings bear witness to the strains associated with her increasingly jaundiced vision of working-class politics. By 1905, when *George Eastmont: Wanderer* – her retrospective of the 1889 Dock Strike – appeared, she was ready to have her eponymous hero consider quitting the city for a rural socialist utopia in the shape of an Owenite farming community. Well before that stage had been reached, however, any last vestige of a distinction between the sentiments voiced by the narrator and those identified with her characters was becoming hopelessly confused. This was not a new problem in Harkness's work and is perhaps most apparent in her fourth novel, *A Manchester Shirtmaker* (1890), which treats the city it names 'Cottonopolis' as a straightforward extension of London's East End, underwriting this effect through the disingenuous claim that the local dialect 'has been translated into English'.[54] In this book, anti-Semitism also looms large, but now it has ceased to be a characterological quirk and has become instead an integral component of the main plot. Harkness resumed her attack on the practice of 'sweating', the hyper-exploitation of labour associated with a subcontractor or middleman – originally taken up in *A City Girl* and a major concern among social reformers and anti-immigrant lobbyists in the 1880s – but here she condenses its evils into a single fantasmatic individual: 'the miserable Jew', Joseph Cohen.

Cowardly, tyrannical, and rapacious, Cohen is the archetypal parasite who fears for his life when his workers gleefully crowd round him waving their scissors and knives and crying '"Sweater! Sweater!"' (58–60). Yet he thinks nothing of confiscating the money that Mary Dillon, a widowed seamstress, has had to pay him for the cloth she must use, or of refusing to pay for the work she has done – an act which finally robs her of her livelihood as an outworker by forcing her to pawn her sewing machine. Once her money has run out, Mary is unable to feed her baby or herself and in the end is driven to murder her own child. Weak from hunger and utterly destitute, Mary repeatedly imagines that she is being haunted by Cohen's grasping presence. In her delirium she fantasises that he is wrenching her wedding ring from her finger, though she has, of course, already had to pawn it. And on the morning after she killed her baby, she seems to see 'the Sweater' again, this time 'followed by a crowd of angry women' (109). Cohen's grotesqueness is heightened by his calculated use of patois – written out phonetically, unlike the other 'translated' accents – rendering him thoroughly alien. A Mancunian by birth and proficient in 'the Lancashire dialect', he has resisted assimilation by electing to speak 'a sort of heathenish gibberish, because he thought that it impressed his hearers with a sense of his importance as an employer of labour' (70). One chapter takes his intransigent words as its title: "No Vork vithout Monish!" As with the 'middle-aged Jewess' who sides with Cohen when the heroine appeals to her for help, standing with hands on hips and showing 'two rows of white teeth in absolute silence', Jewishness is consistently figured as persecutory, aggressive, unfeeling, the embodiment of capitalism at its worst (77–78). It is as if *A Manchester Shirtmaker* were being narrated by Jane Hardy on a return visit to the North.

'Sweating' could scarcely have been more topical in 1890, for in April of that year the Final Report of the Select Committee of the House of Lords on the Sweating System was published. This body had been in session since March 1888, following a controversy that had arisen in the wake of a Report to the Board of Trade in September 1887 on sweating in London's East End. Drafted by John Burnett, a former trade unionist who was the Board's first Labour Correspondent, this analysis had aroused considerable interest, not least among anti-alien activists. Arnold White, together with Lord Dunraven, had co-founded the Society for the Suppression of the Immigration of Destitute Aliens in 1886 and on 15 December 1887, he led a deputation to the Home Secretary in order to reinforce the connection that Burnett had made between foreign immigration and the trade in sweated labour. So it was highly significant that, when the Lords Select Committee began to sit, Dunraven was appointed as its chair. In fact, official and semi-official investigations into the practice of sweating were plentiful in this period. Burnett had also looked into sweating in Leeds in 1887, as had the medical journal the *Lancet* in April and June 1888 (with a study of tailors in Manchester in the April report), and, in addition to a number of essays in prominent periodicals like the *National Review* and the *Fortnightly Review*, there had been several inquiries of a more journalistic nature, such as the two volumes put out under the auspices of the *British Weekly* in 1889, entitled *Toilers in London*, which Margaret Harkness had been involved in editing.

As Norman Feltes has argued, the Lords Select Committee report was a defining moment in the history of sweating because, much to the chagrin of White and others, it reversed the conventional wisdom on the subject.[55] Sweating, as Beatrice Potter told the Committee in her evidence, was not a 'system' at all; it was simply labour carried out in small workshops or at home, where control over working conditions was either weak or nonexistent. Much energy had been expended by the Committee in seeking to define the peculiarities of sweating – almost an obsession with Dunraven – but in the end there had been a coup and the chairman had found his initial report brushed aside. Placed in an impossible position, Dunraven was effectively suspended from the committee while a new report was prepared and the chair passed to Lord Derby. The main casualty was Dunraven's endeavour to gain an official endorsement of his claim that sweating was indissolubly linked to low-cost immigrant labour. When the heavily revised report finally appeared, it was clear that Potter's views had won the day – not altogether surprisingly, given that, as her later account of this episode in *My Apprenticeship* (1926) reveals, she worked hard behind the scenes to influence the views of Dunraven's opponents. Reviewing the report's achievements, Potter (now Beatrice Webb) saw her contribution as twofold: first, employers were made legally responsible for the conditions under which home workers laboured; and second, that the 'idea of the sub-contractor, the middleman, the alien or the Jew being the "cause" of sweating' was completely discredited and consequently 'disappeared'.[56] In an address to the Co-operative Congress in 1892 (quoted extensively in *My Apprenticeship*), Potter told the meeting that before she had 'studied the facts of East London industries for myself I really believed this horrible creature existed'. But her investigations showed that 'either he was a myth, or that the times had been too hard for him, and that he had been squeezed out of existence by some bigger monster', a monster which was 'in fact, the whole nation', insofar as everyone was now enmeshed in the social relations of capital. In those predominantly Jewish areas of manufacture like 'the coat trade' or 'the low-class boot trade', where middlemen could still be said to exist, Potter found that these individuals 'work as hard, if not harder than their sweated hands' and often 'earn less than the machinists or pressers to whom they pay wages'.[57]

From Potter's perspective, the figure of 'the miserable Jew' found in Harkness's work represented a rearguard attempt to resurrect and substantiate the mythological creature that history and reason were threatening with extinction. But Harkness did more than perpetuate a simple category-error: her entire narrative lent support to Lord Dunraven's Tory paternalist vision in which it was the political duty of the great and the good to protect the British working class against the depredations of the alien. In *A Manchester Shirtmaker*, there is no one who will take the side of the heroine: the garment workers are a sadistic but ultimately ineffectual mob while, on the other side, a philanthropist idly complains of the problems caused when a 'hereditary class of vagabonds' is allowed to breed, two doctors discuss social philosophy and their careers while the heroine dies, and the only assistance she receives from a local millionaire is the silk handkerchief which she uses to take her own life (144). As elsewhere in Harkness's fiction, the novel hollows out a space for political agency and reflection, but leaves it vacant. Beatrice Potter came to think of Harkness as politically unprincipled, noting in her diary that her cousin Margaret lacked 'the masculine standard of honour and integrity' so essential to a campaigning woman in the public sphere.[58] Harkness's attachment to the myth of the sweater helps to explain why these two women writers, who had once shared similar socialist beliefs, found themselves increasingly at odds with each other at the beginning of the 1890s.

Contrary to Potter's claims, the Select Committee's final report on sweating did not banish 'the sweater' from political discourse, least of all in its alien or Jewish incarnations. Sweating continued to play a vital part in the bestiary of the anti-immigration lobby until well into the Edwardian era. Barely two years after the Lords had published their report, for example, W.H. Wilkins's *The Alien Invasion* referred to the sweater as 'the bloated human spider, who ... sucks the life-blood of his victims', appropriately pictured 'in the pages of *Punch* as a gorgeously-apparelled, champagne-drinking, cigar-smoking Hebrew', laughing as he rakes in his gold.[59] Indeed, the figure of the alien sweater returned with a vengeance in the proceedings of the 1902–1903 Royal Commission on Alien Immigration. "Mr B", whose evidence was cited earlier, had been one of the original witnesses before the House of Lords Committee in 1890 and now thought the entire proceedings had been a waste of his time. 'The result,' he declared curtly, 'was nothing'. There was no improvement in the conditions of the boot and shoe workers until they left their home-based 'sweating dens', joined forces with their fellow English trade unionists, and successfully fought for 'indoor workshops' and union rates of pay. In a series of tense exchanges with Major Evans-Gordon (who was clearly annoyed at having an ally publicly rubbished), "Mr B" singled out Arnold White's role in orchestrating testimony before the House of Lords Committee as particularly blameworthy, because he had brought Jewish workers to give evidence immediately after their shifts, when they 'had been sweated all night' and were still 'dirty', and so had made them appear as less respectable witnesses than they might otherwise have been.[60] In fact, "Mr B"'s resentment was only the tip of the iceberg. The House of Lords Committee had been a personal disaster for White and had severely dented both his reputation and his wallet. Carried away by the rectitude of his cause, White had descended into abusive and libellous statements, based upon grossly misleading information that he had failed to check, and the considerable sums of money that he spent in searching out evidence had been frittered away – a lesson White never forgot.

Despite the support it was able to muster, the first phase of anti-alien agitation of the 1890s must be judged a failure. Its leaders, Lord Dunraven and Arnold White, were effectively blocked from achieving their aims in the House of Lords Select Committee on the Sweating System, and a parallel committee in the Commons to look at immigration fared no better, again in no small measure because of White's ineptitude. In May 1891, desperate to repair the damage to their cause and eager to take advantage of worsening economic conditions, Dunraven and White launched a new pressure group, The Association for Preventing the Immigration of Destitute Aliens. This organisation was a significant improvement on its predecessor. By drawing on the support of public figures as various as the Bishop of Bedford and the dockworkers' leader Ben Tillett, Dunraven and White ensured that it received substantial press coverage. Yet in spite of its high profile, the APIDA failed to make the sorts of inroads into the East End that would have given it a popular base, primarily because its leaders never fully appreciated the complexity of local political conditions. Contrary to its popular image, the East End in the 1880s and 1890s was far from being a zone of unrelieved poverty and casual employment and its patterns of political affiliation were likewise extremely variable.[61] As Marc Brodie has observed, between 1885 and 1914, 'only four of the eleven constituencies within the East End … voted Conservative in any consistent way' and of these, Mile End and Stepney 'were overwhelmingly the wealthiest in the area'.[62]

At the same time, other images of East End life were beginning to find an audience. In 1892, Israel Zangwill published *Children of the Ghetto*, creating the first Anglo-Jewish bestseller, and was promoted as 'the Jewish Dickens'. Commissioned by the Jewish Publication Society of America to write a Jewish version of another bestseller, Mrs. Humphrey Ward's celebrated crisis of faith novel *Robert Elsmere* (1888), Zangwill was determined that his book would be a very different kind of narrative, a fictionalised version of the Jewish East End over several generations, contrasting the immigrant experience with that of their children and grandchildren in the 1880s, and with the affluent world of Jewish West London. While drawing on his own early life in Whitechapel (with the character Esther Ansell as a kind of writerly alter ego), Zangwill also reworked several topical events including the furore surrounding the publication of Amy Levy's novel *Reuben Sachs* in 1888 and the East End tailors' strike in 1889. When the proto-Zionist Holy Land League assembles or the militant workers meet, Zangwill's keen eye for detail and his gift for social comedy provide a measure of the omissions in *Daniel Deronda's* portrait of Jewish life and show much had changed. And though the speeches heard at such gatherings hark back to the debate at the *Hand and Banner*, they contain formulations that have no place in Eliot's novel. Here 'the poet of patriotism and Palestine' can confidently proclaim that 'Socialism is Judaism and Judaism is Socialism' – a sign of the 'Messiah-times' to come.[63]

In a phrase dating back to the fifteenth century, the book's subtitle defined *Children of the Ghetto* as 'a study of a peculiar people', a distinctive, singular, and above all *different* people that had been chosen by God – for, by embracing what is odd or queer as well as special, the word 'peculiar' carries something of the ambivalence associated with 'the uncanny' and is a similarly unstable term. Moreover, in calling his novel 'a study', Zangwill was also associating his thronging narrative with the sociological empiricism typified by Charles Booth's voluminous *Life and Labour of the People in London*. More radically, Zangwill's corrective to hostile or indifferent representations of the Jew should be seen as an example of what James Buzard has usefully identified as 'metropolitan autoethnography', a species of writing that is 'insistently positioned as the outsideness of a *particular* inside', presenting the inner life of a community to a wider public through the interrogatory resources of narrative fiction.[64] Buzard's gloss brings out Zangwill's importance as a mediator of Jewishness within late-nineteenth-century British culture, a point that is reinforced by the way in which his novel tacks between East End and West End settings.

But it is the East End that is privileged in *Children of the Ghetto*: its soup kitchens, jokes, rituals, entertainments, and internal wrangles. And where *Robert Elsmere* had focussed upon a questioning of religious belief through the doubts of a single, agonised individual, the episodic structure of Zangwill's novel follows the ethical quandaries faced by a multitude of characters within the ghetto as they struggle to make their lives in a rapidly changing world. Zangwill was to write of the ghetto's 'slow breaking-up in our own day' and it is this decline, together with the absence of any coherent substitute for the beliefs and solidarities which were irretrievably being lost, that gives the Jewish East End its poignancy.[65] In Zangwill's vision, as expressed in the novel's opening 'Proem', the ghetto is already being 'abandoned' as the old communal ties extending between rich and poor are being replaced by the harsher class divisions of the 'larger, freer, stranger' society into which Jews are increasingly passing. 'In the early days of the nineteenth century, all Israel were one': but no longer (62). In Zangwill's overblown Disraeliesque cadences, 'respectability crept on to freeze the blood of the Orient with its frigid finger, and to blur the vivid tints of the East into the uniform grey of English middle-class life' (67).

Instructively, the novel's second chapter is devoted to 'The Sweater', introducing the reader to Bear Belcovitch (formerly Kosminski), a Polish immigrant who is as many-sided as 'The Pauper Alien' who works for him: Esther Ansell's extraordinarily versatile father Moses, who is introduced more fully under this stereotyped heading a little later. Although in the 'Parliamentary Blue Books, English newspapers, and the Berner Street Socialistic Club', Bear Belcovitch is identified as a sweater, he cuts a very different figure from the man with 'a protuberant paunch and a greasy smile' that the 'the comic papers' like to imagine. He is 'a tall, harsh-looking man of fifty, with grizzled hair', whose appearance belies the 'God-fearing, industrious, and even philanthropic citizen' within, a pillar of his community. Belcovitch can be curiously sentimental as well as austere – in celebration of his daughter Fanny's betrothal he hands over a shilling (in farthings) to a recently arrived immigrant 'greener' – and while he abhors 'waste', his family can be certain that he will not miss his soup, when they plan to give it to the desperately poor Ansell family upstairs without telling him (84–85).

Belcovitch has known better days. In Poland he had owned 'a brass wash-hand basin, a copper saucepan, silver spoons, a silver consecration beaker, and a cupboard with glass doors', whereas in England he settles for 'the simplest and shabbiest' décor and knows how to infuse and re-infuse a quarter of a pound of coffee to make it last a week (84). His generosity is in part a token of his earlier life when he made it his habit to lend money to Polish officers hard-pressed at cards, and now he never hesitates to provide loans to poorer Jews in the ghetto, loans that are hardly ever repaid. As an agent of exploitation, Bear Belcovitch is a most ambiguous taskmaster. He is the workers' enemy during the strike, but after the labour leader Simon Wolf has been marginalised and his party has dropped him, following the intervention of the local Jewish MP (the stockbroker Gideon, said to be modelled on Whitechapel's Sir Samuel Montagu), it is Belcovitch who takes Wolf back into his business and supports him, despite a lifelong ban on employing union labour. When Esther last visits the Belcovitch household towards the end of the novel, the family has moved to a different floor of the house they occupied, but is otherwise unaltered.

Although he believed that the ghetto was dwindling, Zangwill gave scant attention to the relations between Jews and non-Jews or of the difficulties of being accepted as an English Jew – matters which he took up in some of his later stories, like 'Anglicization'. When the aspiring, Oxford-educated editor Raphael Leon tells his hostess at a West End dinner party, 'There are thousands of families in the East End now among whom English is read if not written', the context of their exchange might lull the reader into thinking that the ghetto *was* the East End, give or take a few 'Christian roughs' (309, 349). In fact, East London would have been better described as 'a quilt of contrasts', or extending the analogy, 'a patchwork quilt of settlements with interwoven subcultures'.[66] And to recognise this plurality is also to raise the question of who 'the people' that might be the true East End constituency of the People's Palace actually were. As we have seen, Walter Besant and Margaret Harkness gave very different answers to this question; the British Brothers' League gave another.

"Mr B"'s testimony reminds us that the organisation of industrial action was one instance where inter-communal rivalries were suspended and a new sense of popular solidarity flickered into a life – an insight that is lost in the version of the tailors' strike recounted in *Children of the Ghetto*. Despite these *lacunae*, Zangwill's own career – and especially the immense success enjoyed by *Children of the Ghetto* – was a powerful exemplar of the conversation between others that might be said to be autoethnography's fundamental raison d'être. It would doubtless be too much to claim, as did Zangwill's brother Louis in a letter to the *Jewish Chronicle* in May 1894, that the Conservatives jettisoned their planned Aliens Bill 'under the direct influence of his writings.' Nevertheless, Zangwill's voice was not without effect. When he embarked on a nationwide lecture tour of Britain in the mid-1890s (including the People's Palace), not only could he record houses of 3,000 or so, but the audiences that came to hear him were often 'mainly Gentile'.[67] Yet in bringing the ghetto out of London's East End and into the wider political arena, Zangwill was speaking out as well as speaking to his readers. The forces that Zangwill was speaking *against* form the topic of the next chapter.

CHAPTER 3

Counterpublics of anti-Semitism

In their different ways, Walter Besant, Margaret Harkness, and Israel Zangwill were writers searching for a form of communal solidarity that would address the social and political problems posed by the East End. Ultimately, it eluded them. This difficulty was most marked in Margaret Harkness's writing from the late 1880s, in which her unflinching diagnosis of the need for a socialist panacea extended to an explanation of why such a solution would continue to be unavailable. In areas like Whitechapel, Stepney, or Hoxton, the conditions of industrial labour had destabilised everyday life, creating a social milieu whose population was constantly in flux, struggling to find work, and forced to move on when employment prospects worsened. *Out of Work* and *In Darkest London* each end with scenes of outward migration, but in the latter there is a strong sense of displacement as the 'strong, healthy girls' who sail for the colonies pass immigrant ships arriving daily from Hamburg (219). There is none of the poignancy of Esther Ansell's departure for the New World in Zangwill's *Children of the Ghetto*, only a loud outburst of disgust from the labour-mistress Jane Hardy. This angry loathing, utterly transfixed by the object of its hatred, is not given the name of 'anti-Semitism' here, but the casual, mundane occasions of its expression conform to Adorno's epigrammatic definition of the term as 'the rumour about the Jews', a matter of highly charged stories and fictions that are never quite out of circulation.[1]

The 1905 Aliens Act would have been inconceivable without the complex historical shift through which looser terms like 'Judaeophobia' or 'Jew-baiting' came to be subsumed under the rubric of 'anti-Semitism'. But this was less because of any simple correlation between the modern rise of anti-Semitism and the push to restrict immigration; rather, anti-Semitism was part of a wide-ranging and deeply contested racial imaginary, with its own distinctive debates, polemics, idioms, and practices which formed a cultural matrix that allowed the possibility of anti-alien legislation to become thinkable. In this chapter, I attempt to give substance to this claim by examining some of the contradictory attempts at incorporating the notion of anti-Semitism into British social and political life, moves that intersected with changes in the representation of Jews at a number of important cultural sites during the fin-de-siècle. Imported from Continental Europe, the term was easily disparaged, and this created a powerful vested interest in finessing its meaning so as to make it acceptable to established opinion – a strategy found in grass-roots movements like the British Brothers' League and across the Radical Right more generally. Adorno's aphorism captures the ordinariness of anti-Semitism, but it fails to capture the organizational ambitions that were there from the beginning: more than a rumour, anti-Semitism was always also a slogan and a perverse badge of honour.

ANTI-SEMITISM'S UNRULY INFANCY

In the 1880s, 'anti-Semitism' was a new word to English ears, transplanted from Germany where it was introduced by Wilhelm Marr, a socialist journalist and founder of the political Antisemiten-Liga in September 1879, the first political group to use this label. Like others hostile to the Jews in this period, the League wanted to roll back the legal and civic gains associated with Jewish emancipation which its supporters believed was creating a thoroughly Judaised society. Never particularly successful as an activist, Marr's insistence that the Jews belonged primarily to a racial rather than a religious category encouraged political mavericks like Ernst Henrici and Otto Böckel to openly embrace the anti-Semitic cause. Paradoxically, the impact of Marr's propaganda encouraged religious conservatives like Adolf Stöcker, leader of the Christlichsoziale Arbeiterpartei, to employ far stronger anti-Jewish invective than before.[2]

Initially, few people in Germany would have understood what the word 'antisemitische' meant. Nevertheless, it caught on fast. In the early 1880s, Marr published a series of cheap pamphlets publicising his views, with the new term prominently displayed on the cover. And in 1881, Ernst Henrici's 'freisinnig-antisemitisch' Soziale Reichspartei was the first to advance a classic anti-Semitic political programme, calling for an end to Jewish immigration, the exclusion of Jews from public office, and a special census of the Jewish population. A year later, Henrici presented an anti-Semitic petition containing 225,000 signatures to the imperial chancellor Bismarck, but to little effect. It was not until 1890 that Otto Böckel, leader of the Antisemitische Volkspartei, became the first German politician to be elected on an anti-Semitic platform which included the demand that

Jews should be given a special civic status of their own and governed by 'an Aliens' Law.'[3] However, by the end of the 1880s, the word had already reached other Continental countries and also Russia.

At first, 'anti-Semitism' was used in Britain in relation to these developments overseas. Of the ten news items in *The Times* in the 1880s in which reference was made to 'anti-Semitism,' nine were stories from elsewhere in Europe, chiefly reports on German domestic politics. The tenth was embedded in an East End news story. When the Deputy Chief Rabbi Hermann Adler spoke on the annual prize day at the Jews' Free School in Spitalfields in June 1885, he suggested that the recent peerage given to the School's president, Lord Rothschild, should 'be regarded as a protest against the species of anti-Semitism which still lurked in some foreign countries'.[4] On this view, such forms of prejudice were fundamentally un-British, little more than a European disorder.

Adler had some grounds for optimism. When Adolf Stöcker visited London in November 1883 for a planned speaking tour, he was virtually run out of town. Stöcker had hoped to capitalise on the upsurge of anti-Jewish sentiment at the end of the previous decade, when outrage at the massacre of thousands of Bulgarian Christian insurgents by the Turkish Army was directed against Disraeli's tactical alliance with the Ottoman Empire. Gladstone had inveighed in the press against the influence of 'Judaic sympathies' in foreign affairs, and the historian E.A. Freeman had mischievously described Disraeli's pact as 'a Hebrew policy'.[5] Yet despite the aspersions that had been cast on the patriotism of British Jews, Stöcker found himself howled down, driven from the platform, and obliged to abandon any prospect of being heard in an open meeting. True, the bulk of the opposition came from German liberals and socialists exiled in London – who else would drown out his speeches by singing the 'Marseillaise' or 'Rule Britannia' in German? But Stöcker had faced a largely hostile press, and the attempt by his supporters to arrange for him to share the stage with such local dignitaries as the Lord Mayor of London or Lord Shaftesbury, President of the London Society for Promoting Christianity among the Jews, quickly collapsed under a hail of adverse publicity. According to the *Daily News*, for example, Stöcker's views were 'detested by all sensible Englishmen', and the *St James's Gazette* poured scorn on his contrast between 'intolerant antisemites' motivated by pure hatred and 'tolerant antisemites' (like himself), who believed that Jews might become acceptable if only they would convert to Christianity.[6] Stöcker never returned to Britain.

Talk of 'tolerant' versus 'intolerant antisemites' was part of an early attempt to defend the concept of anti-Semitism against political criticism. At the same time, as the word became better known, it was often extended to include all types of anti-Jewish prejudice, past and present. In an essay published in December 1881 on 'Recent Phases of Judaeophobia' – an intervention in a spirited and at times caustic debate about the Jews in Britain that had been running in the periodical press since 1878 – Hermann Adler noted what he called 'a strange coincidence of argument between the anti-Semites, old and new', slipping effortlessly into the generalised reference that is taken for granted today. Adler's specific target was a recent piece by the former Regius Professor of History at Oxford, Goldwin Smith, who had long argued that the 'tribal exclusiveness' of the Jews prevented them from being true patriots, and who had made provocatively friendly noises towards Adolf Stöcker's cause. In response, Adler castigated Goldwin Smith for attacking Disraeli, 'whose memory all England honours', and associated the historian with 'the head-quarters of anti-Semitism' in Berlin, implying that it was Goldwin Smith and not British Jews who were unpatriotic.[7] Like Stöcker, Goldwin Smith emerges here as another intolerant anti-Semite shielding himself under the mantle of tolerance.

But the phrasing of Goldwin Smith's argument, together with Adler's characterisation of it, left permanent scars, just as Adler's own critical usage was a sign that the word was beginning to take hold. Echoes of the Adler-Smith exchange can be heard in the controversy aroused by Amy Levy's novel *Reuben Sachs* (1889) when an anonymous critic in the *Jewish World* accused Levy of endorsing 'the anti-Semitic theories of the clannishness of her people and the tribalism of their religion', suggesting that a systematic, intellectualised form of racism had been internalised as a form of self-hatred.[8] Nevertheless, 'anti-Semitism' continued to be associated chiefly with the racial turn in German and Austrian politics, until reports of the Dreyfus Affair began to appear in the British press. The furore surrounding the secret trial of a Jewish army officer falsely accused of selling French military information to Germany placed the term in a new national frame, adding to the suspicion with which it was regarded in Britain. Here the mobilisation of anti-Dreyfus groups like the Ligue Antisémitique was seen as a sign that something was amiss in the French national character. Confirmation of this view could be found in some of the extraordinarily toxic publications emanating from the lunatic fringes of the French radical right, among whose titles *L'Anglais est-il Juif?* (1895)

and *La Sémitique Albion* (1898) claimed, for example, that Englishness was invariably a kind of mask concealing Jewish faces.[9]

In fact, by the 1890s, avoiding the accusation of anti-Semitism was becoming a pressing concern amongst those who shared at least some of the beliefs and attitudes of Marr, Böckel, or anti-Dreyfusards like Louis Martin. During what was probably his most active period as an anti-immigrant lobbyist and organiser, Arnold White was haunted by the fear of having his ideas dismissed as those of a crass anti-Semite. Thus, in a letter to *The Times* on 10 July 1894 drawing attention to a potential difficulty with Lord Salisbury's Aliens Bill, White argued that it was vital to recognise that the vast majority of destitute persons who would fall under the jurisdiction of the proposed new laws restricting immigration 'are of one race and one faith' – in other words, that this question had an 'essentially Jewish character', a point on which Salisbury and the Prime Minister had been silent. To escape what he pre-emptively called 'the just charge of anti-Semitism' that might be levelled at the Bill, White recommended the addition of a clause requiring that 'an assessor' belonging to 'the Hebrew faith' be appointed to help each of the chief officers of customs in the major ports to decide which Jews were genuine political or religious refugees and which were not. To underscore the urgency of the problem, White closed his letter with figures purporting to show that 'Jewish poverty in London has doubled' in the last three years.[10]

Elsewhere, White expressed himself less guardedly about the problem that charges of anti-Semitism posed for the nation as a whole. In his book, *English Democracy; Its Promises and Perils*, also from 1894, White noted how circumspect 'the public men of England' now had to be in their statements on social or political issues, taking great care to eschew even 'the imputation' of prejudice against the Jews. Inescapably, according to White, the hither side of this gentlemanly discretion was extensive bigotry in private, 'for nothing is more common, when no Jew is present, than to hear anti-Semitic sentiments expressed with quite as much fervour in England as in Russia', as if acts of self-censorship were practically inciting feelings of hostility.[11] White's chapter on the 'Jewish Influence on Democracy' was ostensibly one of his most positive reflections on the Jewish Question and, like 'the public men' whose enforced hypocrisy he was at pains to lay bare, he studiously praised Jewish intelligence, industriousness, hard-headedness, prudence, dignity, generosity, and subtlety. Yet a deep ambivalence runs throughout this text. In the space of a single page White can argue that 'Englishmen of the Jewish race to-day form one of the most valuable constituent elements in our nation', while a few lines later he will backhandedly claim that 'Jewish character supplies the points in which British character is most defective', implying that Jews were not really British at all – an impression reinforced by his disparaging references to the increasingly numerous 'alien Jews' (163). Ultimately White believed that the very presence of the Jews eroded British national self-confidence by inducing a 'supersensitive timidity' towards them, because the fear of being thought anti-Semitic is so great that 'the charge of being anti-English is accepted as a compliment, being merely equivalent to having cosmopolitan sympathies' (157–158). White warned that worse might follow as the Jews reaped what they had sown: their growing economic influence and social power threatened to lead to an upsurge in *ressentiment*, a backlash in which the Jews became the victims of what sounds suspiciously like a racialised class war.

White's account of anti-Semitism is twofold. Initially, it refers to the casual prejudice of 'public men', aired among themselves when there is no one there to object; in the second phase, in the guise of the anticipated 'anti-Semitic movement of the future', it is the rise – not to say the revenge – of the disadvantaged, enabled by a political system that has given them a voice: 'frantic debtors, starving thousands, and a desperate democracy' on the march, enacting a return of the repressed. In *English Democracy*, White was attempting to change the meaning of anti-Semitism and to give it a kind of national legitimacy so that it would seem natural (the reality behind the polite façade), unstoppable (mere convention cannot touch it), and self-imposed (in large measure it was a problem that the Jews had created), for the upward curve of the graph of anti-Semitism closely followed that of Jewish success. 'These magnates' may be able to secure 'as allies all that brains, influence, legislation, and noble alliances can give', but they cannot avoid what White melodramatically yet evasively calls the 'crucible of pain' that comes from having 'the civilised world … in pawn' (170).

But violent confrontation was just one of several conceivable scenarios. In this book, as in so many of his publications, White was preoccupied with 'the manufacture of the unemployable', with the encouragement of 'the unfit', with 'idleness' as 'a trade', a vision of England's energy being sapped from within by a 'residuum' of outcasts. And into this immoral economy 'the foreign Jewish poor', 'destitute aliens', and 'the incurable paupers who now have free entry into the country from other lands' were constantly flowing (43–46, 211–222). Immigration control was therefore vital. However, at this point in his political career, White regarded a policy of restricted entry as a panacea of only very limited effectiveness. What was required, he insisted, was a re-Christianisation of democracy, a view that might well have met with Stöcker's approval. But unlike German radical anti-Semites like Marr or Böckel, White was firmly opposed to having any truck with socialism. And of course in linking Christianity to democracy White was necessarily placing the Jewish Question at the top of the national-political agenda.

If White's defensive reflections on anti-Semitism failed to rehabilitate or at least neutralise the term, his tortuous account brings out its inherent slipperiness and the unevenness of its development within Britain's political culture and civil society. In *English Democracy*, White sometimes writes as though anti-Semitism were timeless – he refers, for example, to the likely 'recrudescence of anti-Semitism in Great Britain' (44) – but, as this brief history has indicated and as his own book clearly shows, the concept belonged to a new moment in national-democratic politics when a new calculus for winning electoral and extra-parliamentary victories came into being using the emotive and aggressive appeal of racial fantasy. White's ambition was to produce a kind of racial common sense that would alter the climate of opinion in which immigration and pauperism were discussed, nudging it closer towards the putative sciences of race.

Such an aim was much less comprehensive than that of the majority of political anti-Semites in Germany whose goal was, in Geoff Eley's words, to achieve 'a radical-nationalist counter-utopia'. By contrast, White and other members of Britain's Radical Right sought to create what might best be described as a 'counterpublic', a loose formation with a largely oppositional relationship to the main centres of power, whose many-sided activities aimed to expand its base of supporters and sympathisers, drawing in as many people as possible.[12] A given counterpublic cannot be enumerated with any exactness and, as we will see in the discussion of the British Radical Right later in this chapter, its affiliates are often dispersed across a number of distinct special interest groups. As Michael Warner has argued, the reach of a counterpublic is 'in principle indefinite, because it is not based on a precise demography but mediated by print, theatre, diffuse networks of talk, commerce, and the like'.[13] Indeed, to the extent that anti-Semitism was both contested *and* pervasive in Britain in the 1880s and 1890s, it was frequently regarded by the political class as a volatile problem that needed to be managed, as a danger that was symptomatic of democratic or popular excess, rather than a position that deserved parliamentary representation. For many, this was the lesson of the Dreyfus Affair for Englishmen and women.

THEATRES OF PREJUDICE

What ideological resources within late Victorian culture helped to lend credibility to politicians and pundits like White who campaigned on an anti-alien platform? Before turning to the rise of the Radical Right and its relationship to anti-Semitism, this section examines structural and thematic changes in the image of the Jew in a variety of popular fictional and theatrical forms and asks how far the fin de siècle saw a break with earlier and long-standing traditions of representing this troubling and frequently ambiguous figure.

The elaboration of Judaeophobic and anti-Semitic ideologies in the nineteenth century has been heavily indebted to the theatrical codes of melodrama with its heightened, not to say Manichaean, polarisation between good and evil. In his influential study, *The Melodramatic Imagination*, Peter Brooks argues that melodrama – a mode of expression he describes as theatrical, without confining it to the stage – has been the primary vehicle for representing the stakes of moral action in a world in which the traditional certainties of organised religion were being increasingly put into question, on occasion with considerable violence. In making visible the dilemmas of right and wrong, virtue and vice, continually throwing choice and conduct into the starkest relief, melodrama also personalises them: as Brooks puts it, 'good and evil can be named as persons are named', and so the 'ritual of melodrama involves the confrontation of clearly identified antagonists and the expulsion of one of them'.[14] In this respect, melodrama constantly reaffirms the moral order, setting everything to rights once more.

Of course this formulation begs the question of what kind of moral order is being restored. Elaine Hadley has made a strong case for regarding early-nineteenth-century melodrama as moved by a powerful desire to offset the unstable and untrustworthy individualism of a market society by reinstating a solid public world of hierarchy, paternalism, and deference that took its inspiration from the past.[15] However, the theatrical groundwork for this suspicion of commerce had been laid in the eighteenth century through a variety of theatrical entertainments, including comic opera, which used the stage-Jew as a stock figure. Whether a subject of mimicry or moral probity, the depiction of the Jew underwent a series of transformations around a central economic theme: peddler, usurer, moneylender, broker, benefactor. And variants of these stereotypes continued into the twentieth century, passing beyond the theatre into fiction and early cinema. But the questions that these representations pose are focussed upon the city as a proxy for the larger problems faced by the nation-state, and also upon Britain's place within the international state system.

To address the question of continuity, a useful starting point is the extraordinarily popular Irish dramatist Dion Boucicault's four-act play, *After Dark: A Drama of London Life in 1868*, first performed at the Royal Princess's Theatre, London on 12 August of that year, in which 'the Jew' plays a key role. This classic mid-century example of sensational melodrama initially played until May 1869, and productions of *After Dark* were being staged well into the early 1900s, following a London revival in 1891 – a reminder that the social life of melodrama, like other theatrical forms, depends for its economic viability on reproducing itself across time and space. But one can also think in terms of a complex melodramatic *dispositif* or apparatus in which elements of the theatrical experience both draw upon print media like novels and periodicals and subsequently feed back into other cultural forms (silent film being an important example in the Edwardian period). *After Dark*'s themes were hardly new. Boucicault was consciously working within a well-worn tradition of urban narrative that had originally become hugely successful in France with the serialisation of Eugène Sue's *Les Mystères de Paris* between 1842 and 1843, and had subsequently been adapted by numerous authors and transposed to other national or regional centres including Berlin, New York, and San Francisco, as well as London.[16] Whether circulated as cheap novel, *feuilleton*, or stage drama, the genre revolved around an exposé of the modern city's hidden life, its dirty secrets, the buried connections between the idle rich and the destitute inhabitants of the urban streets: in short, the city as a place of conspiracy and concealment. Boucicault's play is no exception and, true to its origins, it displays a fascination with the fluidity of the nineteenth-century city, relayed as a set of outrageous back stories whose exhumation provides the motor of the plot. The final revelations that make the dénouement possible may be damaging, but they purge the city of its injustices, albeit temporarily.

Who or what is 'the Jew' in *After Dark*? Step forward Dicey Morris, characterised in the published acting edition from 1871 as a 'gambling-house keeper', although some playbills used the blunter, more hostile description 'Jew money-lender'.[17] In dress, he looks the part of a vulgar dandy, with his 'showy watch-chain, with charms', 'fancy scarf', 'fancy pocket-handkerchief', and his trademark 'black hat, turned up at the sides, pinched down before and behind, cocked over one eye when worn', together with his 'blue velvet figured vest', 'black cutaway coat', and 'riding trousers' (7). The riding trousers may seem like an odd touch, but they indicate an identification with the leisured classes on whom Morris preys, a point underscored by setting the opening scene in a London railway station with billboards advertising the Crystal Palace and the Paris-Brighton races. Similarly, the walls of Morris's Soho gambling den are decorated with prints of races, prize-fights, and ballet girls, not simply to create the right kind of environment for his wealthy clientele, but also to signify the social world in which Morris likes to see himself moving. Of course his aspirations are in vain. No sooner has one of the play's heroes, the gallant dragoon Captain Gordon Chumley, clapped eyes on Morris than he is dismissing him *sotto voce* as someone who 'looks like a Jew horse-dealer' (12).

Deflated and mocked behind his back, Morris is an intrinsically comic character – which is to say that he is to be *laughed at* – and therefore a figure whose villainy is to be taken with a pinch of salt. His wiliness has definite limits. Sharp enough to secure an agreement by cutting a cheque in half to delay full payment, Morris's methods are too slipshod to prevent his being defrauded when a gambler doubles his credit by borrowing from different employees using the same collateral. But as an incarnation of evil, Morris pales beside his partner in crime, Richard Knatchbull – sometimes literally so. When Knatchbull reveals that he plans to use the subterranean exit from the Elysium Music Hall, which Morris also owns, in order to place the drugged Captain Chumley on the underground railway line and bring about his death, Morris is 'put … in a cold shiver' (34). Nevertheless, it is Morris whose capital and remorseless business sense keeps the plot in motion, hatching schemes to get his hands on other people's fortunes and acting as the cultural impresario whose properties provide the stage sets for the commissioning of crime.

As often happens in 'mysteries of the city' narratives, identities are virtually free-floating and names turn out to be mere devices for enabling suspense and surprise. Thus, in one twist, 'Old Tom' (Frank Dalton), a former soldier turned semi-employed drunkard who once saved Chumley's life in the Crimean War, prevents a young woman from drowning in the Thames, little knowing that she is his daughter, Eliza (Fanny) Dalton, whom he has not seen since his wife was seduced by 'that fiend Knatchbull' while Tom was away serving his country (36). Not only will Tom be reunited with his daughter, but he is on the brink of moving up in the world, for Eliza is loved by society heir Sir George Medhurst (who is, in turn, being blackmailed by Knatchbull and Morris).[18] The play shifts rapidly between the mean London streets that Tom now calls home and the new-found affluence of sudden inheritances and unexpected bequests – money that can be lost at the gaming tables in a second – in a dizzying panorama of coincidences whose stark contrasts and instant reversals preclude any possibility of finding a secure middle ground. Will Eliza find happiness with Sir George, or will he marry his family's choice, the upper-class Rose Egerton? Can Sir George escape Morris and Knatchbull's wicked designs, or will he be dragged down into the gutter? Could a drunken old tramp prove to be the agent of justice?

Convoluted biographies are therefore very much the melodramatic rule in *After Dark*, complicated pasts that threaten the ever-precarious present. Many circuitous routes lead into and out of the city of dreadful night: Richard Knatchbull is a criminal who was once transported to Australia where he became an infamous bushranger (and was arrested by Captain Chumley), after which he enlisted in the Confederate Army in New Orleans and fought in the American Civil War before returning to London where he operates under the name of Chandos Bellingham.[19] But the one character who needs no history, and who is required to be exactly what (or no better than) he seems, is Dicey Morris – indeed, the futility of this meretricious parvenu's ambitions is essentially what makes him a figure of fun. Dicey represents a fixed point amid the fluctuating tides of concealment and disclosure, and his duplicity – like his Jewishness, with which it is here closely aligned – is quite blatant, not to say banal. The only other figures in the play to be typecast by their '*fancy* vests and coats' – in a related, yet subtly different kind of racialised baseness – are Jem and Josey, the two 'Negro minstrels' who sing and dance on a miniature stage at Morris's music hall (7, my emphasis).

The ineffaceability of Morris's Jewishness may help to explain a tantalising note included in the playscript's inventory of traits and idiosyncrasies defining this character. The 'personator' playing this part is urged to 'study it up', for, at the Princess's Theatre, 'Mr Dominick Murray's imitation of the salient peculiarities of the low-lived London Jews' speech and mannerism ... strengthened the attractions and made a perceptible proportion of the audience be of that race' (7). The precise nature of Morris's appeal will never be known, but perhaps the fact that this stage villain need not be taken too seriously, being so plainly the trite vulgarian and the comic foil to the decidedly more sinister Knatchbull, brings him nearer to the indulgent realm of mimicry and caricature than the protocols of melodrama would usually allow. As we will see, there are signs that the stock figure of the "Jew money-lender" became increasingly menacing later in the century. Here, in the person of Dicey Morris, he is a pathetic, and finally an abject, individual, ineffectually insisting when the evidence is against him that he is 'a respectable householder … a payer of rates and taxes, and a member of the westry' – altogether too *bourgeois* to be transported to Australia (38). This is the money-lender as *schlemiel*. But it is the sadistic Knatchbull who has the last laugh, who encourages the audience to enjoy seeing Morris's discomfort, and who ultimately re-inscribes the line of racial difference when he hands over the Australian reward on his head to the arresting police officer on 'one condition; that you expend half of it in sending out that cowardly cur there.' Knatchbull takes his punishment like a man; 'the Jew' is just 'a cringing hound' (38–39).

After Dark was not the last word on the Jew as money-lender. By the turn of the century, more insidious versions of this figure were beginning to appear. To assess the pervasiveness of this caricature, I want to turn from the analysis of an individual play and look at some examples of drama presented at a single venue at the turn of the century. From the 1880s onwards, commercial theatre had begun to follow the increasingly dominant business model of the music hall, with capacity seating and luxurious fittings and design, and the (typically) grandiloquently named Imperial Theatre at Bordesley in Birmingham was no exception. When it opened its doors on 30 September 1899, it offered popular drama on a weekly basis to the relatively affluent working-class public in that area. Opulently furnished, this was one of the new breed of provincial theatres where audiences of up to 2,000 people could go to see a play like *After Dark* performed, as they did during the week of 6 August 1900. Yet, economically, the Imperial was always overshadowed by the competing attractions of the music hall, and in August 1903 this was precisely what it became, when it was relaunched as the Bordesley Palace, a 'theatre and stage circus of varieties'.[20]

Theatre programmes and posters give a good sense of the kinds of productions the Imperial was mounting. 'Mysteries of the city' were amongst the most regularly staged entertainments and, following the example of *After Dark*, London was the generic city for most of these plays, although other urban locations were sometimes possible, such as New York in the famous American actor Joseph Jefferson's *Shadows of a Great City* (17 March 1902). And, as in Boucicault's popular classic, Jewish characters were an integral feature of these melodramas and were invariably defined in terms of their still overly familiar financial roles. Jefferson's Abe Nathans was listed as 'a pawnbroker', but most such figures were described as 'Money Lenders', regardless of the setting or subgenre in which they were inscribed. Thus Abram Shabner in Mat Wilkinson's

Saturday Night in London (12 March 1900) was a 'Money Lender', as was Gordon Isaacs in Max Goldberg's *The Bank of England: An Adventure in the Life of Sherlock Holmes* (23 December 1901), whereas the following week, Ikey Moss and Solomon Jacobs in John Douglas's *No Man's Land* (30 December 1901) were, respectively, 'a Broker' and 'a young Broker.' The name or context generally conveyed dubious or pejorative connotations, but sometimes the moral function of the character was unequivocal. In the 'sensational musical comedy-drama' *The Hand of Iron* by M. Roy Jackson and his No.1 Company (21 July 1902), 'Solomon Isaacs Silver' was rather superfluously identified as 'a Bad Lot' and no further particulars about his vocation were felt to be necessary.

Mat Wilkinson's *Saturday Night in London*, subtitled 'The Powerful Drama of Modern Life in the Great Metropolis', is a good example of how the tradition of urban melodrama was hardening. Set in Whitechapel, and keenly alert to the district's renewed reputation for crime and destitution, Wilkinson's play was representative of the kind of gritty theatre that had long been popular in the East End, yet which also travelled extremely well. If the name of its stage Jew, Abram Shabner ('a Money Lender and City Shark'), can be traced back to that of Hawksworth Shabner, a character in William Moncrieff's earlier and immensely successful stab at the genre, *The Scamps of London* (1843) – and said to have been an inspiration for Boucicault's Dicey Morris – Wilkinson's revamped reprobate is made of far sterner stuff.[21] Shabner is indubitably the chief villain of the piece, and the play climaxes with his death following a thrilling 'struggle on the housetops'. Once he has been dispatched, there can be 'freedom at last from the perils and dangers of Saturday Night in London.' Scenes from London life – 'Fast Life', 'Busy Life', 'Whitechapel Life' – provide the backdrop for such moralising vignettes as 'A Woman's Love and a Father's Wrath', 'The Curse of Drink', and the possibility of harmonious relations between Jews and Gentiles ('Peace and Good Will to all'), epitomised by the contrast between Shabner and his daughter Sarah, a variation on the common nineteenth-century trope of the good Jewess and the depraved father (even included in Eliot's *Daniel Deronda*).[22] For all its London associations, *Saturday Night in London* evidently went down well with Bordesley audiences and the play was brought back to the Imperial in November 1901.

If Wilkinson's melodrama reflected the changing national image of East End life, updating earlier themes in light of the recurrent racialised fears of 'Darkest London', two even more sensational productions from 1900 each put the ubiquitous moneylender to work in imperial narratives designed to rally support for British troops. John F. Preston's *Soldiers of the Queen; or Briton and Boer* (30 April 1900) and Arthur Shirley's *The Absent-Minded Beggar; or For Queen and Country*, performed five months later, were essentially militaristic stage shows, spectacular melodramas that brought the heat of battle, including the latest technology of war, to the urban auditorium. Shows of this type dated back at least to the Eastern crisis of the late 1870s and had long been a staple of the music halls. By placing the thrill of the machine at the centre of the drama, these extravaganzas followed in Boucicault's footsteps, but the substitution of an army relief train in *The Absent-Minded Beggar* for *After Dark*'s fearsome underground locomotive gave a new patriotic accent to the sensational rescue scene. Indeed, in a very real sense, the machine takes over. As *The Times* reviewer of Shirley's drama disappointedly observed of the 1899 London production: 'It is really a Maxim gun's play'.[23]

Soldiers of the Queen proudly paraded its verisimilitude, being 'founded on Actual Facts and Incidents that have occurred in South Africa from Majuba Hill Disaster to the Present Day' and closing with a 'Grand Tableau, illustrating The Relief of Ladysmith'. Given that the play sought to instruct as well as to entertain, the role of Solomon Levi, 'a Jew Financier, Agent, etc.', was grossly tendentious, because in the first act it is made clear that he is prepared to pay to have the heroic Captain Forrester of the 95th and his entire family shot – a gesture set against the image of gallant soldiers standing shoulder to shoulder against overwhelming odds in the 'Massacre at Majuba'. Majuba was very much a rallying cry during the 'Khaki Election' of 1900; one of the catchy slogans that helped to get Major William Evans-Gordon elected Conservative MP for Stepney was "Remember Majuba, and vote for the Major".[24] *Soldiers of the Queen* aimed to offset British humiliation in the first South African War in the 1880s by celebrating the victories of the then-current war, showing that Britain could win. To drive the message home, the poster promised 'a new and original Patriotic Song', entitled 'Revenge Is Sweet'. The play was hugely popular and constantly returned to Birmingham's theatres long after the Boer War was over. As late as August 1910, it could still be seen at the Metropole, alongside other military and naval dramas, at a time when the question of Britain's preparedness for war was again moving to the forefront of national debate.

The more spectacular but no less homiletic *Absent-Minded Beggar* was inspired by Rudyard Kipling's poem of the same name, specially commissioned in 1899 by Alfred Harmsworth for the *Daily Mail* in aid of a variety of military charities centred upon widows, orphans, and wounded veterans. The play was part of a formidable burst of merchandising during which Kipling's verse was marketed in every conceivable format, from public readings by the wife of the celebrated actor Beerbohm Tree to the sale of crockery and handkerchiefs on which the poem was reproduced. But Shirley's play was concerned with generating a more immediate and emotional mode of involvement. At the end of the third act, British prisoners are rescued by the thrilling 'ARRIVAL OF THE ARMOURED TRAIN WITH NAVAL BRIGADE AND MAXIM BATTERY', and the play later ends with a bayonet charge that pays back the Boers for their treachery, 'leaving the house filled with gunpowder fumes and the audience with frenzied feelings of patriotism and joy.'[25] In this spectacular melodrama, unlike Preston's *Soldiers of the Queen*, the Jewish moneylender Levi Winklestein is there to provide light relief rather than to function as the enemy within. The reviewer for *The Times* thought that 'the comic Jew' was 'really funny', the 'best piece of acting' in the play's London 1899 debut, which was otherwise viewed with scepticism and some distaste (in part because of the disorderliness of the house, with wags in the gallery poking fun at the portrayal of the villainous stage Boers in a potent mixture of theatricalised mockery and ideological bravado).[26] But perhaps this rather unthreatening Jewish character was not so surprising. The official patrons of Shirley's 'patriotic' melodrama included not only royalty (the Princess of Wales), the military (Lord Roberts), and politicians (Joseph Chamberlain), but also two important Jewish businessmen (the banker Alfred de Rothschild and the mining magnate Alfred Beit). Under the circumstances, it was only to be expected that Levi Winklestein would differ substantially from Preston's Solomon Levi. Yet together the two Levis represent alternating modes for staging the figure of the Jew: those of menace and ridicule. These are not necessarily distinct, and indeed a charge of aggression runs through both, although the direction in which this violence flows varies significantly. While strictly speaking there are no pure cases – laughter may accompany the Jewish villain's come-uppance, for example – by the turn of the century, figures like the moneylender were becoming appreciably more threatening to the imagined community of the nation-state.

To this line of development, a new figure had been added to the bestiary of Jewish malfeasance between 1894 and 1895: Svengali. The popular actor Herbert Beerbohm Tree's legendary stage recreation of this role crested on a huge sales "boom" on both sides of the Atlantic generated by George Du Maurier's bestseller, *Trilby* (1894). Almost any item or performance, no matter how loosely connected with the novel, had become instantly marketable, instantly commoditised, including shoes, sweets, and musical scores. Paul Potter's dramatisation of Du Maurier's book was a huge success when it opened at London's Haymarket Theatre on 30 October 1895, playing for six months before going on tour.[27] However, the play took considerable liberties with the novel and left some critics dissatisfied. Clement Scott, drama critic for the *Illustrated London News*, felt that the character of Trilby, the vivacious grisette and artist's model who becomes a great singer, had lost much of the charm that Du Maurier's original had conveyed. Equally disappointing, the young artist Little Billee with whom Trilby falls in love was now an insipid and unconvincing figure, indeed little more than a cipher.

These criticisms point towards a major change of emphasis. In Potter's version, the tragic story of the two star-crossed lovers was overshadowed, and in fact largely displaced, by Tree's 'superb performance' as Svengali, the down-at-heel Polish Jew whose mesmeric power turns the tone-deaf Trilby into a star, a pitch-perfect singing sensation, and also – as 'La Svengali' – into his wife.[28] This was not Tree's achievement alone. He worked closely with Potter on the final shape of the play, consulted with Du Maurier, and continued to make important substantive alterations to the script based on audience responses.[29] Svengali's death is a dramatic tour de force, in contrast to his initially unnoticed heart attack in the novel, where it is obscured by the simultaneous "death" of Trilby's singing voice to the sound of 'laughter, hoots, hisses, cat-calls, cock-crows' from the working-class members of the packed house in Drury Lane, now that Svengali is no longer in control of her.[30] So powerful was Tree's rendition of Svengali's death at the close of the third act that the fourth and final act seemed like a terrible anticlimax, and when Trilby also dies in the final moments of the play, any possibility of a happy ending dies with her. Conscious of the dangers of frustrating the pleasures of theatrical melodrama, Tree – and other, lesser performers – would sometimes end the play with Svengali's sudden demise, leaving the newly reunited Trilby and Little Billee in each other's arms, secure in the knowledge that any danger from the heroine's Jewish master has been completely exorcised.[31] Tree would take a bow after Svengali's last appearance on stage, and it seemed quite natural to abandon the fourth act thereafter.

As George Taylor has shown from a careful study of Tree's own annotated prompt-copy of the play, the actor's lasting contribution to the perpetuation of this evil-magus figure was to intensify Svengali's Jewishness by adding a Faustian speech in which Svengali defies the 'God of Israel' and then, when he starts to experience the first pangs of a weak heart, show Svengali pleading pathetically for his life – thus producing another highly melodramatic variant of the cowardly Jewish stage villain. Tree also reinserted an eerie mesmeric speech in which Svengali compels Trilby to imagine herself as a corpse lying in the Paris morgue, a vivid intimation that his hypnotic gifts hold the keys to life and death.[32] But much of the credit for this larger-than-life Svengali should rightly be given to Paul Potter. As Du Maurier himself acknowledged, it was Potter who stripped away any remaining trace of the novel's gossipy verbiage and digressive subplots, allowing Svengali to move to centre stage; and it was Potter who turned the dead Svengali into a spectral Wandering Jew, stalking the Paris streets by night, 'a big greasy creature, with a worn overcoat and muffler that half concealed his face … carrying a large parcel' that contains the painted portrait (shades of *The Picture of Dorian Gray*) that will once again mesmerise Trilby and so hasten her death.[33] In the novel, by contrast, Svengali's *photograph* is not delivered by the dead hand of its former owner, but comes by a circuitous postal route 'out of some remote province in eastern Russia – out of the mysterious East!', immediately qualified as a 'poisonous East – birthplace and home of an ill wind that blows nobody good.'[34] Potter's rewrite makes the Jewish presence no less deadly, but reimagines it as a Gothic form of power, a mesmeric mode of influence that is unfathomable, supramundane, and certainly not to be dissipated or brought down to earth by 'the feel of that long, thick, shapely, Hebrew nose being kneaded between … gloved knuckles', when Little Billee's friend Taffy leaps to his defence (219).

Du Maurier's Jewish Faustus was built upon recognisable stereotypes. Like the 'hideous' Jewish theatre manager with his 'greasy ringlets' and 'soiled shirt' who amused and appalled Wilde's Dorian Gray, Svengali is 'very shabby and dirty', with 'thick, heavy, languid, lustreless black hair'.[35] But the way his hair falls 'on to his shoulders, in that musician-like way that is so offensive to the normal Englishman' marks him out as a deliberately repulsive incarnation of the bohemian artist, shamelessly cajoling and begging for his rent-money, and the antitype to the hearty but rather prudish British bohemians represented by Little Billee and his companions (10). Svengali is also a true bohemian in caring only about his art, or rather about 'himself as a master of his art', regarding others, even his closest associates, as mere means to his own ends (37). In the play, one symptom of Svengali's monomania and of his brazen disregard for human suffering is the revelation that he is an unregenerate wife-beater, a trait considerably softened in the novel, where the ironic caveat that Svengali is incapable of playing 'the highest and best' music is no less important a failing (38). In Potter and Tree's *Trilby*, Svengali's monstrosity and sinister genius go hand in hand; both are signs of his overweening power and indicate that he is not to be confined to the middlebrow or the merely second-rate. The growing horror of the play depends upon the awareness that Svengali is capable of anything.

Svengali needs other vessels to realise his ambitions, and when he takes over Trilby, he invades and subjugates her psychically – indeed, in Svengali's hands, the Trilby that everyone had known and loved is effectively 'dead' – or, in the words of Svengali's violin-playing companion Gecko, she has been transformed into 'a singing-machine', a pure instrument of Svengali's desire, '*un écho, un simulacre*', without a life of her own (275). Alongside this image of petrifaction, the play also picks up on one of Du Maurier's most lurid illustrations and has Trilby compare Svengali to 'a big black spider' that traps, immobilises, and devours its victims.[36] Under the pretext of relieving the pain in her eyes, Svengali is physician, occult professional, and then predator. In the novel, this 'most unclean' figure is still more nightmarishly complex, 'a sticky, haunting, long, lean, uncanny, black spider-cat, if there is such an animal outside a bad dream' – but the garrulous excess of Du Maurier's prose, tumbling over itself in its search for a striking phrase, has a dismissive mockery, an impatient strain of comedy, that the dramatic *Trilby* lacks (66). On stage, Svengali may be admired as 'a genius' who 'can make divinest music out of a common streetsong', yet also be feared and shunned for being 'as bad as they make them'.[37] He is never to be ridiculed or underestimated.

For all its theatricality, the depiction of Svengali redoubles the malevolence of Jewish villainy, imagining the Jewish artist as manipulative and self-seeking, the creator of false impressions and deceptive pleasures. Despite ostensibly belonging in a tale of the 1850s, Svengali is a version of the shiftless itinerant Jew who lives off his wits, the competitive, unassimilable 'alien' of contemporary discourse from the 1880s and 1890s. Unlike Boucicault's parvenu Dicey Morris, whose criminality is intimately connected to his desire to secure a place in English society, Svengali has no nation and no aspiration to be part of one, and it is significant that Du Maurier has him moving between Poland, Germany, France, and England. Svengali's name entered the English language as national loyalties were coming under pressure again especially in relation to the Boer War. To be sure, *Trilby* also inspired parodies and pastiche, encouraged by the light-handedness of much of Du Maurier's own writing and the effervescent consumerism of the Trilby 'boom'. But in the theatre and the music hall, the line of continuity ran from the stock character of the shady

Jewish entrepreneur to the chilling intensity of Tree's ruthless impresario. So when, in May 1904, Israel Zangwill rightly noted 'that the germs of anti-Semitism are always being fostered by the synonymousness of Jews and the money-lender in fiction', he was only telling part of the story.[38]

To provisionally draw together some of the strands in this specimen genealogy, I want briefly to consider a slightly later fiction that both dramatises the impact of East European Jews on East End life and combines the figure of the Jewish usurer with the excessive potency of Svengali. When John A. Steuart's novel, *The Hebrew: A Story of the Time*, appeared in 1903, an anonymous reviewer for the *Times Literary Supplement* was struck by the book's melodramatic power – 'no one can read through *The Hebrew* without feeling some sense of the horror which the author would have him feel' – but deplored the author's unrelentingly 'rhetorical manner' the aggregate effect of which was to turn the narrative into 'a sermon'.[39] An extended sermon is precisely the form taken by this Manichean tale, because Steuart addresses his readers as members of a 'Christian nation', who have averted their gaze from the 'cankerous, devastating evil' in their midst.[40] Evil is of course brought into focus through the eponymous Jewish figure at the centre of the novel, the banker Israel Herstein, who, in a grim variation on the themes of money-lender and sweater, squeezes the last farthing of profit out of his wretched East End tenants. Herstein is the future that alien immigration is putting into place, as the following reminiscence reveals:

His mind went back to the day on which a certain youth shook the dust of a foreign ghetto off his aspiring feet and set his face resolutely towards the New Jerusalem, which is to say the capital of the world; also to the night on which a certain alien immigrant, ignorant alike of English speech and English ways, was taken in by a Jewish Board of Guardians on the banks of the Thames. (35)

England is imagined as 'the New Jerusalem' and it has become a land of rampant parasitism that 'throve on affliction, grew fat and sleek on poverty, [and] flourished like a fungus on social disease and distress' (214). As in the mysteries-of-the-city narrative, here combined with the slum romance for which Steuart was best known, this threat is present at every level of the imperial capital's social structure, from bourgeois heights to sordid depths, and hence Herstein's sinister (and partially hidden) influence extends from the Standard Metropolitan Bank, unblinkingly described as 'a typical English institution', to the East London slums (36). Young immigrant Jews act as housing agents forcing desperate clients to pay more than they can afford, and if they refuse, they are promptly replaced by the 'frowsy foreign Jews chattering guttural Yiddish' who queue on the stairs 'exhaling all the malodours of Jewry' (200). Below these would-be tenants lies an underworld represented by the 'group of startled black-bearded men' later glimpsed in 'a coiners' den', Polish Jews whose 'growl [is] as of beasts of prey for blood' (337). Such alien figures bear the marks of Svengali with long, greasy black locks and the evil eye 'glaring with the ferocity of a hyena' (338).

Yet, cutting across this invective, is another kind of discourse, which at some points contradicts the religious world-view that frames the novel and at others enters into a complex – and occasionally confusing – engagement with it, epitomised by a wealthy American slum visitor's observation that 'in slumdom the Darwinian principle out-heroded Herod in ruthlessness of slaughter' (349). Thus the violence of the metropolis is systemic, bringing about the demise of its most vulnerable city-dwellers – not only slum children, as in the untimely death of little Peter'j'n – but also those like the Rev. Perceval Emmet who literally works himself to death trying to raise money to help the poor. In naturalist vein, the city is depicted as a voracious animal, 'a blind monster' that chews its inhabitants 'limp' and spits them out 'as refuse', as though in the struggle for survival London represents the most dangerous, the most predatory of species (201). Translated back into the religious register, it is 'the cruel pagan city', cruel because insufficiently Christianised, or, once again in the language of race, London is the place that is falling into the hands of the devious Jew who is 'too complex to be read by the downright, simpleminded Saxon' (167). In an extraordinarily heterogeneous catalogue, the 'rare brain' of 'the Hebrew' – the 'intellect of his race' – is said to be as 'alert as the lynx, subtle as the serpent, practical as a Yankee, trenchant as a Moslem lance in the dawn above Hebron, and withal mystical as a Hindoo seer' (168). What these powers of mind can never be is English.

How is such an unyielding text to be brought to a satisfying conclusion? According to the cultural logic of *The Hebrew*, the ending will necessarily be twofold, even if this closure pulls back from the novel's rhetorical excesses. In the first place, the English must rise up 'in a fury of shame and indignation ... and put an end to the barbaric cruelty of harrying and plundering' (476). Popular justice is now the prerogative of the vigilante: Israel Herstein is attacked in his own home by a masked intruder and is so badly beaten that he is left a helpless invalid, in body and in mind. His assailant is not named, but the reader is left in little doubt as to which denizen of 'slumdom' is the culprit. The second element in the novel's conclusion combines restitution with assimilation. Herstein has a daughter Rachel, 'a young lady of Oriental profile and the gleaming hair of the daughters of Judah', who is also known within English high society as 'the prettiest and cleverest girl in London' (38, 170). Not only does she become a slum visitor, but, once she has discovered the truth about her father's misdeeds, she uses his ill-gotten gains to turn one of his properties into a home for the destitute. As an icon of Christian charity, of the love of one's neighbour that is enjoined upon 'a Christian nation', Rachel the good Jewess partly occupies the place of the convert. Nevertheless, her primary duty is to care for her now emasculated father: immured within the family home, 'hers was not to be the lighter lot' (481). If *The Hebrew* envisions a future for the Jew, it seems to be caught between confinement and terror. This is not the only time these forced alternatives will appear.

Taken together, these case studies suggest that the second half of the nineteenth century saw a substantial rescripting of the kinds of meanings traditionally associated with the stage-Jew. Firstly, the money-lender or broker begins to meld with the latter figure of the financier or plutocrat. The Jew as speculator was not a new development; in fact, one could say that in a certain sense it had been perfected much earlier in the person of Augustus Melmotte in Anthony Trollope's *The Way We Live Now* (1875), *except* that, like everything else about this elusive character, it is entirely unclear whether he actually is a Jew. As Jonathan Freedman has argued, in the creation of Melmotte, Trollope deployed all the cultural signifiers that swirled around the image of the Jewish plutocrat in order to intensify the social magic of high finance, while deliberately withholding the marks of individual identity.[41] What Melmotte represents, then, is the rumour of Judaized capital, whose phantasmatic reality is coarsely substantiated in the character of Israel Herstein more than a quarter of a century later.

Secondly, where the identity of the Jew is filled out, it is the experience of the migrant that increasingly supplies the main attributes of otherness. Thus Svengali is portrayed as a sort of footloose musical entrepreneur, the marginal *Ostjude* seeking to insinuate himself into the heart of Europe, whose designs on a young Irishwoman is stoutly resisted by an Englishman, a Welshman, and a Scotsman.[42] In a melodrama in which everyone's nationality tends towards a parodic stage presence, Svengali is weirdly cosmopolitan: it is said that he 'fears neither God nor man, and blasphemes in sixteen languages', and in the flesh he shifts forcefully between French, German, and English – in contrast to the more haphazard attempts at French by the British.[43] But his flowery, yet touchy, courtesy quickly slips into the incessant boast that he will make millions once he has trained Trilby to sing. Like Herstein, Svengali's is a rags-to-riches story of success in a foreign land in which this extraordinary cultural operator is able to orchestrate the fates of others (which is, of course, followed by a fall in each case). For while Svengali is at times regarded with a mixture of fear and awe, he is – especially in the early chapters of Du Maurier's novel – the subject of utter contempt, condemned for being dishonourably poor, egotistical and vain, and 'both tawdry and dirty in his person', a parasite who lives off others, including his own family in Austria (37). These attitudes have a considerable pedigree: when Goldwin Smith defended Adolf Stöcker in the 1881 essay on 'The Jewish Question', he claimed that it was the 'Jewish antipathy to labour' that went against Stöcker's 'Christian Socialist' principles.[44] Worse still, Goldwin Smith implied that the traditional faith of the Jews had been replaced by the love of money.

ANTI-SEMITISM AND THE RADICAL RIGHT

At its inception, "Antisemitismus" was an inherently political concept, the stuff of leagues, parties, and conferences: the Deutsche Antisemitische Vereinigung or the Ligue Antisémitique. Britain had no organisations that were able to openly raise the banner of anti-Semitism understood in this specific sense, and during the term's early introduction into the English language it was used with some caution in order to avoid the stigma of its dubious Continental origins. As we have seen, avoiding the attribution of anti-Semitism became an important political tactic in its own right. What, then, was the relationship between hostility to the Jews as an aspect of a general cultural chauvinism and those activists and pressure groups which sought to bring questions of race and ethnicity to the forefront of British political life? More precisely, to what extent can anti-Semitism be said to be a driving force in making an Aliens Act politically possible?

One difficulty in answering these questions stems from the existence of markedly anti-Jewish attitudes right across the political spectrum in Britain at the fin-de-siècle. On the Left, leaders as diverse as Henry Hyndman of the socialist Social Democratic Federation, the radical Liberal MP John Burns, and Ben Tillett, General Secretary of the Dock, Wharf, Riverside and General Labourers' Union, all voiced anti-Semitic sentiments during this period, variously targeting rich Jews, pauper aliens, and the machinations of ' "Ikey Mo" in Pretoria' (in Burns's abusive phrase).[45] As a more stylised example, consider the following verses on the South African conflict, inspired by J.A. Hobson's article on the De

Beers mining company, both of which appeared in the Liberal weekly *The Speaker* early in February 1902:

> Regersbach and Mosenthal
> Gazed beyond the river Vaal;
> Saw a land of peace and plenty,
> Dreamed of ten per cent, or twenty,
> Looked and sighed and longed for war,
>   "This," they said in perfect Yiddish,
>   "Must undoubtedly be British. –
> Should have been so long before."
>
> Bernheim, Hirschhorn, Peiser, Beit,
> Wisely didn't stay to fight.
> Only when the blows are ended
> And the broken crowns are mended
> After this Imperial war,
>   Joseph, Abrahams, and Joses,
>   Britons by descent from Moses
> Will be richer than before.[46]

The accusatory tone of this extract, the insistent rhythm of the list of names ('Bernheim, Hirschhorn, Peiser, Beit') mixed with burlesque ('Mosenthal') and sarcasm ('Britons by descent from Moses', echoing a similar refrain in the first verse), shows it to be, in essence, a more literary statement of Burns's attack on '"Ikey Mo" in Pretoria'. In these verses, capitalism in its most lethal form is Jewish and patriotism is just a sham, an excuse for warmongering and profiteering.

At the other end of the political spectrum, calls for restrictions on 'alien immigration' by Conservative and Unionist candidates during the so-called khaki election of 1900, at the height of the Boer War, were immediately understood as a direct attack on Jews by opponents and followers alike. When Thomas Dewar, prospective Tory MP for St George's East and Wapping, told 'a crowded and enthusiastic meeting' that 'hordes of these pauper immigrants' had been 'dumped down in the streets', and then asked 'what would that district be in another five years' if nothing was done, a voice called out 'Jerusalem' to the sound of 'loud laughter.' Dewar protested that 'he was not decrying the Jews as a race,' but it is significant that when he addressed 'a very large meeting' of Jewish voters a few days later, the issue of immigration control (which he had promised to make 'his speciality') was never mentioned.[47] Managing anti-Semitism for political ends always required deft footwork.

Dewar's appeal to a sense of 'national crisis' in his speeches was of course very much of its time, but his words also resonated with a much broader critique of British politics emanating from the more intransigent sections of the Conservative and Unionist bloc, elements that have been identified by some historians as the party's 'Radical Right'.[48] Whether or not one accepts this label as entirely apt, what is not disputed is the complex nature of their dissatisfaction with Arthur J. Balfour's stewardship and their wish to see a substantial change of direction within conservative politics. At its most truculent and assertive, this Radical Right was – in G.R. Searle's words – 'a collection of super-patriots' who sometimes dreamt of setting up a new party to replace the one that they believed was failing their country. Although this idea was passed around during after-dinner conversations and served as a shibboleth among those in the know, it was at certain critical moments advanced as a very serious option, as in August 1911, when the landed aristocrat Lord Willoughby de Broke began to argue that almost everyone he knew thought that founding a new right-wing party was a real possibility.[49] Yet, despite their intense disillusionment, these malcontents were ultimately contained by the Conservative Party, from within which they launched, or associated themselves with, a wide array of initiatives – in the form of campaigns, pressure groups, and parliamentary and extra-parliamentary caucuses – as well as an endless stream of argument and invective. And it is the interaction between these formal and informal activities that constitutes the Radical Right as a counterpublic whose broad aim was to steer British society onto a fresh course. But the question of whether their party should be abandoned was never resolved.

A preliminary list of the bodies founded to promote the kinds of causes and policies that loosely defined the Radical Right illustrates the restless energy and organisational resilience of this wing of the Conservative Party. Numbered among them would be the National Service League, the Imperial Maritime League, the Radical Plutocracy Enquiry, the Anti-Socialist Union, and the British League for the Support of Ulster and the Union, their very names revealing the characteristic mode of address that its political leaders favoured. And, although it is a rather different example, the British Brothers' League should be added to the inventory too. As their names also suggest, the concerns of the Radical Right were largely conjunctural, changing over time, moving from issue to issue, and failing to develop a coherent alternative programme either within or outside their party. Thus Lord Willoughby de Broke's British League for the Support of Ulster was a symptom of the escalating Irish Home Rule crisis from 1912 and leaned ominously towards plans for armed resistance in the northern counties. However, most of these campaigns were small in scale and their inner histories highlight the dangers of over-hasty schisms. The Imperial Maritime League broke away from the older and better established Navy League in the winter of 1907–1908 because of fears about British naval defence capacity. However, despite enthusiastic support from Rudyard Kipling and Willoughby de Broke, its membership was tiny – a mere 1,500 – whereas the Navy League quintupled in size (to a total of 100,000 supporters) in the four years after the split with the Imperial Maritime League, and had local branches all over Britain.[50] Probably the most impressive campaign to attract a following from among the Radical Right was the Tariff Reform League, but while this organisation provided ideological shelter for such leading figures as Leo Amery, Willoughby de Broke, and George Wyndham, it was hardly their creature. With more than 600 branches by 1910, the League was a useful vehicle for Radical Right activism, but because it was immensely popular throughout the Conservative and Unionist bloc, the League was far too large to be a mere satellite of any one clique.[51]

The Radical Right was always keen to encourage popular forms of political participation – its attempt to promote Tariff Reform among trade unionists being a good example – but its strength lay less in organisational innovation than in its fashioning of a cultural idiom that combined strident anti-liberalism with an uncompromising reassertion of the primacy of Empire. Because of the feeling that the country had been betrayed by a weak and insipid Conservative leadership, these calls for renewal were often couched in the language of national and racial regeneration. As in all counterpublics, networking and the creation of forums for debate were crucial in building a critical mass of support, and these activities were greatly assisted by the presence of several exceptionally well-placed journalists and publicists within its ranks.

Many of the key figures in the group gathered around Leopold Maxse's monthly *National Review* which effectively became the house journal of the Radical Right and a thorn in the side of the upper echelons of the Conservative Party under Balfour. The *Review*'s circulation climbed steadily after Admiral Maxse acquired it for his son in 1893 and its monthly sales had reached around 7,000 copies per month by 1905, a figure that had risen to 10,000 by 1908. In addition to Maxse, other major journalists included Leo Amery, who became a long-standing Conservative MP in 1911, and the editor of the *Observer*, J.L. Garvin ('a remarkably able fellow', Amery wrote to his mother).[52] There were close links between these writers and important politicians from the dissident wing of the Conservative and Unionist Party, such as the Tory aristocrat Lord Willoughby de Broke, the colonial administrator and self-styled 'race patriot' Lord Alfred Milner, and the former chief secretary for Ireland, George Wyndham; and, as we saw in the case of Amery, the boundary separating professional journalists from professional politicians tended to be quite porous. In addition, there were a variety of energetic individuals outside these exalted circles who also made their mark. For example, the writer and veteran campaigner Arnold White and the Unionist MP for Stepney Major William Evans-Gordon were men whose spheres of influence lay at some remove from the fashionable drawing rooms and London clubs frequented by the likes of Milner and Maxse, but both published in the *National Review* and compensated for their lack of social cachet by the determination with which they pursued their chosen projects. However, not all of those whose views found a home in the *National Review* could easily be placed on the conservative spectrum. The former New Zealand politician William Pember Reeves, who wrote on immigration control in Australasia, was a New Liberal sympathiser and friend of the Liberal MP Herbert Samuel.

Activism among the Radical Right falls into two main periods. At its most intense during the years of opposition following the Liberal landslide in the 1906 election, the Radical Right reached a climacteric in 1911–1912 during the Home Rule crisis and Lloyd George's moves to curtail the powers of the House of Lords.[53] Once this moment was past, the Right became wholly preoccupied with the growing certainty of war and its patriotic agenda began to lose its distinctiveness. However, even while the Conservatives were still in office at the fin-de-siècle, the Radical Right was already starting to find its collective voice. Its origins can be traced back to the final years of Queen Victoria's reign and perhaps particularly to the disquiet aroused by the initial setbacks in the Boer War in December 1899 when the 'Black Week' led to widespread concern that Britain and its empire were no longer capable of meeting the challenges that faced them. As early as April 1900, Maxse saw signs of political failure all around him and asked despairingly: 'Can any substitute for an outworn Party System be devised?'[54] Balfour's appointment as Prime Minister in 1902 did little to appease Maxse and he was soon openly attacking the new leader whenever he could. In April 1905, for example, Maxse criticised the weakness of the Conservatives in Parliament, complaining that – among other lapses – the Balfour administration had no real intention of passing the much-needed Aliens Bill, given that they had ineptly allowed their first attempt to fail the previous year.[55] From these seeds grew a powerful sense of a nation betrayed by its leaders, which became a powerful theme within the Radical Right throughout the Edwardian period and continued into the postwar era.

For the majority of those on the Right of the party – and others too – the one man who appeared to offer a plausible alternative that would revivify both nation and Empire was Joseph Chamberlain, the leader of a Liberal faction that had entered into a coalition with the Conservatives in the mid-1880s after breaking with Gladstone over Irish Home Rule. Between 1895 and 1903, Chamberlain held the post of Colonial Secretary and in May 1903 he put forward an ambitious set of practical proposals that provided a new imperial framework for rethinking the Conservative Party's political and social mission in a way that also had implications for the question of immigration. Originally announced as a system of Imperial Preference but subsequently better known as Tariff Reform, Chamberlain's policies were designed to re-balance the terms of trade between Britain and the Empire by shifting the burden of import duties to non-imperial goods. Not only were these plans designed to bolster economic integration between Britain and its overseas possessions, but Chamberlain thought that they would create an untapped stream of revenue that could be used to fund social welfare schemes at home, while strengthening British industry and binding the new working-class electorate into a more concrete identification with the Empire by promoting what he had earlier called 'the ties of sentiment, the ties of sympathy – yes, and the ties of interest'.[56] Immigration control was not originally part of Chamberlain's initiative, but the racialising rhetoric in which he couched his advocacy of Tariff Reform meant that it could easily be incorporated into his social imperialist agenda. The *National Review* was quick to draw the two together, arguing that the invasion of 'our home market' by imported manufactured goods was 'closely connected' with 'the question of the pauper alien, which has long been a crying scandal', especially in 'the congested districts of London'.[57]

Chamberlain's ideas were rapturously received by some of the up-and-coming figures on the far Right of the party. Leo Amery recalled that Leo Maxse 'waltzed me around the room as he poured forth a paean of jubilation at the thought that, at last, there was a cause to work for in politics'.[58] In July 1903, the Tariff Reform League was launched to campaign for the implementation of Chamberlain's proposals, and on 9 September he resigned his cabinet post on the grounds that he could 'best promote the cause I have at heart from outside'.[59] Generously funded by business and commanding a remarkable level of popular enthusiasm, the League had 'over six hundred branches' at its peak in 1910, some of them with 'well over a thousand members'.[60] But there was always a tension within the movement between those who saw it as essentially a programme of economic protectionism and those who wished to place the emphasis firmly on the imperial dimension of Chamberlain's plans.

For Chamberlain, ties of sentiment were also ties of blood, a point he made forcefully in a speech at Newcastle-upon-Tyne on 20 October 1903 – just a few weeks before the Conservatives took the decision to press ahead with a new Aliens Bill, in the wake of the final report of the Royal Commission on Alien Immigration. Chamberlain reminded his 5,000-strong audience that they were members of an imperial fraternity comprising some 'eleven millions of white men, flesh of your flesh, blood of your blood, of the same religion, and with the same reverence for the British Empire, claiming to share its history and its glorious past; they are willing to unite their future to yours' – and his words were loudly and fervently cheered.[61] This 'glorious past' was quintessentially a history of military endeavour that brought the British people into full consciousness of themselves as a nation and enabled them to grasp where their true loyalties lay. As he had emphasised to a Unionist audience in West Birmingham earlier that year, 'here, in the United Kingdom, we have different races but one people'; the Scot and the Englishman might 'feel differently' about the battles that had once been fought between them, but 'both … may be equally proud of having had their full part in Waterloo or the Alma'.[62]

The terms 'tariff reform' and 'imperial preference' provided a kind of fiscal shorthand that could be deployed as slogans to rally and unite a people whose social and political cohesion had been fractured by the effects of free trade. In arguing that his programme was the only reliable remedy, Chamberlain was telling his audiences exactly what they wanted to hear: that trade unionism and free trade were incompatible and that, according to the economics of tariff reform, the 'sweater' and the 'blackleg' were 'enemies of the human race' because they forced wages down, whereas among proponents of free trade such men were regarded as the 'benefactors' of mankind.[63] It therefore made no sense for his opponents to attack him as a protectionist and then to argue that alien immigration should be stopped.[64] Controlling the movement of peoples was at one with regulating the flow of commodities and raw materials. Chamberlain's most graphic speech on this point was delivered, not coincidentally, in East London on 15 December 1904. The relevant parts of this address were reprinted as a pamphlet by the Tariff Reform League, under the title 'Alien Immigration'.[65]

The extent to which Tariff Reform arguments could be given an anti-Semitic inflection depended very much upon the imagined addressee and the style of the address. So, if one turns to the cartoons and drawings used to illustrate the Tariff Reform League's pamphlets, such as the sketches of 'The Man We Import' or the 'Entrance for Foreigners', then it is immediately plain just who the bogeymen were, whether or not they have explicitly been labelled as Russian or Polish Jews. Nonetheless, as Thomas Dewar's performance on the hustings indicates, politicians were often careful to distance themselves from crude anti-Semitic statements, and with good reason. Moreover, the social composition and interests of the Tariff Reform lobby were too various for the movement to become a simple anti-Semitic tool, and the same was true of the Radical Right more generally. Certainly Thomas Dewar was not mistaken in appealing to the patriotism of East End Jewish voters. High on the list of the Tariff Reform League's financial backers, for example, were businessmen who had made their fortunes in South Africa, including Jews like Alfred Beit who, like Chamberlain, wanted to see the Empire strengthened. Leo Amery, who wrote a regular column for *The Times* under the pseudonym 'Tariff Reformer', was descended from 'a distinguished and intellectual family of Hungarian Jews' on his mother's side and had spent several years as a child in Germany.[66]

However, attitudes towards the Jews within the pages of the *National Review* were never completely settled, and Maxse's own allusions to the Jewish Question were plagued by inconsistencies. On the one hand, Maxse shared his father's pronounced Francophilia and unashamedly rallied to the Dreyfusard cause in the *Review*, publicly defending Dreyfus against his accusers throughout the 1890s. Yet Maxse was to make some lamentably ill-considered judgements in the kind of writing about Jews that he allowed into the journal, most conspicuously in his decision in 1902 to invite Edouard Drumont, the notorious anti-Dreyfusard and author of *La France Juive*, 'to explain the anti-Semitic movement in France' to the *Review*'s readers.[67] Nor was this the first time Maxse had given comfort to anti-Semites. In 1897, for example, Maxse's columns contained questionable remarks about 'cosmopolitan rapacity' in Lombard Street in the City of London. 'The smiling prospect presented to the greatest Empire the world has ever seen', Maxse sneered, was to be at the beck and call of 'a streetful of moneylenders.'[68] Similarly, and despite his own Jewish background, Leo Amery maintained the kind of snobbish dislike towards 'the

Jews in Poland and Russia or those who have just come from there' that was sometimes found within upper-class Anglo-Jewry, believing them to be 'still in a very real sense a separate nation'. As Amery wrote in 1917, 'an Anti-Semitism which is based, partly on the fear of being swamped by hordes of undesirable aliens from Russia, etc., and partly by an instinctive suspicion against a community which has so many international ramifications' could only be 'much diminished' by the achievement of a Jewish homeland.[69]

The nationalist critique of cosmopolitanism alluded to by Maxse could take a number of forms and, even when it was not an attack on Jewish 'plutocracy' per se, the Jews were typically cited as chief offenders. But these arguments sometimes had contradictory results. Consider the case of George Wyndham, ironically described by Amery as 'a romantic Tory with a Disraelian outlook, a Coningsby born into a later age', whose support for Tariff Reform was primarily an imperial rather than 'an economic creed'.[70] At the height of his influence in the Conservative Party, Wyndham set out his vision of the future of the British Empire in a 1904 Address that he gave as Lord Rector to the students of Glasgow University, entitled *The Development of the State*. There he attempted to identify the principles that led to a flourishing polity and argued that the most important factor was what he called 'pride of Race', understanding 'Race' to mean 'blood lineage' rather than seeing it as 'co-extensive' with the more subjective sense of nationhood – that is, the feeling of 'attachment to a particular territory'.[71] It was 'Race' that connected us to the glorious achievements of our forefathers – shades of Monsieur de Sidonia's 'All is race' in Disraeli's *Tancred* (1847) – and it was 'Race' that inspired us to build upon the past.

As a politician who prided himself on being a man of letters, Wyndham commended the 'old humanistic arts of History and Literature' to his audience for its role in enabling students to grasp the racial tradition to which they belonged. But he also extolled the 'new humanistic sciences of Ethnology and Folk-lore' for laying bare those 'facts of Race' that deserved the closest study; and, when he discussed examples (like Switzerland or Poland) where nation and state failed to coincide with race, he contrasted different 'Aryan stocks' with descent from 'a widely alien non-Aryan broad-headed race' that could be recognised by making careful 'head-measurements' (43–47). 'Facts' allowed a nation to learn about and thus to tolerate otherness, including respect for those 'non-Aryan Races' with which a modern state will necessarily come into contact and 'must embrace' (47). Wyndham rarely referred to particular 'Races' by name, preferring to rely upon the more generalised Aryan/non-Aryan dichotomy to indicate the main lines of racial division, but in this part of his Address he specifically mentions the Jews, whose civilisation was once more advanced than that of 'our ancestors', yet who 'have remained a race', despite having briefly 'played a part in State-building' (48).[72]

Given the uneasy relationship between race, nation, and state, Wyndham argued that there were two dangers or 'excesses' that the institutionalisation of racial difference must avoid (56). On the one hand, an over-emphasis on racial pride may give rise to an inward-looking provincialism; on the other, an 'Empire-State' that forgets its racial roots can produce a 'vapid' cosmopolitanism and become prone to 'civic apathy and decay' (36, 49). Throughout his lecture, Wyndham conducted a running critique of cosmopolitanism, tracing it back to first-century Rome where the ideal of being 'a citizen of the world' was initially fashioned by Greek and Jewish writers, men who were 'aliens by origin' and unable to appreciate the true greatness of empire: it was they who made Rome 'the emasculated prey of virile races' (7–8). Resorting once more to the analogy between politics and physics that was woven into his talk, Wyndham portentously imagined the cosmopolitan future as a Wellsian vision of a dying world in which 'an extinguished sun' presided over 'a frozen earth', while 'the whole solar system' drifted 'through the night of space towards the dark resultant of a like catastrophe' (10). Just as entropy extinguished the life of the universe, so cosmopolitanism would bring 'death to the State', as it had to the imperial state of Rome, reversing 'the force of Political Gravitation' (11, 33). And, though in a different key, his warning to the present was no less poetic and no less striking:

Perhaps, at a time when facilities of transit are being multiplied and cheapened until they fascinate our imagination and seem to speak with the very voice of the Spirit of the Age, it is of cosmopolitanism that we should most beware. The Spirit of the Age is seldom prophetic. A life of polyglot restaurants and international sleeping-cars does not conduce to civic virtue. It laps us in the listlessness of cosmopolitan luxury. It makes for satiety and slumber; and slumber, if unduly prolonged, invites a rude awakening. (57)

Cultural, not to say racial, inmixing was becoming effortless in a more mobile world and had resulted in a society grown worryingly lax and soft. In later years, Wyndham's attack on cosmopolitanism was to focus not on food and railways, but on 'cosmopolitan finance and polyglot "Society" and dining off truffles and imitating the Yiddish pronunciation of the letter R with a guttural growl'.[73] Among family and close friends like Hilaire Belloc, Wyndham's structuring opposition between Aryan and non-Aryan races took a more overtly anti-Semitic turn, driven by his disgust over what he saw as the fashionableness of the Jew within the upper classes. 'How good it is that I and you,' he wrote in doggerel to Belloc, 'Are sure that nothing matters/If this, or that, obsequious Jew/ From Mirth, or Terror, chatters.'[74]

In a fanciful aside in his 1904 Address, Wyndham speculated that tales of fairies, goblins, or gnomes were a political phenomenon in that they arose among aboriginal peoples driven out to the margins of the land by conquering races. Fairy stories, ballads, and legends offered a kind of compensatory magic to those who had been vanquished and, in an odd use of Darwin's theory, Wyndham argued that this kind of folklore enabled 'the fittest' of them to survive defeat (54). He was not alone in reading such superstitions in political terms. In January 1906, two years after Wyndham's speech, Rudyard Kipling began to publish his own imaginative version of the relationship between fairyland and history when the stories that became *Puck of Pook's Hill* started to appear in the *Strand* magazine. When the book came out in October, Wyndham read it and was entranced, particularly with the stories dealing with the end of the Roman Empire, which he read as a parable for the present. He wrote at once to Kipling to express his enthusiasm, and in reply Kipling confirmed that he 'didn't mean to write parables – much – but when situations are so ludicrously, or terribly, parallel, what can one do?'[75]

Kipling was highly regarded by leading members of the Radical Right, some of whom he knew well and whose views he shared. His circle of friends and acquaintances included, to name some of the most prominent, Cecil Rhodes, Alfred Milner, Leo Amery, and Leo Maxse. After 'seeing something of Joseph Chamberlain' between May and December 1900, Kipling became a keen supporter of that 'mighty interesting man': 'He is about the only one of our crowd who ever handled a business and he is worth his weight in diamonds for that cause alone'.[76] Kipling's reference to 'our crowd' is particularly revealing. When Chamberlain suffered the debilitating stroke in July 1906, which effectively brought his political career to an end, Kipling hoped – as did Amery – that Lord Milner might be persuaded to take a more active role in politics.[77] This loss only compounded the Liberal electoral victory earlier that year, a setback that for Kipling, as for others on the Right, was profoundly depressing and led him to receive news of the illness of the new Prime Minister, Campbell-Bannerman, in November 1907 with glee ('As a premier he is better extinct.').[78] These politically-inspired emotions were part of the Radical Right's embattled and intransigent structure of feeling and for its adherents it was as though Kipling wrote in a code that only they fully understood. Leo Amery spoke for many of his associates when he described Kipling in Biblical cadences as 'a prophet with a vision and a preacher with a message; a message not for the world, but for his own people; for him, as for the prophets of old, a chosen, if oft back-sliding people'.[79]

Puck of Pook's Hill is, if not prophetic, at least didactic: a 'message' for the English in the aftermath of the Liberal landslide, a reminder of what will endure. In these stories Kipling narrates an extracurricular syllabus to two upper-middle-class children in Sussex, outlining the buried lore of their native land. The stories are largely told by representative historical actors in their own words – here a Norman knight, a Roman centurion, a craftsman from the Renaissance, and finally a Spanish-born Jewish physician from the reign of King John – under the guidance of the eponymous Puck who stage-manages this series of encounters with the past. To ensure that Dan and Una learn their lessons properly, the spirit Puck commands the magic of 'Oak, and Ash, and Thorn' so that what the children have seen and heard is not so much forgotten as transformed into a composite racial memory, a national unconscious that will pervade the very being of these unformed and uncorrupted children.[80] And the stage for their instruction is set and solemnised by a ritual of possession in which the children take 'seizin', a piece of turf that Puck cuts from the meadow as a sign that they are 'lawfully seized and possessed of all Old England' (48).

The closing story, 'The Treasure and the Law' – interestingly, a late addition to the collection that goes unmentioned in Kipling's published letters – belongs to Kadmiel the Jew. Although he is not the most recent inhabitant of Sussex that the children meet, Kadmiel's narrative nonetheless recapitulates a key moment in the coming of modernity, since it is a secret history of the signing of Magna Carta. What this event inaugurates is, in Kipling's telling, the rule of law, underwriting the possibility of peace and commercial prosperity for England. But Kadmiel's influence is not a manifestation of that concern with 'order and obedience' which Matthew Arnold famously identified as the essence of 'Hebraism' in *Culture and Anarchy*.[81] By bribing the Barons and surreptitiously denying gold to the King, Kadmiel manipulates the relative strengths of these two feudal opponents in order to curb the King's power and in the long run protect the Jewish people from further persecution. In fact, treasure *is* the source of the law, for Kadmiel tells Puck how, through a payment of 'two hundred broad pieces of gold to change those narrow words', it was he who secured a significant alteration to the letter of the charter and made its provisions apply to all men, and not just free men. In a double-edged compliment, the priest who bargains with Kadmiel on the Barons' behalf observes: 'Jew though thou art, the change is just, and if ever Christian and Jew come to be equal in England thy people may thank thee' (204). And so Kadmiel fulfils the 'Prophecy' given at his birth, that he 'should be a Lawgiver to a people of a strange land and a hard speech' (200, 206).

But while he is shrewd and far-sighted – he looks beyond the limited horizons of his kinsman 'Elias of Bury, a great one among our people' who clings hopelessly to royal patronage – Kadmiel is a liminal presence, one who walks 'between the living and the dead', having journeyed 'to the East to find my Kingdom' where none was to be found (201). His visit to Bury St Edmunds is a continuation of that unsuccessful search, and England becomes his home. In contrast to the other characters in these stories, Kadmiel remains an outsider and never achieves the stature that he might have done 'if we Jews had been a people' (205). Instead, this sometime physician operates behind the scenes, capitalising on his knowledge of 'how the earth's gold moved – that wonderful underground river' which he claims for 'we Jews' as a special province: 'The Secret River of Gold' of the story's prefatory poem, which 'Shall be shown to thee and thy Race' (195, 200, 203). Kipling is thus identifying Kadmiel with what Marx called 'the worldly cult of the Jew' – that is, with '*bargaining* and *money*', making his role as much conspiratorial as it is financial.[82] Of necessity, Kadmiel works by subterfuge and trickery in order to avoid persecution, but unknowingly he is the instrument of a larger imperial destiny, because the gold bars he uses to alter the balance of forces in the Barons' favour are the spoils of a raid on the African coast by the intrepid Norman knight Sir Richard Dalyngridge. If Kadmiel guarantees the liquidity of these assets, he is also the power that quite literally liquidates them by casting the gold into the sea.

In 'The Treasure and the Law', the Jewish money-lender is an integral part of the nation's collective biography, narrated by a succession of solid historical character types. Uniquely, however, Kadmiel has a half-seen doppelgänger from the present day to represent the fruits of his political labours. Framing and punctuating the telling of Kadmiel's story is the sound of 'the cruel guns' of a pheasant-shooting party led by a local land-owner (197). In 'his new yellow gaiters, very busy and excited,' Mr. Meyer is the vulgar Jewish parvenu who has bought himself a place in the Sussex countryside and tries to act like a member of the gentry, though he cannot shoot properly (he injures one of his own beaters and pays him a sovereign in compensation) and aims at rabbits instead of pheasants (207). This clumsy charade, Kipling seems to want to add, is what equality before the law has finally come down to: 'A Prince without a Sword/A Ruler without a Throne ... In every land a guest/Of many lands a lord' (196).

The before-and-after structure of 'The Treasure and the Law' was a recurrent feature of attempts to bring the Jewish Question into national politics. In his book *The Modern Jew* (1899), for example, Arnold White sought to distinguish between the old and the current form assumed by the Jewish Question, between rank anti-Semitism and what should be regarded as 'legitimate anti-Semitism', between the earlier, 'beneficial' effects of the right of asylum and the creation of 'a Jewish imperium inside the English Empire' under present-day conditions.[83] For White it was the elective affinity between the Jews and the spirit of modernity that made 'the waxing power of the Jewish race' seem so urgent a problem, one that threatened to 'master and mate other questions of international concern' (ix). At times White wrote as though it were modern capitalism that was elaborating a new definition of what it meant to be Jewish, since 'neither origin, race, nor faith' seemed as important as it once did (4). *The Modern Jew* exonerated Captain Dreyfus of all charges and exempted England's Jewish aristocracy and 'the good anglicised Jew' from criticism, applauding these more traditional sections of the upper class for having 'done most to prevent the outbreak of anti-Semitism in England', work that was being undone by newer arrivals (5–6).

The most consistent theme of White's sprawling and contradictory tract is the corrosive effect of Jewish money-making, described in phrases that anticipate Kipling's Kadmiel as 'a river of materialism' or as 'waves of materialism', metaphors that leak into the depiction of Russian immigrants as 'a torrent of Jews' (xi, 14–15). Swept along in the rip-tide of his own invective, White stresses the irresponsibility of the Jewish nouveaux riches, who flaunt their wealth without any awareness of the social obligations that come with advancement and are consequently 'the class which is the cause of coming danger' (8). The argument not only recapitulates that from his book *English Democracy* written five years earlier, but repeats some of its sentences practically verbatim. Anti-Semitism is therefore laid squarely at the door of the Jews because in its 'modern' form it is said to be 'due to the new appreciation of the growing financial power of the Jewish race' (200). While money-lenders and destitute aliens appear to be confined to separate chapters, this separation quickly breaks down, overwhelmed by the swelling numbers ('the hard facts') conjured by White's overheated prose: 'Hundreds and even thousands of the Jewish aliens who settle in this country become, or hope to become, traffickers in money', and so 'the avenues leading to the money-lending trade are crowded with Jews' (166). In White's account, any distinctions that can be made regarding Jewish people as a whole seem difficult to maintain, mere temporary phenomena that quickly pass away as the Jews revert to type. Elsewhere, for example, White argued that it was impossible to distinguish 'refugees' from 'chronic, incurable paupers', and so the definition of the category of the undeserving poor tightens.[84]

White essays a cautious, defensive approach to anti-Semitism, objectifying it as another name for the Jewish Question or citing it as a symptom of an urgent social problem that impacts upon the indigenous working class. But circumspection was not his only mode, and a comparison of his less prudent utterances with the unabashed anti-Semitic prejudice of his Continental peers is revealing. Edouard Drumont's essay on 'The Jewish Question in France', published by Maxse in the *National Review* in January 1902, is a case in point. For Drumont too, the Jewish Question in modern society has nothing to do with religion, but is determined by economic and social factors. In particular, Drumont sees the Jews as *the* principal destabilizing force within the market, the source of all its turbulence and its crises: 'When Opportunism was once enthroned, then began that unforgettable series of discomfitures, failures, catastrophes and financial scandals which finally exhausted the resources of France. ... In all these crashes invariably appeared the sinister figure of the Jew, who was never on the losing side, but always a winner – a duper of dupes'.[85] The Jews are a threat to the Republic, corrupting its ideals and undermining its prosperity. Everywhere they are able to penetrate, the Jews destroy the social fabric, ruining their competitors and at the same time creating 'a State within a State, a nation within a nation'. This latter tendency Drumont regards as a sign of 'their unsocial instincts', in which the self-interested cultivation of social contacts is combined with a marked 'aloofness' and a carefully maintained sense of distance (697).[86] Once again, the fault is said to lie with the Jews themselves, and so 'it is the fury of their victims [that] generated the Anti-Semitic movement, and keeps it alive to-day' (693).

Although Drumont and White concurred in viewing the Jewish Question as, in Drumont's words, 'one of economics, but ... also a national question', they also saw it as 'universal' (695, 698). However, while Drumont approvingly quotes Herzl's contention that the Jewish Question ought to be considered 'a world-wide political question, to be settled by the concert of civilised nations', he clung to the belief that anti-

Semitism was the deepest form of racial antagonism and could be found 'in every latitude, in every religion, and in every race' (695, 699). White's position seems to be less elemental, at least in some of his writings. For example, in arguing for immigration controls in Britain, White insisted that the problem of the destitute alien could not be successfully tackled solely at the national level, and therefore that 'Europe must deal with her Jews as a whole', with talks involving Russia.[87] Like Herzl, White favoured a diplomatically negotiated resettlement of East European Jews, preferably in the Near East, as a way forward. But he held out little hope that Palestine could fit the bill (he thought Armenia was a much more viable option) and, with a smack of satisfaction, pronounced 'the political Zionistic movement' to be 'irretrievably doomed'.[88] Similarly, while he had no qualms about asserting that 'cosmopolitan finance is only another name for Jewish finance', White's language rarely descended into the open display of phobia characteristic of Drumont's invective where 'cosmopolitan nomads' are quickly transformed into 'cosmopolitan vermin' that are 'eating [France] up' (697, 702).[89] In Drumont's ideology there is a kind of racialist metaphysic at work, according to which the Jewish 'craving for lucre and domination ... seems to be in their blood' (697). That this is no casual figure of speech can be seen from its extension into the realm of ideas, which 'the Jewish and Judaising world handles ... precisely as it handles bills': 'The Jew is not only a dealer in dishonest money, he is likewise a dealer in dishonest thoughts, and as he circulates bogus shares which are not worth the weight of the paper on which they are printed, he also circulates ideas which are misleading and mendacious caricatures' (691).

Compared to Drumont's uncompromising racism, White's comments are more guarded, and when he discusses 'the anti-Semitic movement' across Europe, it is clear that he would not wish to include himself within it. Nor does he follow Drumont in essentialising Jewishness. The final paragraph of *The Modern Jew* is a good example of White's paradoxical use of developmental arguments, for he concludes his book with the pious hope that the feminising influence stemming from 'the growth of the woman's movement' will lead to a diminution in the unremitting harshness of 'Jewish materialism'.[90]

'THE ANTI-ALIEN CRUSADE'

Arnold White was among those sitting on the platform in the Queen's Hall of the People's Palace when the newly formed British Brothers' League held its 'Great Public Demonstration' against alien immigration on 18 January 1902. Founded early in the previous year, the British Brothers' League was the most visible and the most vocal of the anti-alien associations that came into existence between 1880 and 1914, and its working-class base in London's volatile East End gave it some prominence during the hearings of the Royal Commission on Alien Immigration in 1902. As a grass-roots extra-parliamentary campaigning body that claimed to have reached a membership of 12,000 by October of that year, the BBL's profile was significantly different from most other movements built around the issue of immigration, though its relatively brief existence makes the scale of its influence difficult to assess.[91] Colin Holmes has argued convincingly that the BBL should not be considered in isolation because it had strong connections with Conservative and Unionist Party branches in East London which also sponsored the more parliamentary-focused pressure groups like the Londoners' League and the Immigration Reform Association during the same period.[92] Local councillors, MPs, and civic dignitaries were all well represented at the People's Palace demonstration, whose smooth organisation was in the capable hands of 'the Conservative and Unionist agent for Bow and Bromley'.[93] This was a showcase event for the BBL, and the choice of venue was intended to lend it respectability and a community presence that would ensure its leaders had the maximum political leverage. According to the headline in the *East End Observer*, the rally marked the start of an 'anti-alien crusade' (the word 'crusade' carrying a historical allusion to Jewish persecution). However, reports were not confined to the local press, and the demonstration was clearly intended to be a moment when one of the most uncompromising and strongly proletarian counterpublic voices made itself heard in the wider political culture.

The opening speeches and statements of support included 'a long letter from Miss Marie Corelli', the bestselling popular novelist, who demanded that 'British workmen, British wages, and British homes' should be the government's first priority and called for branches of the League to be formed all over Britain as 'a firm bulwark … against constant foreign invasion of our land and our trade interests'.[94] But it was Arnold White who proposed the first motion, calling for the prevention of immigration in order to solve London's housing problem.[95] In his speech, White argued that aliens, who came to England 'not … because they were persecuted' but 'because they wanted our money', were putting the 'riches and wealth and magnificence of this great Empire' at risk. Returning to the themes of *The Modern Jew*, he asserted that the reason nothing had been done was because 'the people who invented key-money in East London belong to the race of whom the majority are poor, but of whom some are very, very rich, and the very, very rich financiers are the financiers of Europe'.[96] White did not have to name this 'race': those in the gallery who responded with cries of "Wipe them out" and "Down with them" knew who he meant. If there were any doubts, other speakers like the London County Council member for Stepney (and member of the BBL), A.T. Williams, whose bravura display of rhetorical questions and posture of plain speaking ('That was not the time to mince matters or words') whipped the crowd into a revivalist frenzy, eliciting the condemnations that were already on many lips:

[A]s I walk about your streets, I see names have changed; I see the good old names of tradesmen have gone, and in their place are foreign names – the names of those who have ousted Englishmen into the cold (Loud cries of "Shame!" and "Wipe them out!") What about the men who worked seven days in the week? What about Sunday labour? (Loud and continued cheers, and a voice: "Give it them thick.") What about the people who lived eight in a room? ("Jews!")

Once generated, however, this aggression had to be contained. And so the call and response of the crowd was inserted into a larger, almost dialectical structure of incitement and disavowal.

When a speaker issued a disclaimer, however, it had an edge. Harry S. Samuel, the new Conservative MP for Limehouse, was insistent that this was not 'an anti-Semitic movement', but added that without immigration control, 'the future boded ill for the Jewish race in England'. David Hope Kyd, the Tory candidate for Whitechapel, also declared that 'it was not a movement against the Jews. But it was a movement in defence of Englishmen'. Such statements outraged the 'few isolated foreigners' who were present and led to their summary expulsion, as though the meeting were seeking a symbolic prolepsis of the deportations that it had been convened to bring about.[97] This pattern of incitement and disavowal was also characteristic of the BBL. For example, when A.T. Williams gave evidence before the Royal Commission on 15 May 1902, the Chairman taxed him with using the word 'Jew' too freely as a synonym for 'alien' or 'immigrant' and asked whether 'you are positively anti-Semitic and wish to exclude all Jews from this country?' – a suggestion Williams quickly denied. Yet a moment later, while explaining how the Antcliff Estate had changed hands, Williams produced a plan 'marked in red' to indicate which houses 'have been bought by Jews, and mostly by foreign Jews' since 1895.[98] In fact, the charge of anti-Semitism seems to have been a source of real difficulty for Williams and in a later speech he repudiated his association with the BBL precisely because of what he called its 'anti-Jewish position'; nor was he the only BBL member to do so.[99]

The BBL's public utterances were racked by ambivalence, as though they were unsure how far they could go. In February 1902, just weeks after the 4,000-strong meeting at the People's Palace, the BBL brought out a pamphlet in both Yiddish and English warning the public not to be 'deceived by people who are trying to make you believe that "alien" means "Jew". It does not! Alien means "foreigner".'[100] Yet in April 1904, the League passed a resolution which it forwarded to Father Creagh in Limerick, thanking him 'for the noble work he has undertaken to prevent a class of undesirable aliens … from demoralising the nation and bringing misery into the homes of our Irish Brothers and Sisters through their inborn instinct of greed, usury and arrogance' – a message of support that could have had no other target than the Jews of that city.[101] Earlier that same month, William Stanley Shaw, the BBL's founder and former president – he had left the League ostensibly because of its anti-Semitism in summer 1902 – wrote a letter to the *Daily Express* urging Catholics and Protestants to avoid taking sides in 'the alarming state of affairs now prevailing in the city of Limerick'. It was not a case of 'religious persecution', he argued, but of 'fair-dealing' Jews being lumped together with 'the guilty'. He then turned his attention closer to home: 'In East London, how many small British shop-keepers have been ruined through being Boycotted by Jews? The bulk of the Hire-Furnishing Companies in London are run by Jews under British names. – Schlesinger becomes Sinclair, Sigenberg becomes Stuart, Slobererbosky becomes Gordon. – What have their "clients" got to say?'

It is a mark of the perceived need to handle expressions of anti-Semitism in the public sphere with some care, at least in moments of political turbulence, that the *Express* declined to publish the letter. Unabashed, Shaw had it printed up as a poster and asked sympathisers to pin it to their walls or windows. Appended to the slogan was the declaration: 'The only real solution of the Jewish Problem is the ZION MOVEMENT'.[102]

The year 1904 was a pivotal moment in the history of anti-Semitism in Britain. At the beginning of the year, the riots against the Jews in Limerick provoked widespread condemnation and, as this unsavoury episode rumbled on, fanning out into the countryside around the city, even the *Daily Express* felt moved to denounce the police for their failure to protect 'the victims of Limerick race-hatred'.[103] The shift from sudden irruptions of violence to a generalised boycott of Jewish traders in the area indicated a degree of planning and local organisation that went beyond spontaneous expressions of hostility. The boycott lasted for months and, as late as July, attacks against individual Jews were continuing to occur. By early 1905, Jewish families were starting to move out of Limerick.

The violence against the Jews coincided with the Conservative government's first attempt to bring in anti-immigration legislation – the First Reading of the new Aliens Bill took place in March, although by July the Bill had to be abandoned. The letter columns of the press were heavily preoccupied with 'the alien question' and much of the discussion reads like an extended series of footnotes to the 1903 Report of the Royal Commission, with several of the Commissioners expanding on their individual views. In *The Times*, for example, Major Evans-Gordon reintroduced the bogey of the 'sweater' into the debate, arguing along Tariff Reform lines, that 'the unrestricted importation of cheap labour' could only result in '"sweated" conditions all round, cheap goods cheaply made by one set of "sweated workers" for another, who could afford nothing better'.[104] By May, the fear that the Aliens Bill would be undermined by the charge that it promoted race-hatred was being taken seriously enough for the Conservative Prime Minister Arthur Balfour to issue a statement insisting that no such 'rise and growth of any anti-Semitic feeling in this country' was taking place.[105] The following day, Israel Zangwill promptly wrote to *The Times* to disabuse Balfour of this mistaken belief.

Zangwill was particularly angry because when Balfour referred sceptically to 'the epidemic which rages everywhere against the Jew', the unattributed phrase that he placed in quotation marks was Zangwill's own. Whatever Balfour or his government's intentions might have been – and Zangwill was careful to deny any suggestion of anti-Semitism within the Cabinet – 'the Aliens Bill was inspired by anti-Semites and will reinspire them'. Nevertheless, Balfour's sensitivity about the Bill missed the point which was that 'the whole of the country shows signs of infection', as evidenced by 'Jew-baiting in Wales, Jew-boycotting in Ireland, and anti-Semitic pamphleteering in Scotland.'[106] Four days later, in a letter to the jurist A.V. Dicey, Zangwill suggested that 'it might help to stave off' what he called 'the coming Anti-Semitism' if, in his capacity as Vinerian Professor of English Law at Oxford, Dicey were to write 'to *The Times* or in some other weighty medium' pointing out the threat that lay ahead. Citing the BBL's endorsement of Father Creagh's agitation as 'holy work', Zangwill stressed that 'the danger is not trivial' and to clinch his case he enclosed an anonymous letter he had recently received for Dicey to see, a sign of 'what germs are in the air'.[107]

A few years later, when the 1905 Aliens Act had become law, Zangwill's position had become noticeably more pessimistic. On 25 April 1907, in a reply to a fellow activist, Zangwill expressed his doubts about the value of holding a meeting in opposition to 'the growth of anti-Semitism in England'. According to Zangwill – perhaps reflecting upon his own bitter experience – anti-Semitism was simply the wrong kind of sociopolitical phenomenon to be tackled by raising a public outcry. Unlike the specific acts that offended against the Jews, anti-Semitism was 'an indefinite thing', notoriously difficult to target or pin down: 'you might as well protest against the fog or the rain,' he wrote dismissively. While never going quite so far as to suggest that anti-Semitism was as natural as the weather, Zangwill seemed to hold firmly to the liberal view that people were entitled to their opinions, however distasteful one might find them to be. Like Herzl, he had now come to believe that 'there is no radical remedy for the Jewish situation except acquiring a territory of our own'. And, with a touch of that waspishness for which he was renowned, he insisted that, in line with their own teaching, Jews should expect to be 'tried by a higher standard than the rest of the population'; indeed, it was good that they should be pressed to live more principled lives than those around them, allowing them to set an example to everyone. Better by far that Jews strive to remove 'the faults in our people which provoke hostility.' If they could demonstrate that 'the Jews [did] not deserve anti-Semitism', then they could 'at least despise it'.[108]

CHAPTER 4

Writing the 1905 Aliens Act

Whether one starts from the avalanche of numbers that thundered through the headlines of the popular press – "SIXTY THOUSAND COMING!" – or from the more cautious tallies kept by bodies like the Jewish Board of Guardians, behind the brute statistics of immigration lay the actual experience of the journeys undertaken by families and individuals.[1] Migrants were rarely given the opportunity to speak publicly about their passage, but occasionally stories surfaced that revealed the hardship they had to endure, a plight for which they were frequently held to be responsible. This chapter examines some important examples of migration narratives and considers the ways in which such stories formed a backdrop to the introduction of a law to restrict the numbers of immigrants entering Britain. As the aforementioned headline implies, these narratives often fanned the fear of immigration as the root cause of a cluster of refractory urban problems whose persistence threatened to bring the country to the brink of disaster. But the prospect of immigration *control* was also a source of fear, variants of which were emplotted in fictional anticipations of national disgrace and even imperial decline. In a sense, the fitful progress of the legislation reflected the necessity of charting what members of the Tory cabinet hoped would be seen as a reasonable and arguably moderate course between these larger contradictory narratives, whose consequences were pushed to extremes in some of the popular fiction of the period.

'AN INQUIRY ON THE SPOT'

Travelling in steerage, without the benefit of a cabin, had long been thought to be as sordid as it was cheap – everyone 'condoled together over the food and the vileness of the steerage', as Robert Louis Stevenson wrote during his voyage to America in 1879.[2] But for East European Jews at the turn of the century, conditions were particularly bad. On some of the Danish ships sailing between Libau and London, migrants were crammed into the space between decks and in one instance where the main cargo consisted of horses – more than twice as many horses as passengers – the animals' urine and faeces ran into the passengers' already squalid quarters. Complaints had been made to the Danish Consul by the medical authorities for the Port of London but to little effect, as the officer in charge, Dr. Herbert Williams, told the Royal Commission on Alien Immigration in the evidence he gave on 19 June 1902.[3]

This was an extreme example of the commodification of space in commercial sea travel. According to Williams's testimony, agents would book space on board ships measured in cubic feet and then maximise their returns by selling as many tickets as they could. On the *Riberhuus*, the ship referred to in Williams's testimony, it was calculated that there was only 4.12 square feet per person, and Williams added that this was by no means the smallest area he had encountered. Not all ships treated their passengers as inhumanely as these Danish vessels did. Yet when representatives of two of the shipping companies were interviewed by members of the Commission nearly a year later, it was apparent from their vague and defensive answers that no substantial improvement had occurred. The London agent for Denmark's United Steamship Company immediately sought to distance himself from any knowledge of the migrant's journey from Libau to London, emphasising the independent role played by local firms in arranging contracts to transport Russians and Poles to England, chartering accommodation in steerage and then organising their food and passage. 'The steamer has nothing whatever to do with them except to receive them and reserve the room', the agent said of the migrants, when questioned. From the outset he had insisted that 'the carriage of these immigrants is a matter of small interest to me, personally', and then, in an extraordinary statement, he all but conjured them away, as though their very existence were a matter of chance, and certainly an unwelcome embarrassment: 'They happen to be on board the ships that come to London. We have nothing whatever to do with them; we have nothing to do with their passage, and have nothing to do with them when they arrive. Really I have not anything to do with them at all, so that I have no information to give about them'.[4]

Ultimately, the lack of concern for the migrants was a function of their status relative to other profitable goods in Libau's busy export trade, alongside grain, wood, eggs, and ponies. Major Evans-Gordon, the Unionist MP whose inveterate campaigning had done much to bring the Royal Commission into existence, reported a conversation with a ship's captain at Libau regarding the ventilation of his steamer under adverse weather conditions when the hatches had to be battened down. The captain claimed that he would always 'turn the vessel's head to the wind and wait till the sea moderated.' To close the hatches would be to risk the death of the ponies. "And the people?" asked Evans-Gordon. "Yes," replied the captain, "and the people" – a response that the MP decided was 'evidently an afterthought'.⁵

This exchange occurs in *The Alien Immigrant* (1903), Evans-Gordon's account of his own unofficial investigations into 'the Alien Question', including his travels in Russia and Eastern Europe. The trip was undertaken on his own initiative in the autumn of 1902, when the Royal Commission was not in session. As he told the other Commission members with disarming frankness, as someone who 'was presenting one side of the case' only, he had felt that it was 'essential ... to find out all I could'. Evans-Gordon clearly saw his role within the Commission as partisan, but he must have been worried about his credibility and about how best to strengthen the argument he wished to press upon the government. At any rate, his uncompromising and yet intensely fastidious stance during the Commission's meetings put him in the odd position of acting as both judge and expert witness, contributing detailed papers to the Commission on the condition of the Jewish people in the countries he had visited, on immigration into the United States, and on the vagaries of the Russian system of passports. However, Evans-Gordon was never cross-questioned. The Chairman adroitly suggested that his evidence might be discussed at a later date – an option that, despite Evans-Gordon's own eagerness, was never taken up.⁶ *The Alien Immigrant* was an expanded version of the various reports that Evans Gordon had handed in to the Commission the previous year, and was intended to ensure that his voice would not be muffled by those who sought to outmanoeuvre him.

Evans-Gordon's journey – what he pointedly called 'an inquiry on the spot' – was by no means unique.⁷ The myriad journeys outwards from Eastern Europe led to a number of high-profile expeditions in the opposite direction by concerned individuals drawn from a variety of political and professional backgrounds. Few achieved much success. In 1886, to take possibly the earliest example, the merchant banker and Liberal MP for Whitechapel, Samuel Montagu, had visited Russia, stoutly insisting to the authorities there that it had become impossible for 'any more of our people ... to maintain themselves in London, owing to the depression of trade'.⁸ Montagu's outspoken views made him so unpopular that he was summarily expelled from Moscow for falling foul of the laws restricting the movement of Jews. The following decade saw the novelist Hall Caine travelling to Eastern Europe in 1892 to investigate the plight of the Jews, a trip sponsored by the Chief Rabbi Hermann Adler, but a cholera epidemic prevented him from going beyond the Russian border. Meanwhile, Arnold White made no less than five trips to Russia in the 1890s, under the auspices of the philanthropist Baron de Hirsch, with the aim of examining conditions on the ground and trying to persuade the tsar to support a South American colony for impoverished Russian Jews. White subsequently testified before the Royal Commission that these visits had been instrumental in changing his thinking on the problem of immigration. Initially, he had thought it a 'matter of mere local economics', but he soon came to realise that 'the crux of the problem is primarily racial and international'.[9] Like his ally Major Evans-Gordon, anecdotes drawn from his Russian trips formed an important part of White's evidence and also featured prominently in his political journalism. Evans-Gordon's book on immigration was therefore the latest instalment in a long line of fact-finding expeditions that continued into the twentieth century. Yet the facts these investigators found varied considerably. In May 1903, the *New York Journal* commissioned the Irish politician and crusading journalist Michael Davitt to travel to Russia to report on the Kishinev pogroms. His book, *Within the Pale: the True Story of Anti-Semitic Persecution in Russia*, was published during the same year that Evans Gordon was arguing in *The Alien Immigrant* that, so far as religious tolerance was concerned, the Russian Jews were 'better off than their Catholic fellow subjects.'[10]

In an unpublished article entitled "The Problem of the Russian Jew", Davitt wrote that he had 'come from a journey through the Jewish Pale a convinced believer in the remedy of Zionism'.[11] But other reporters came to very different conclusions. In an early example of the genre, a journalist from London's *Evening News and Post* was instructed to 'Go to Hamburg to-night, collect facts about the emigration of paupers from that port to England, and come back as a destitute alien'.[12] This was the same route described by the labour-mistress Jane Hardy in Margaret Harkness's 1889 novel *In Darkest London*, and like that fictional account, the *Evening News* correspondent emphasised the predominance of young female workers among the Russian and Polish Jewish migrants. In both narratives conditions on board ship are disgusting, but in the newspaper story the insanitariness of life below deck shades into displays of rank indecency and moral turpitude, the base reality that everyone involved in the trafficking of migrants, from German officials to Jewish support networks, are depicted as furtively attempting to conceal. According to the *Evening*

News, only a blanket refusal of entry would put an end to the subterfuge through which 'pauper aliens' were brought into England through a confidence trick involving borrowed clothes and borrowed money.

To produce these reports, the *Evening News* correspondent also had to resort to disguise, passing himself off as an impecunious wanderer, travelling in steerage – though at one point he was taken to be a man of loose morals in search of an easy lay. But mistaken identity was an occupational hazard in the kind of investigative exposé that became the stock-in-trade of the New Journalism, where no human interest story was complete without a frisson of voyeuristic horror and fascination at transgressing conventional barriers of class, culture, and taste. Within this journalistic framework, migration narratives thrived and improvements in mass visual reproduction meant that these feature stories were increasingly backed up by glossy illustrations or photographic vignettes to drive home their point. The series of photo-essays by the Punjabi writer and performer Olive Christian Malvery, originally published in *Pearson's Magazine* between 1904 and 1905 under the title of "The Heart of Things" and later released in book form, is a good example of how Jewish migrants were invidiously contrasted with the indigenous poor. With her theatrical talent for disguise, Malvery sought to make the lived experience of London street hawkers, tramps, pea-shellers, and barmaids accessible to her readers, whereas East European Jews were treated as stubborn exceptions to this personal approach. Not only was she unable to cross into Russia, but her attempts to gain admission to the Poor Jews' Temporary Shelter in Whitechapel in order to photograph the conditions inside met with a hostile response. Following this tense stand-off, the East End Jews were depicted as a problem and a threat, requiring vigilant policing, denied the kind of sympathetic hearing that would bring them into the national imaginary.[13]

Malvery's articles on 'the Alien Question' need to be seen as part of a rising curve of similar stories during the period from August 1903, when the Royal Commission on Alien Immigration reported, through to the early months of 1905, when the Conservatives decided to make a new Aliens Bill one of their two key pieces of legislation for the coming Parliamentary session. By this time, the sheer accumulation of 'facts' about immigration led to a new focus on how these data were to be understood and whose interpretations of these narratives of exit and entry were to take precedence. Moreover, the resort to a Royal Commission in order to cool the political temperature with a dose of rational deliberation actually gave the issue greater prominence and undoubtedly stimulated more adverse publicity. Nor was the pressure relieved by the Commission's majority recommendations in August 1903, which urged that 'the immigration of certain classes of Aliens into this country be subjected to State control and regulation' and also that any districts which had become overcrowded as a result of migrant settlement could be 'declared ... a prohibited area' and barred to incoming foreign workers and their families.[14] Although there were sometimes heated disagreements during the hearings, the pressure of tendentious questions made it difficult for dissenting views to be heard. In the press and in political debate, the migrant's voice was either suppressed – the Royal Commission's proceedings were a rare but only partial exception – or relayed in a highly mediated form. In fact, those who were called upon to represent this experience typically belonged to an older generation, those who had lived in Britain for ten or twenty years. The sole 'distressed English Jew' to speak before the Commission was born in Manchester and had been a British resident for two decades – instructively, the usual adjective 'destitute' or 'pauper' was replaced by a more genteel designation, perhaps because he was not, *strictu sensu*, an alien and therefore did not warrant the standard pejorative phraseology.[15]

As Michael Davitt's account of his visit to Russia concluded, the main alternative perspective available came via the Zionist movement since this provided an organised platform through which the concerns of East European and Russian Jews could be expressed within the public sphere. But in defending Jewish interests, the Zionist leader Theodor Herzl was necessarily promoting a possible national future for Jews that at least some British restrictionists could support – hence the complex multiparty investment in inviting Herzl to address the Commission. The idea of Britain underwriting a Jewish homeland had apparently been floated by Joseph Chamberlain, following representations from Herzl's English supporters in Birmingham, much to the consternation of Lord Rothschild.[16] In fact, most British commentators found Herzl a striking and impressive figure – as they were clearly intended to do – and failed to mark the internal divisions that were simmering below the surface of the movement. The Fourth Zionist Congress in London in August 1900 had been sufficiently well received in the press to heighten British awareness of the Zionist cause and strengthen the powerful sentiments it could elicit. Indeed, Herzl was keen to win as many British supporters to his cause as he could, Jew and gentile alike, with a view to outflanking the rather disdainful response he had received from the Anglo-Jewish establishment. When Herzl told his audience that England was the one place in the world where 'God's ancient people were not detested and persecuted', he was flattering a wider public outside the meeting hall, and when he added that further immigration into England by his fellow Jews would be a disaster, he was telling those who sympathised with the anti-alien lobby exactly what they wanted to hear.[17]

Flattery did not stop reports of the Congress from sliding into the gross caricature, with Herzl rising above the excitable throng like some latter-day Svengali or vulgar matinee idol:

There were tall, dark Jews, with jet-black beards, flowing robes, spectacles, and skull caps; diminutive plump Jews, with grey, shaggy whiskers, who shouted "Yah!" with gurgling vehemence when any speaker scored, rising from their seats and nearly clapping the skin off their hands; then, in bright colours and coquettish headgear, was a row of pretty Jewesses, who took down the utter-ances of Dr. Herzl verbatim, only pausing in their task to wave handkerchiefs frantically when the president beamed on them; and lastly there was a heteroge-neous array of Zionists in the galleries – dark-haired men and women, presum-ably linguists – for all the speakers, save one, and he used two languages, spoke in their own tongue.

'The scene was often a lively one,' observed the *Westminster Gazette*'s cor-respondent, noticing the heckling that sometimes broke out. Expressive, colourful, and, in this column, rather absurd, the Congress opened onto a world that the reporter seemed ultimately to find quite baffling, an enigma epitomised by the 'strange signs' appearing in the delegates' copious notes, signs 'which might have stood for secret condemnation and disgust, for all the Christian knew to the contrary.' Although the touch is light, there are undertones of conspiracy in the *Gazette*'s sly portrait, an implication that Zionism was some kind of secret society, impenetrable to an outsider, despite its official front.[18] Nevertheless, Zionist themes became integral to the public and parliamentary debates around the 1905 Aliens Bill, and arguments about the future of Zionism formed an important backdrop to the way in which "the Jewish Question" was posed during the early years of the twentieth century.

Zionism crops up in one of the last and most contested journalistic accounts of migrant journeys, a series of thirteen articles that appeared in the *Standard* in January 1905 under the general heading "The Home of the Alien". Written by the paper's own 'exceptionally qualified and impartial Special Commissioner', a title that would have reminded the reader of the recent Royal Commission, this collection of pieces was in fact the work of Robert H. Sherard – a man who boasted of travelling with a com-plete three volume set of the Commission's Report in his portmanteau.[19]

Sherard, a great-grandson of Wordsworth, was a novelist, biographer, and critic who wrote books on Daudet, Wilde, and Zola as well as sensational investigative tracts like *The White Slaves of England* (1897) and *The Cry of the Poor* (1901). The series immediately provoked outrage in the *Jewish Chronicle*, and Sherard was soon obliged to reveal his name when defending himself in its letter columns. The cycle of rebuttal, defence, and counter-accusation continued into late March.

In format, Sherard's articles resembled those that had appeared in the *Evening News and Post* in 1891. But, unlike the *Post*'s "Commissioner", Sherard did not take the role of the alien and instead relied upon the police, emigration officials, newspaper editors, and shipping company managers to give his reports the stamp of authenticity. The opening sentence of the series set the tone for what was to follow. 'One monstrous fact can be ascertained here in the course of a one-minute's conversation with any official at the Emigrants' depôt', wrote Sherard, 'and that one monstrous fact is in itself alone … the entire justification of Mr. Chamberlain's policy'. This putative 'fact' was that three-quarters of all Jewish emigrants from Hamburg carry what by 'euphemistic convention' are known as 'the loathsome diseases.' Sherard's bizarre claim served as a point of departure for a litany of allegations over the following days and weeks that included lack of hygiene, criminality, overcrowding, parasitism, and exploitation, gathered under such lurid subheadings as 'The Shameless Greed of Parasites', 'Russia's Refuse', 'Only Waste Products for England', or 'A Tale of Worse than Mean Streets'.[20] While the details varied, the alarmist tone was unwaveringly maintained as Sherard moved from Hamburg to Bremen and on into Russia (Alexandrovno), before ending his journey and his column in Poland (Warsaw).

Sherard's consistency of tone was not matched by consistent argument, and the *Jewish Chronicle* quite effectively pilloried the series by printing his conflicting claims side by side, allowing them to self-destruct. The further the *Standard*'s Special Commissioner travelled into Russia and Eastern Europe, the more likely he was to acknowledge the suffering of the Jews and to contradict his earlier assertion that 'Anti-Semitism appears a myth, or rather a legend, to be found only lurking in the Paris offices of Monsieur Edouard Drumont'.[21] Overall, however, his reports read like a commentary upon (or annex to) the Royal Commission, sounding out German or Russian officials on its recommendations and interviewing informants mentioned by Evans-Gordon. To be sure, the final articles were written under the shadow cast by the *Jewish Chronicle*'s patient demolition of his case, telegraphing its own correspondent in Hamburg to check Sherard's figures and revealing 'that only one per cent of all emigrants passing Hamburg were found ill, of which 3/4 Jews and 1/4 Christians'.[22] When Sherard argued that, were the Aliens Bill to become law, Russia might be forced to 'treat her millions of Jewish subjects like human beings' and 'the Jewish question would be settled in a day', he was attempting a last defiant response that he hoped might salvage the raison d'être of his series.[23]

Zionism comes to the fore in an interview with the Rabbi Dr Rosenak in Bremen. Sherard arrived to find the Rabbi reading a report of Joseph Chamberlain's December speech in Limehouse, which had argued that the idea of a Jewish home in East Africa – a proposal that Chamberlain had earlier discussed with Herzl – could provide 'an asylum for these persecuted people' and thus 'the solution of the [Jewish] question'.[24] The Rabbi praised Chamberlain as 'a Zionist', but was doubtful whether a territory could be found. Instead, he believed that there was 'plenty of room in England for the alien Jews there and to come', so long as this population was properly dispersed and the English were prepared to spend 'some money' on them. The function of the Rabbi in this report is to illustrate the delusions, but also what Sherard calls 'that entire want of altruism' of the Jews with regard to 'their destitute fellow-countrymen.' The Rabbi's belief that his co-religionists were hardworking, skilled labourers who were rarely a burden on the community is cited; and yet, no sooner has he left the room than his beliefs are thoroughly contradicted by 'an Israelite gentlemen' who has also been present and who works in shipping. This unnamed interlocutor argues that it would be cheaper for the British government to pay the emigrants' fare to America and asks whether, by refusing to consider this step, the government is not using the 'thousands' of destitute London Jews as 'an object lesson' in order to gain electoral support for the Aliens Bill. Sherard was unimpressed. Only 'the sternest and most radical measures' can deal with a 'parasitism of so aggressive a nature', he told his readers.[25] His words might have stood as an epigraph for the entire "The Home of the Alien" series.

Nevertheless, the 'Israelite' informant's reported comments touched on an issue that bedevilled discussion of "the Alien Question" from the very beginning and was to form a key component of the Parliamentary debates in 1905. Estimates of the size of the immigrant population settling in Britain were always clouded by the much larger number of arrivals who were transmigrants, those who came into the country en route to other destinations, predominantly the United States. For dogmatic opponents of alien immigration, the claim that many migrants were simply passing between ships and that Britain merely served as a stepping stone in a far longer journey was either a cover under which East European Jews could slip into the country unnoticed or an idle wish entertained by those who were in fact too destitute to travel any further. In each case, the transmigrant label would have been a misnomer. Unsurprisingly, critics of immigration control were unconvinced by such alarmist claims. In their view, anti-alien campaigners were deliberately inflating the real number of immigrants by adding in those with no intention of making their home in Britain.

AN ALIEN CASTAWAY

The ambiguous figure of the transmigrant lies at the centre of the most deeply felt of all migrant narratives from this period – Joseph Conrad's short story "Amy Foster", written between May and June 1901. Originally serialised in three weekly instalments in the *Illustrated London News* during the latter half of December, it was longer than was usual for such pieces – initially more than 9,000 words; but then, as Conrad told his literary agent J.B. Pinker, 'the subject is big too'.[26] Described by Edward Said as 'the most desolate of his stories', this tale of a man who escapes one death only to succumb to another has been rather neglected by Conrad scholars, although Conrad evidently regarded "Amy Foster" as one of his 'most highly finished' pieces.[27] It is also in essence very close to his own personal history as an outsider – the *Times Literary Supplement* once called Conrad 'this alien of genius', overlooking the fact that he had by then been a British subject for more than twenty years.[28] Indeed, the story has been read (auto)biographically by Said on more than one occasion as a fictional representation of the exile's fear that separation from home will be sealed by the finality of a lonely death in a foreign country, perhaps a recognition of 'how his own experience of exile converged with Conrad's'.[29] An early title for the piece, "A Castaway", nicely captures the migrant's sense of abjection and abandonment, and when Conrad incorporated the phrase within the text, he revised this part of the story several times.[30] However, the wider political context ought also to be borne in mind here. "Amy Foster" was written during a phase which saw a marked rise in organised hostility towards 'aliens' – that is, during the months between the official foundation of the British Brothers' League in Stepney on 9 May and the setting up of the Parliamentary Pauper Immigration Committee on 31 July 1901, two pressure groups arising from opposite ends of the sociopolitical scale.[31]

Moreover, from 1894 to 1898, a bill seeking to reduce alien immigration had been brought before Parliament nearly every year. If Jósef Teodor Konrad Korzeniowski ever ceased to think of himself as a foreigner, it would not have been in 1901.

The protagonist of "Amy Forster" is 'a poor emigrant from Central Europe bound to America' in the hope of making his fortune when the ship on which he is travelling is hit by another vessel desperately trying to escape a storm.[32] Both ships go down and this man is the sole survivor, but his existence is only discovered after the bodies of the dead have been washed ashore. And so, by chance, on an 'awful, blind night', he becomes a reluctant transmigrant, a man whose life is suspended between an irretrievable past and an unknown (in this case unattainable) future – 'separated by an immense space ... and by an immense ignorance', in the words of Conrad's country doctor's narration – and condemned to remain permanently in transit, stranded in a coastal village in south-east Kent (161, 168). Gradually the man, whose name is Yanko, gives up the idea of travelling on to America, for he cannot afford a ticket and, after the shipwreck, he has become afraid of the sea. Instead he marries Amy Foster, a stolid local girl who cares for him, and fathers a son on whom he dotes, believing that the little boy will now provide him with a real companion, a soulmate who will learn his language and his customs and come to know him as he truly is. Yet finally Amy turns against him too and, when he falls ill, she runs away, taking the child with her. Sick, neglected, and bewildered, Yanko dies alone.

The use of the shipwreck as a device to intensify the survivor's isolation and dramatise his unpreparedness for a life of exile raises an important question: to what extent do the details of this emigrant past resemble those of the alien immigrants about which Arnold White or Major William Evans-Gordon or Robert H. Sherard wrote? At first sight, the parallels are close. Characteristically, Conrad's alien is a rather peripheral European, originating from 'the eastern range of the Carpathians' or from 'the more remote provinces of Austria', and speaking neither English nor German or French (161). In a 1902 letter to his French translator, Conrad referred to his 'castaway' as 'an Austro-Polish highlander' ('un montagnard autrichien-polonais') and the man's repetition of the Polish word 'góral' to indicate that he comes from a mountainous region is mistaken for his surname by the uncomprehending English villagers.[33] He is rechristened Yanko Goorall, literally 'John the mountaineer'. This is one of several, often painful cultural misunderstandings that harden into what is, at best, a grudging tolerance – at worst, a beating.

As one would expect from an experienced mariner, Conrad's account of Yanko's journey is precise and pointed, confirming the miserable over-crowded conditions revealed by the Royal Commission and other inves-tigations. Again, this part of the narrative was among those most heavily revised by Conrad and he evidently took considerable pains to convey the confusion and vulnerability of the migrants, taken first by train to Berlin ('large and lofty and full of noise and smoke and gloom, and clang of iron') and then on to Hamburg where they are 'driven below into the 'tween-deck and battened down' – like prisoners – 'from the very start' (155–156). In these passages, Conrad's impressionism is stark and claustro-phobic, like a nightmare from which it is impossible to awaken: 'People groaned, children cried, water dripped, the lights went out, the walls of the place creaked, and everything was being shaken so that in one's little box one dared not lift one's head' (155). As Gail Fraser has noted, Conrad deliberately defamiliarizes his descriptions, describing both steamships and railway engines as 'steam-machines' in order to emphasise the gulf 'between an industrial society and the peasant's world'.[34]

By making events strange, Conrad's narrative obliquely moves the reader closer to the disturbing formative experience of the migrant, but also further away, as the ordinary becomes bizarre or odd; and this dis-tancing is mirrored in the frame narrative through which the telling of the story takes place. Like the earlier *Heart of Darkness* (1898–1899), 'Amy Foster' consists of a tale within a tale, a story told to the unnamed initial narrator by Kennedy the country doctor and former naval surgeon who is also reporting (and commenting upon) what Yanko has told him. As in *Heart of Darkness*, there is a kind of indistinctness in the portrayal of certain events whose nature and causes are left for the reader to speculate upon. Amy Foster's change of heart towards Yanko resists explanation and consists of '*unreasonable* terror' or '*unaccountable* fear', and once he is dead we will never know whether the past sometimes appears before the 'white screen' of her mind (174–175, my emphasis). But the distancing effect is social and cultural too, for the device of the shipwreck effect-ively removes the migrant from the metropolitan crucible in which 'the Alien Question' is posed, the very place where Yanko might have encoun-tered others who speak the same tongue. Instead he is marooned in the heart of the English countryside, maximising his difference from those around him.

If this ploy can be defended as perfectly justifiable poetic license – the most economical method of representing the migrant as a challenge to Englishness in its purest, ostensibly least troubled state – Conrad's

reliance upon atypical circumstances does not stop at this point. For in
'Amy Foster' the defining characteristics of the alien's foreignness are
also blurred, making it an open question how like or unlike the English
he actually is. Yanko is, for example, a Christian, but a very un-English
Christian, for his naive devotion casts a satirical light on the faith of the
good people of Colebrook who refuse to treat their new neighbour as their
brother. It is a mystery to Yanko why the local churches are 'kept shut up
on week-days' or why they are so poor when there is 'so much wealth' in
the community (168). In fact, Yanko does not at first believe that he has
fallen among Christians and only 'the steel cross at Miss Swaffer's belt'
showed that 'he was in a Christian country at all' (166). On their side,
the local inhabitants are so dismayed by his wild and swarthy appearance
that they find it difficult to think of him as a Christian and at one point it
is suggested that he is 'a bit of a Hindoo' (164).

However, there is another, more disquieting way in which Yanko's simple Christian piety is thrown into relief and which is used to underscore
his status as luckless victim. For it turns out that his whole journey has
been based on an act of deception or misrepresentation. Yanko's decision
to travel to America is based on the belief that he will quickly become rich
and will then be able to send money to his family. But it is made obvious to the reader that this is nothing but a confidence trick devised by
predatory Jews who prey upon these gullible Central European peasants.
Arriving 'in a peasant's cart' on market-day, these Jews dress themselves
up to resemble 'Government officials' and 'in the next room, so that the
common people shouldn't hear, they kept a cunning telegraph machine,
through which they could talk to the Emperor of America'. After much
negotiation, the Jews relay an offer from 'the American Kaiser' of 'three
dollars a day' with 'no military service to do', which is eagerly accepted by
those 'young men of the mountains' who are able to raise the fare and are
not afraid to travel (157). Yanko's father sells land and livestock to pay for
his son's passage.

This is not the only reference to predatory Jews in "Amy Foster" – Jews
are also typed as cheapjack market traders, for instance. But in each case
what is set in play is the notion of them as a 'parasitic', commercially venal
class, 'exploiters of the peasantry' who are always ready to gull the unwary,
the same pejorative characterisation that was rife in Eastern Europe and
was used to justify the persecution of the Jews.[35] However, the English villagers know nothing of Yanko's past. To their eyes he appears variously as
'a hairy sort of gipsy fellow', 'an unfortunate dirty tramp', a 'nondescript
and miry creature', and possibly 'an escaped lunatic' – alternative ways

of putting a name to what is threatening in an outsider (159–160). Yanko never escapes these attributions, and elsewhere in the story, even though the grime has been removed from his person, Conrad's descriptions exaggerate and generalise his foreignness in ways that seem to deny any claim to social acceptance he might conceivably make. Yanko is always a 'foreigner' or a 'stranger', 'so different from the mankind around' him (153). Where the innocence of the shipwrecked children's bodies on the beach is marked by the fairness of their hair, Yanko is distinctively 'swarthy', his "olive pallor", "little black moustache", and "big, black fierce eyes" indicating divergent, almost orientalised racial origins, whether Romany or Asiatic (164, 168). An earlier portrait of him "parting with his black hands the long matted locks that hung before his face, as you perhaps part the two halves of a curtain" also seems to point in the same direction, suggesting something stealthy or mysterious, 'the dread of an inexplicable strangeness' (160). Though Yanko's deracinated ethnicity preserves a certain air of elusiveness, it remains at bottom stubbornly incontrovertible. 'His foreignness had a peculiar and indelible stamp', remarks the doctor, a specialist presumably well versed in reading the idiosyncrasies of the body (168). It is not so much that Yanko represents all foreigners, ambiguously Eastern and Western at once, as that he stands for a moment of difference so stark that it nullifies any possibility of trust.

In the end, it is the ineradicability of that 'inexplicable strangeness' that condemns Yanko. While the villagers grew accustomed to the sight of him, they 'never became used to him', and it is as though the slow-witted Amy Foster also starts to become unused to him, as her affections modulate from love to repulsion (168). This reversal is presented in terms of the chemistry of raw emotion. "Physiologically, now," muses Dr Kennedy, "it was possible. It was possible" (172). More bluntly, an anonymous notice in the *Academy* described the story as having all the force of a dream that administers a rude shock to the senses. Cutting through 'any kind of sentimentality', the reviewer wrote, Conrad confronts the reader with 'bare life' – 'life … bare to the nerve'.[36] Here the phrase 'bare life' refers to the immediacy of unguarded or uncontrolled feelings, released from the restrictions imposed by social convention, but in recent years the expression has acquired considerable political weight as a concept used to denote those who fall outside the protection of the law and thereby become subject to unlimited state control. In Giorgio Agamben's analysis of how systems of government have developed in the West, what the ancient Greeks called *zoē* – that is, the mere fact of being alive (as opposed to the identity that is conferred through participating in a specific way of life) – has been brought 'into the sphere of the polis' and this 'politicization of bare life as such' is '*the* decisive event of modernity'.[37] In making this claim, Agamben is arguing that the ultimate political sanction which can be imposed upon those who are judged not to belong within a given nation-state is to be denied access to legal consideration or legal redress. Such a denial is signified by the removal of such stigmatized populations to a physical space that is 'outside the normal juridical order' – a work camp, an internment camp, a transit zone – in which they are 'stripped of every political status and wholly reduced to bare life'.[38] His examples are various, but they range from the persecution of the Jews in Nazi Germany in the 1930s and 1940s to, closer to home, the treatment of illegal Albanian immigrants in Italy in the 1990s. While the origins of this crucial event – or whether it can properly be said to constitute an event at all – remain open to dispute, Agamben's emphasis upon the exclusionary nature of what he has called 'this no-man's land between public law and political fact' directs attention to the blind spots of modern democracies.[39]

Clearly 'bare life' has a somewhat different meaning in these two contexts, but their coincidence is not entirely fortuitous and each illuminates the other. In 'Amy Foster', one might say that the political forms the backdrop to the physiological, but it would not be true to say that Yanko's difficulties are a product of his being excluded from the civil rights available to British subjects. Yanko's precise legal status is never directly broached, but what we do learn about him is consistent with changes in the position of aliens brought about by the 1870 Naturalisation Act. In law, there was no barrier to a marriage between Amy and Yanko; however, as a government review of naturalization noted in 1901, 'a woman who is a British subject ceases to be a British subject by marrying an alien', and Yanko's death would have done nothing in itself to alter this fact.[40] Importantly, the 1870 Act had made it possible for a 'foreigner' like Yanko to own property, so that he could accept the wedding gift of a cottage and an acre of land from Mr Swaffer, his employer. In both instances, Yanko's encounter with the legal system publicly ratifies a personal bond: the gift, which offers him a livelihood, is a token of Swaffer's gratitude to Yanko for having saved the life of his granddaughter after she has fallen into a horse pond. The deed is processed by the child's father, Mr Willcox, who happens to be a solicitor and also Colebrook's Town Clerk. Yanko, of course, has no knowledge of British law and regards Swaffer as if he were a landowning Polish patron and benefactor. While their relationship is modern and contractual in form, Kennedy is right when he describes it as 'curiously feudal' in substance (171).

In doing relatively little to regulate the lives of resident aliens, British law generally left them to sink or swim in civil society, guaranteeing a bundle of rights and responsibilities among nominally equal subjects who were otherwise free to follow their own inclinations. 'Amy Foster' depicts the hither side of this legal fiction. Wary of foreign intruders – Yanko is never a casualty or refugee – the villagers instinctively view Yanko as not only less than their equal, but less than human, his language sounding to their ears 'so disturbing, so passionate, and so bizarre' (172). Instead of welcoming this marooned 'creature', Yanko is at first confined in a wood-lodge, where he reminds even Kennedy, his most humane interlocutor, 'of a wild bird caught in a snare' – bare life indeed (164). In death, the figure of the nonhuman returns: staring at the migrant's body, Kennedy is once more put in mind of 'a wild creature under the net; of a bird caught in a snare', an impression that the doctor also associates with Yanko's son, like some inherited taint, when he looks down on the child, lying helpless in his cot, a perception that provides the story's final image (175). Conrad was later to describe the theme of 'Amy Foster' as the 'essential difference of the races'.[41] But it is Yanko's minority status, signified by his unassimilated creatureliness, 'the narcissism of minor differences' with a vengeance, that leads to his perishing 'in the supreme disaster of loneliness and despair' (175).[42]

TROUBLE IN STEERAGE

'Amy Foster' might serve as an epitaph for what was thought by many in nineteenth-century Britain to be a *right* of entry. By the time that Conrad's story was republished in *Typhoon and Other Tales* in Spring 1903, the Royal Commission on Alien Immigration was nearing the end of 49 days of hearing evidence in which 175 witnesses had been examined. It issued its report in August of that year and, after a major controversy within the Conservative party around the question of tariff reform which resulted in Joseph Chamberlain's resignation from the front bench, Arthur Balfour's reshuffled Cabinet decided in November 1903 to bring forward a Bill to regulate alien immigration – the fifth such Bill in a decade.[43] Not everyone in government was in favour of such a measure. As early as December 1901, Arthur's brother, Gerald Balfour, then-President of the Board of Trade, had written a nine-page Cabinet memorandum casting a sceptical eye over the evidence used to support the restrictionist case and arguing that a system of passenger inspection was likely to be ineffectual, as he believed the relative failure of far tighter laws in the United States had already demonstrated.[44]

The 1904 Aliens Bill foundered: announced as the first item in the King's Speech in February, it was badly drafted, badly handled, and had to be withdrawn in the first week of July. The government had been weakened by the split on Tariff Reform and was scarcely prepared for the fierce Liberal attack during the Second Reading. There is still doubt as to why Balfour then took the unusual step of sending the Bill to the Grand Committee on Law, a procedure expressly designed for complex but uncontentious legislation requiring expert attention. Was it a desperate effort to circumvent Liberal censure (in which case it failed miserably)? Or was it, as the young Winston Churchill, among others, believed, a ruse that threw an already damaged Bill to the Liberal wolves in order to place the blame on them (in which case Balfour might still be suspected of having snatched defeat from the jaws of victory)? Either way, the Bill suffered death by a thousand amendments in frequently noisy sessions in which Churchill played so obstructive a role that he was angrily accused by Evans-Gordon of acting at the behest of Lord Rothschild and other 'powerful Jewish' interests.

There would be no blunders the second time around. On 18 April 1905, the government introduced a new, more robust Aliens Bill and by early August it had cleared the House of Lords and received the Royal assent. After the previous year's disastrous dress rehearsal, Balfour was determined to move the measure briskly through the Commons, keeping to a strict timetable. On the fourth day of the Committee stage, after the Liberals had pressed hard, but largely unsuccessfully, to amend the Bill, Balfour intervened to propose a series of deadlines to expedite its progress through the House, under the pretext – as before – that there was nothing controversial about the intended legislation. In the face of a Tory majority, the Liberals were powerless. The Third Reading took place at the duly appointed time on 19 July, and the Bill passed by ninety votes. Henceforth foreign steerage passengers arriving in the country by any one of fourteen major ports were liable to inspection and could be denied entry.

Precisely because it was procedurally so messy and took place at a moment when tensions within the Conservative-Unionist bloc were coming into the open, the parliamentary discussion of the 1904 Aliens Bill is far more revealing than its successful sequel and deserves greater attention from historians than it has hitherto received. By 1905, positions on both sides were well entrenched and the truncated debates seem curiously anticlimactic after the heated exchanges only a year before. The extended speeches that brought the Act into being sound like elaborate set-pieces, their terms already set in such moments of high theatre as the Khaki election hustings, the People's Palace rallies, and the sessions of the Royal Commission, ghosts of arguments and counterarguments that had been in play for a decade or more. But in 1904, the Aliens Bill that the restrictionists had so long desired was now, as the veteran Liberal spokesman Sir Charles Dilke noted, the principal government business of the day, and the debate quickly became argumentative, intemperate, and, at times, raw. There was nothing in 1905 to compare with the proto-socialist John Burns' tub-thumping, rancorous attack on 'rich Jews' for 'bringing upon this country untold harm which poor Jews would not do if they could'. 'The rich Jew suborned judges and corrupted Parliaments, made raids, organized rebellions, and did not hesitate to do things to make himself still richer', and it was these men alone that ought to be kept out, Burns had asserted. So, when Harry Lawson, the Liberal Unionist MP for Mile End, complained in 1905 that there was 'more denunciation of Jews' to be found among Radicals and Socialists than on his side of the House, he doubtless had the memory of Burns's 1904 speech very much in mind.[45]

The central issue for the Liberal opposition in 1904 was the question of asylum, which they linked to Britain's national character. In the past, they argued, Britain had taken in and benefited from many who had been fleeing persecution and it was this humanitarian recognition of the value of freedom of thought that made it unlike any other country in Europe. In his opening statement of the Liberal case, Dilke listed some of the important political exiles who had found sanctuary in Britain, a roll-call that ran from the Communards to Prince Kropotkin. And, during the Second Reading, he gave examples of how refugees had escaped persecution, referring to some twenty-eight Spanish men who had entered the country in July 1897 after being 'improperly charged as anarchists' and 'tortured in defiance of the law' by the Spanish authorities.[46] According to the Liberal party leader Sir Henry Campbell-Bannerman, the very notion of 'keeping foreigners … out' amounted to 'a new constitutional practice and principle'.[47] Equally worrying was the arbitrary power that the 1904 Bill would have placed in the hands of the Home Secretary. For, while the draft legislation contained a loose checklist of the types of aliens that would be barred – including prostitutes, persons of bad character, those unable to support themselves, and the diseased – the decisions as to which ships, at which ports, would be liable to inspection, and which categories of passengers might be detained and possibly deported, lay entirely within the minister's discretion. Better, then, to try to address what were real problems by less draconian legislation, the Liberals argued. Their strategy was to try to replace immigration control by laws that concentrated on sweating. But they were careful not to concede too much. Exploitation in the labour market was not the result of immigration and so immigration control was irrelevant, insisted Dilke. Shifting the argument from race to gender, he claimed that sweating was the result of nonunionized female labour being brought in at lower rates of pay, rather than of Jews driving out non-Jewish English workers.

But the Liberal position on immigration and asylum was never quite as straightforward as this direct rebuttal suggests. At the same time as they were fighting the Aliens Bill, the Liberals were also mounting a campaign against the recruitment of indentured Chinese labourers to work in the Transvaal mines, a scheme that had been sponsored by the Tory Governor Lord Milner. Originally brought in to meet the shortfall of mineworkers in the aftermath of the Boer War, Milner's Labour Importation Ordinance was reviled for undercutting the position of white workers emigrating to South Africa, for promoting appallingly brutal working conditions, and for encouraging sexual immorality in all-male compounds. In a letter to his wife on 22 February 1904, the recently elected Liberal MP Herbert Samuel observed that the morning papers were full of the Chinese labour question and in his diary on 4 March he again noted the scale of the agitation.[48] On 26 March, just three days before the First Reading of the Aliens Bill, the Parliamentary Committee of the TUC organized a rally in Hyde Park to protest against "Chinese slavery", attended by an estimated 80,000 people at its peak.[49] The Liberal party seized on this issue as a means of embarrassing the government in the name of the dignity of labour. But their language was anything but dignified.

The politics of "Chinese slavery" formed a kind of ideological counterpoint to discussions of the 1904 Aliens Bill, a source of populist slogans that could be thrown into the face of Tory jingoism.[50] At the beginning of his first speech, Dilke wasted no time in taunting his opponents:

It was an extraordinary fact that they should be called upon to consider a measure of this description which, for the first time, was going to prevent European white men from coming, at their own cost, as free men to a free country, at the very moment when the very same Government were engaged in sanctioning the importation of yellow men by Government intervention and under servile conditions into the Transvaal.[51]

Writing in a more academic vein in the *Contemporary Review* the following month, Herbert Samuel was no less direct. Contrasting the entry of 'Eastern Europeans' into England 'on a comparatively small scale' with the global movement of the Chinese who 'number a fourth of mankind' and can 'flourish in any latitude from Canada to Singapore', Samuel argued that the latter 'can never be assimilated by the whites.' His case was in essence the same as that made by the Conservatives against Russian and Polish Jews: that their 'excessively low standard of living', 'their narrow, tireless industry' constituted a form of unfair competition with indigenous workers, and that their racial and cultural differences ('their addiction to gambling', 'their secret societies', their 'peculiarly degrading vices') meant that they were incapable of being 'absorbed' into the community. In short, the Chinese were the threat that the Tories feared the Jews were becoming.[52]

To cries of dissent from the Government benches, Dilke told his opponents that the Russians described by Evans-Gordon in *The Alien Immigrant* were 'of a stock which, when it mixes with our own in course of years, goes rather to improve than to deteriorate the British race'.[53] As A.J. Balfour pointed out, Dilke's rhetoric put 'the question of race' at the centre of the debate, and it was the Liberals who often drew attention to the fact that the bulk of the immigrants under discussion were Jewish because this was integral to their argument regarding the need to uphold the right of asylum on religious as well as political grounds.[54] The Conservative approach oscillated between defensively declaring that race was irrelevant – Evans-Gordon liked to say that their wish was 'not to exclude undesirable aliens because they are Jews but because they are undesirable aliens' – and deploring the Judaisation of local constituencies.[55] In the Second Reading on 25 April 1904, for example, Samuel Forde Ridley, the Unionist MP for SW Bethnal Green, told the House that 'he represented a constituency which was entirely alien, and where they would hardly see the English language written either in the newspapers, posters, timetables, or in any other printed matter, but where Yiddish was the universal language and where they might just as well be in Palestine as in London'.[56]

Forde Ridley's punch line was a commonplace of Edwardian anti-Semitism. One finds virtually the same sentiment expressed in the epigrammatic quip made by the eponymous dandy in Saki's early sketch, 'Reginald at the Theatre', when he drolly informs 'the Duchess' that 'the great Anglo-Saxon Empire ... is rapidly becoming a suburb of Jerusalem.'[57] In a less facetious idiom, this vision of cultural annexation was a staple in the platform of the British Brothers' League and drew 'loud cries of "Shame!" and "Wipe them out!"' at their 'Great Public Demonstration' in January 1902.[58] Indeed it was a position also voiced by Liberal restrictionists like Henry Norman (MP for South Wolverhampton and a powerful speaker at the People's Palace rally) and Sydney Buxton (Tower Hamlets, Poplar), each of whom spoke on this theme during the Second Reading of the 1904 Aliens Bill. Evans-Gordon seized upon this fear and shrewdly turned it into a countervailing right to be set firmly against the right of asylum, "the most elementary of all their rights, namely, the opportunity of earning a living in their own land".[59]

Race was therefore a vital ingredient in the arguments both for and against an Aliens Bill. When Sir Charles Dilke and Herbert Samuel made their case on immigration, neither of these two temperamentally very different kinds of Liberals was prepared to argue that restriction was entirely unjustifiable. Before going on to savage the Conservative case, Dilke deliberately emphasised that he had never been an advocate of 'laissez faire', whereas, in his major speech on the 1905 Bill, Samuel – who a few years later was to be the first practicing British Jew to obtain a Cabinet post – was careful to state that he was 'not opposed to the regulation of immigration in all cases on grounds of principle'.[60] Hovering in the background of the debate was a notion of racial eligibility which on occasion slipped into racial entitlement, as when Samuel asserted later in the same speech that it was 'universally agreed that the Jewish race are a sober, industrious, domesticated, quick-witted people and easily assimilated'.[61] Who then could be more deserving of the protection afforded by a right to asylum?

Restrictionists were placed in an uncomfortable position. They could deny the relevance of Jewishness to any rational assessment of the necessity for immigration control, which would have forced them to drop their argument that English culture was being eroded in parts of the metropolis and in other urban centres. Or they could insist upon the pernicious nature of Jewish immigration and risk the damning accusation of anti-Semitism. One well-worn way out of this dilemma was to claim that an Aliens Bill would prevent the rise of an anti-Semitism that was already dangerously close. This was a claim advanced at all levels of the Conservative and Unionist bloc from Harry Lawson to the Home Secretary, Aretas Akers-Douglas. Likewise, at the close of the Second Reading on 2 May 1905, Prime Minister A.J. Balfour sought to distance the Bill from any hint of anti-Semitism by categorizing 'the Jewish question' as an unwelcome foreign concept that should not have been allowed into the debate. It was, he maintained, a term that rightly belonged 'in Continental Europe, and especially in Eastern Europe'. With a probably unintended pun, he insisted that immigration control was 'a question wholly alien to and wholly distinct from the Jewish question' and really had to do with national character. Attempting to trump the notion of a right of asylum, Balfour proposed a formulation which differed from Evans-Gordon's 'right' to earn a living in one's own land, by insisting that 'who is to be added to its community from outside, and under what conditions ... is a final and indestructible right of every free community'. In a reworking of the cultural annexation argument, he imagined the ultimate effect of 'a substitution of Poles for Britons' to be the creation of a 'new nationality', un-British and unwanted, one that we would not wish upon 'our heirs through the ages to come'.[62]

When he came to wind up the Third Reading on 20 July 1905, Balfour's final words on the Aliens Bill again touched on the two main issues that had polarised discussion during the eight months in which draft legislation had been before Parliament. Referring to the right of asylum, the only significant area where the Liberals had been able to secure any concessions, he reminded the House that 'hospitality' was 'a virtue' but in no way 'obligatory upon individuals or upon nations' and ought never to be abused. Then, taking up the fear of anti-Semitism one last time, he told his opponent Stuart Samuel that if immigration were to be ignored, there was 'a real danger that some of the difficulties from which the Continental nations now suffer might arise' in this country. In each case, a distinction was being drawn between Britain and the rest of the world. Part of the problem, argued Balfour, was that other nations were acting inhospitably, either by being too restrictive about who might enter or by meting out 'harsh treatment' to those already there.[63] The tenor of his remarks and the whole thrust of anti-alien populism are indicative of an insular turn in Edwardian culture running from popular invasion novels like Erskine Childers's portrayal of the German menace in *The Riddle of the Sands* (1903) to the Liberal Party poster for the 1906 election that sought to discredit Joseph Chamberlain by depicting him with a long Chinese pigtail.[64] It was one of the abiding paradoxes of this inward-looking stance that condemnation of the illiberal attitudes of Britain's Continental neighbours was often couched in racial terms.

Nevertheless, notions of a sharp divide between Britain and its Continental neighbours on questions of race persisted. In his feverish Chinese invasion novel, *The Yellow Danger* (1898), for example, M.P. Shiel likened Paris to a hysterical woman foaming at the mouth, citing the Dreyfus riots as her most recent, most destructive outburst. Indeed, implicit in Balfour's rhetorical strategy of playing up the differences between Britain and Europe and his suggestion that the Aliens Bill would keep that divide in place was a disturbing question: what would an England that had succumbed to the unthinkable excesses of Continental anti-Semitism have looked like? As the brief reference to the work of M.P. Shiel suggests, it was in the pages of fiction that explorations of these extreme counterfactual states could most frequently be found, stretching the logic of statecraft in unexpected and deliberately provocative directions. In the final section of this chapter, I examine two works which attempted to imagine the future that an Aliens Act might bring into being: *A Modern Exodus* (1904) by the little-known author Violet Guttenberg, and *The Four Just Men* (1905), the first book from the spectacularly successful thriller writer Edgar Wallace. Written as the new restrictionist legislation was being drafted and debated, each of these novels sought to sensationalise the forms that the law might take in order to draw out its pitfalls and the dangers it posed to the country. In place of the reasonableness which the government's official rhetoric had tried so assiduously to foster was a new escalation of the all-enveloping sense of crisis that had long been the press's stock-in-trade.

EXILES AND ENEMIES: TWO LEGAL FICTIONS

Much of the interest of Violet Guttenberg's futuristic novel *A Modern Exodus* lies in its vision of a Britain in which uncompromising anti-Semitism has been given an officially sanctioned existence, institution-alised as the law of the land. In Guttenberg's hypothetical social world, the words 'alien' and 'Jew' become entirely synonymous, rendering these subjects stateless by a linguistic sleight of hand, verbally expelled from membership of their own country as a prelude to their physical exile. However, the story is precipitated by a moment of pure contingency: the sudden death of the Prime Minister and a crisis of succession. For the fact that this man was famously philosemitic and the certain knowledge that he will be replaced by the influential demagogue Athelstan Moore who already has a formidable reputation as a 'rabid Jew-hater' – the word 'rabid' being used repeatedly and exclusively about him throughout the book – means that these are dangerous times for English Jews.[65] Although the novel is ostensibly set in an unspecified time beyond the present, the pol-itical situation Guttenberg describes is clearly a dark pastiche of England circa 1903 when anti-alien legislation is in prospect, taking an incalculable step into the unknown. In this parallel Edwardian universe, the 'Alien Immigration question had reached a crisis which would have to be settled at Parliament's next session', with the outcome entirely dependent 'on the unreliable temper of the Government' (16). Athelstan Moore's leadership brings matters to a head by affirming what he regards as the necessary incompatibility between Englishness and Jewishness. His first act is to bring a Bill before the House that will authorise the deportation of '*all* the Jews, both English and foreign, rich and poor', extending from 'the sweaters and aliens of the East End' to 'the upper and middle classes of Jewish society' (18, 87). There is a period of grace of fourteen months, but in the interim the civil and political emancipation of British Jews is annulled. Renting or purchasing new property is forbidden, money-lending is banned, Jewish marriages are made illegal, and those Jews holding civic appointments lose their posts with immediate effect. Moreover, alien immigration is completely brought to a halt – of course only the 'foreign Jew' is mentioned – and even transmigrants are prevented from entering en route to their final destinations (130).

The chief opponent of the Bill is Lionel Montella, a young Oxford-educated MP from an old and respected Sephardic family who emerges as the parliamentary spokesman for the Jewish community. In a last desperate attempt to defeat the Prime Minister's plan, he makes an impassioned speech pointing out that English Jews are law-abiding, productive, and loyal citizens whose business acumen has contributed substantially to the nation's prosperity during the Victorian era – Lionel's words echo those later spoken by Herbert Samuel in the 1905 debate – but his 'lucidity' can make no headway against the prejudice he faces (91). Athelstan Moore's Bill is successful, partly because of the sheer force of his personality – he is variously compared to Cromwell, 'Napoleon the Great', and (shades of Walter Besant!) a heartless Pharaoh – and partly because the current state of public opinion in the country, aided and abetted by a hostile press, is strongly against 'the Jew' (51). In one scene, a mass traffic-stopping march by 'the great body of the unemployed' wends its way through the capital, its 'ragged' and 'emaciated' demonstrators carrying placards that read "British workmen thrown out by aliens" or "Boycott foreign Jews" (71). Indeed, 'the whole of the working-classes supported the Bill', and it is this democratic mandate that ultimately sways the House. 'Public feeling' is 'always ready to rush to extremes' and can be relied upon to ally itself 'conclusively on the side of the anti-Semites' (51). Moore is also able to make political capital from the collapse of a trust run by 'South African Jews' causing financial ruin to hundreds of investors and leading to rumours of an elaborate swindle perpetrated by the directors (50). From the very beginning, the new prime minister has the newspapers, the trade unions, and the music halls on his side.

There is one possible compromise, but it is only available to British-born Jews or those who have been naturalised for at least five years. Recent arrivals are ineligible 'and foreign labour in Whitechapel was thereby done away with' (132). Provided that they agree to swear an oath declaring that they are Jewish 'by birth only, and not by religion', that they will put aside all Judaic rites and practices, and that they will observe the calendar of Christian festivals, those who wish to stay can obtain 'a certificate of assimilation' that will allow them to remain in the country. The thinking behind this alternative is spelled out by the framer of the amendment. British Jews are no longer Jews in the old 'Oriental sense of the term', he argues, despite the persistence of 'an element of Hebraism' in their 'moral and intellectual nature'. These residual traits have been largely displaced or overlaid by more typically 'Occidental' forms of self-understanding, recapitulating a modified Arnoldian account of cultural tradition. 'Do you think your forefathers, when they left Palestine and lived in the West, were not affected by the influences of Hellenism, of Chivalry, of the Renaissance, of the Reformation, and of the Christian ethics in general, with which they came into contact?', Lionel's interlocutor asks (134). Lionel's response is to fall back on the indelibility of his Jewish formation, to claim that 'once the blood of an Israelite flows in a man's veins, it is impossible for him to forget his heritage' (135). This confrontation between race and culture is a pivotal, but never fully resolved, moment in the book. As Lionel observes, the prime minister is a very modern Judeophobe, because his visceral hatred is directed at 'the Jewish race' rather than at 'the Jewish religion' (88). Indeed, by the end of the book, this anti-Semitism, always obsessive, has tipped over into debilitating mania.

In the face of a repressive, forced mode of assimilation, Britain's diasporic Jews depart for Palestine where, unlike earlier Jewish settlers, they flourish and their success causes a precipitous decline in the economy they have left behind. Lionel becomes Governor of Haifa, but his liberal views incur the enmity of the more traditional Jews led by Ben-Yetzel, the Chief Rabbi of Palestine. Lionel's wife, Lady Patricia Byrne, is an aristocrat who renounced her Anglican beliefs and became a Jewess, but one of Ben-Yetzel's spies discovers that she has attended a Christian service while on a visit to Jerusalem and now wishes to return to her old faith. The strain on their marriage that ensues forces them to separate, leaving their son in Palestine under Lionel's care. However, as is so often the case, the private sphere provides a providential corrective to the public world of politics. On her return to England, Lady Patricia visits an

American friend who is married to the prime minister and while there she undertakes to nurse the Moores' sick daughter through an attack of diphtheria. But, in reality, she has two patients, because Moore's anti-Semitism has become a kind of sickness too. As the fear for his child's life begins to dissipate, Moore begins to listen to Lady Patricia's arguments and undergoes a change of heart that is described both as a conversion and a cure. As a whole-hearted Christian, the prime minister knows he must rescind his Expulsion Act and, in a reversal of what might be read as a *Deronda*-like motif, he brings about the return of the exiled British Jews with their entrepreneurial skills.[66] Lionel Montella and Lady Patricia are then reunited, this time with their separate faiths intact. But having conjured up this nightmare scenario, Guttenberg finds herself unable to banish its destabilising traces from her novel's apparently reassuring conclusion.

In her preface, Guttenberg described her novel as 'a story of the impossible' – impossible because in Edwardian Britain, 'the attitude of our country towards her Jewish subjects is that of justice, toleration, and friendliness'. *A Modern Exodus* is intended to be 'a warning' against the insidious way in which anti-Semitism can insinuate itself into a nation's heart and mind, although there is nothing 'subtle' about its progress here (v). The freshly converted prime minister triumphantly tells Lionel that 'Anti-Semitism doesn't answer in England, and it never will' (328).[67] Yet when the Jews' Expulsion Act is repealed, there is one important exception: Parliament is 'too wary to fall into the old error of allowing unrestricted immigration, and determined to keep the pauper alien away from English shores'(317). This exclusion should come as no surprise since it has been trailed from the start. Contemplating the harm that Athelston Moore might do, Lionel tells his political colleagues that 'it's the impolitic and regrettable behaviour of the immigrants themselves', which has led to the rise of 'anti-Jewish feeling among the masses', although he has always voted against immigration control – for not to do so would be to side against his own people (18). But his sympathies are with the unemployed demonstrators because their livelihoods are being destroyed by 'the influx of pauper Jews' who 'can live on next to nothing' and whose 'clannish' attitudes 'are a clog on the wheel of national progress' (72–73). When he speaks out against Moore's Bill, Lionel for the first time publicly accepts 'the undesirability of pauper alien immigration' (91). Post-expulsion Britain may no longer accept 'the pauper alien' – again, the alien simply *is* the Jew – but because Palestine is now at least a partial homeland, a welcome still remains for them in this newly prosperous settlement. And so, Guttenberg's omniscient narrator predicts, 'the term "pauper alien" would soon be as worn out as the dodo' (317).

Asylum has only a vestigial role in *A Modern Exodus* and the actual word is practically elided. Lionel Montella seems to recognise its importance, citing it as the reason why he has always resisted anti-immigration Bills. But his own view suggests room for a certain scepticism, namely that he must vote as he does 'especially *when I am told* that owing to persecution abroad they come here to try and regain their self-respect' (73, my emphasis). The novel provides an implicit justification for discriminatory treatment by emphasising the differences among Jews and insisting that it is 'a fatal mistake' to think of them as 'one nation of one unvaried character' (12). This is certainly true when considering 'the English Jews' and 'their poor Polish and Roumanian brethren' who look down upon each other when they arrive in Palestine, as though they could never occupy the same space (141–142). There may be a place of refuge for East European Jews, but it cannot be in England.

By contrast, Edgar Wallace's thriller *The Four Just Men* (1905) takes a rather more robust stand on the question of asylum, at least so far as political refugees are concerned. As we saw, during the 1903–1904 and 1904–1905 parliamentary sessions, the notion of a right to asylum was the rallying cry in the Liberal attack on anti-alien legislation, and in 1905 their major advance against the Tories in the Committee stage was a concession that allowed entry to those endangered by *religious* persecution.[68] But in Wallace's counterfactual narrative it is as if those debates had never taken place. At the start of the novel, an Aliens Extradition (Political Offences) Bill is on the verge of becoming a reality despite divisions within the country, a measure which would ensure that those activists now living in Britain who have organised resistance to repressive regimes will be handed over to their oppressors. As in *A Modern Exodus*, it is not the machinations of parties or governments that are putting British traditions of tolerance and fair play at risk; once again, the threat comes from a highly placed political maverick, here an inflexible Foreign Secretary who, having once made his decision, is impervious to the views of others in his party and incapable of changing his mind. In *The Four Just Men*, however, the struggle against arbitrary power is taken to its logical conclusion: those who provide assistance to tyrants are ipso facto themselves tyrants and there is more than a suggestion in the offending Foreign Secretary's un-English-sounding name – Sir Philip Ramon – that the country is becoming aligned with foreign despots. So desperate is the situation facing Britain that the task of defending the country from itself has passed to outsiders.

'The Four Just Men' of the title are outsiders in a double sense. Although their names and identities are clearly European – Manfred, Gonsalez, Poiccart (the fourth member, Clarice, has already been gunned down by the police in Bordeaux before the novel begins) – and although they take the side of national political movements like the Spanish Carlists whose leader is threatened with deportation from Britain (and is, curiously, at one point even associated with anarchism), their mission is unswervingly internationalist. The adversaries of the 'just men' are typically capitalists, speculators, and tyrants of all kinds and they hunt down 'sweaters', degenerates, swindlers, and gangsters across the globe, from Russia to Venezuela. Significantly, the novel opens in Cadiz – perhaps another political nod towards the Spanish anarchists favourably mentioned by Dilke in his March 1904 speech – though, no less importantly, the men meet in that city's Café of the Nations. Through their language and their actions, the 'Four Just Men' represent a global manifestation of the desire for popular justice, enforcing a radical political morality where individual states fall short or fail to act. Yet in the popular imagination they are identified only as the 'deadly foreign anarchist' and 'coward alien', known for their facelessness and clandestine organisation, their use of the 'infernal machine' (a threat made with a defused bomb), and their refusal to recognise any jurisdiction or authority other than their own.[69] As a sometime *Daily Mail* reporter, there was little Wallace did not know about the power of labels and catchphrases and the orchestration of public attitudes by the "*Daily Megaphone*" in the novel is a reflection of his own experiences in the press corps. At the same time, Manfred, Gonsalez, and Poiccart are never unambiguously aligned *with* the people. In order to secure the withdrawal of the Aliens Extradition Bill, the 'Four Just Men' threaten to kill the Foreign Secretary if he does not comply with their demands, and this sets the stage for a duel between the 'deadly anarchist' and the police, in which the public are reduced to the status of massed voyeuristic bystanders, a 'crowd … growing in volume every hour', 'a mob', 'a cruel thing, heartless and unpitying' (137–138).

The climax of the novel is a variation on the classic locked room mystery as Sir Philip Ramon stubbornly waits in what the police describe as his 'anarchist-proof' study in a vain attempt to escape the final sentence that Wallace's vigilantes have pronounced on him (133). Because *The Four Just Men* was originally conceived as a competition, with cash prizes for correctly showing how the Foreign Secretary met his end, his death is necessarily a foregone conclusion. And given that Sir Philip dies in very mysterious circumstances, the reader can only assume that his Bill dies with him. So, just as the Foreign Secretary cannot be safe in the midst of 'a great sea of black helmets' ('the whole vicinity was black with police'), Britain too cannot hope to be 'anarchist-proof' (136). Freedom of movement remains inviolable to the very last in a narrative that is described as having been written 'long after the event' (136). Indeed, the easy passage of Wallace's 'anarchists' from one country to another is in many ways a throwback to the heyday of nineteenth-century liberal principles. This, and not the fate of the Jews in Britain, is the real focus of the novel, quite unlike that of *A Modern Exodus*. True, Jews do receive an occasional mention here, but they are usually stock figures with a relatively minor role to play – for example, a master tailor killed for sexually exploiting his female employees is 'a sweater of a particularly offensive type' whose real name is Bentvitch, and Billy Marks, the South London pickpocket and informer who threatens the 'just men's' plans by stealing Poiccart's watch and pocketbook, is in all likelihood a Jewish criminal too (18). And on another occasion 'Andrew Cohen, financial agent' is among the cover stories employed by the 'just men' themselves when setting up their new hideout in Carnaby Street (42). But Wallace skirts round the issues raised by these allusions, concentrating instead on making the elusive figure of the alien a cipher for violence and terror, while giving the reckless law-defying exploits of 'the four just men' a positive spin. In this early phase of his career, Wallace was closer to the older, mid-nineteenth-century 'mysteries of the city' tradition associated with Eugène Sue and G.W.M. Reynolds in which criminal acts can sometimes turn out to be restitutive.

In their very different narratives, Guttenberg and Wallace each invoke the spectre of anti-alien legislation only to have it swept aside and, in this respect, *A Modern Exodus* and *The Four Just Men* both belong to a historical moment when immigration control could still be regarded as unthinkable, an initiative that could never last. If Conrad took up the inner isolation of the migrant, the racialisation of the alien adrift in a hostile or indifferent civil society, Guttenberg and Wallace each drew their readers into a version of a manipulative, overweening political system whose decisions had the power to shock. The scandal at the heart of these stories stems from the palpable fragility of those virtues that defined the nineteenth-century liberal state and were integral to what might be called the liberal structure of feeling – civic toleration, freedom of conscience, freedom of movement, individual liberty – principles that were deeply embedded in the political rhetoric of the opponents of the Aliens Bills in 1904 and 1905. However, this was a transient moment, one that was quickly brushed aside by an upsurge in social and political militancy during the years leading up to the Great War. As we will see in the next chapter, only three years later, Wallace's sequel to *The Four Just Men* adopted a far more conservative stance, a sign that the nature of the debate had already begun to change.

But in 1904 and 1905, the very idea of an Aliens Bill could be treated as belonging to a near-Manichaean universe, the fact given humorous recognition by Wallace when he has an exasperated Sir Philip Ramon accuse the 'four just men' of making 'the atmosphere … like that of a melodrama' (83). Even when the narrative was at fever pitch, Wallace deployed his theatrical skills with a light touch, leavening the drama with satirical portraits of newspapermen and parliamentarians, and always conscious that he was putting on a grand spectacle; whereas Guttenberg maintained her ethico-religious seriousness throughout, with little variation in tone. Ultimately, neither of these novels exactly qualifies as a considered political intervention, and both writers looked on the role played by populist sentiments in representative democracies with suspicion, shown by the sense of social distance that is inscribed their modes of address. In *A Modern Exodus*, the narrator's remarks on the extremism of the demos, where rank prejudices pass back and forth between the music hall artiste and the man in the street, has much in common with the characterisation of the crowd as a heartless mob at the climax of *The Four Just Men*, capped by Sir Philip Ramon's heartfelt cry: 'God save me from the people, their sympathy, their applause, their insufferable pity' (139). Yet what is finally the most misleading feature of these novels is their overly optimistic sense of closure. To the contrary, the problems that came to the fore when the Liberals were obliged to administer the Aliens Act after gaining power in 1906 suggested that there was much unfinished business here, particularly to the Radical Right. As the controversy about what the Act was *for* rumbled on, a new crop of narratives centred on the politics of immigration began to appear. It is to the Act's afterlife that we now turn.

CHAPTER 5

Restriction and its discontents

In 1906, the political tide turned dramatically and the Tories suffered a massive defeat in the national election. By the beginning of February, the Liberals had won slightly more than two and a half times as many seats as the Unionists and Conservatives, giving them an overall majority of 243.[1] Coming just a month after the Aliens Act had become law, this was hardly an auspicious beginning and its supporters feared the worst. Indeed, the election campaign suggested that immigration had peaked as an issue, for neither party, with a few local exceptions, tried to put it at the centre of the contest. For the Liberals, the Aliens Act was associated with a phase of parliamentary setbacks and best avoided. Although they did continue to exploit Conservative embarrassment around Chinese migrant labour in South Africa very effectively – with some nasty racial undertones at times – the Liberals' chief strategy on the hustings was to rely on traditional themes like free trade and Home Rule for Ireland, as well as bringing forward new plans for poor law reform and pensions. On the Tory and Unionist side, the Aliens Act was among a number of measures that candidates stoutly defended, but it was quite low on their list of priorities – appearing only in around one-sixth of Conservative election addresses – and it was fiscal and foreign policy, including the need for a strong army and navy, which dominated their agenda.[2]

Before turning to the problems that the implementation of the Aliens Act raised for different interest groups – the main focus of this chapter – I want to consider the scale of the Conservative defeat in a little more detail. The extent to which the political weather had changed can be seen most clearly in the election results for the East End – the heartland of calls for restricting immigration. In 1906, six of East London's eight Conservative MPs, anti-aliens to a man, lost to incoming Liberals, and Major (now Sir) William Evans-Gordon (Stepney) and Claude Hay (Hoxton) were the only Unionists who kept their seats. Little more than six months before, even the majority of East End Liberal MPs had felt sufficiently nervous about support for the Aliens Bill in their constituencies to have pressed their party leaders to support a modified version of it in May 1905, Stuart Samuel being the sole exception.[3] Moreover, some individual Liberals had publicly associated themselves with the British Brothers' League, like Sydney Buxton, MP for Poplar, whose anti-alien pedigree went back to the days of the APID.

Loud calls for tough immigration controls no longer made a candidate electable – quite the reverse. In his desperate campaign against Stuart Samuel in Whitechapel in January 1906, David Hope Kyd told voters that there was 'no subject of political interest' that 'can compare in importance with the scandalous and disgraceful abuse of our hospitality to the foreigner', and in his official election address he argued that the Aliens Act needed to be strengthened.[4] In one leaflet, Kyd attacked Samuel's voting record as (in heavy red bold type) 'PRO-ALIEN!' and pilloried him as 'a man who stands up in this way for the <u>foreign</u> Jews.' In another handbill, he drew attention to the fact that Samuel's brother Herbert had just been appointed Under Secretary at the Home Office, asking his readers: 'Can you, under these circumstances, trust Mr STUART SAMUEL'S party to <u>administer the Act honestly</u>?'[5] This dual emphasis in Kyd's electoral platform is very revealing. On the one hand, his claim that the Act provided a legislative framework, but did not go far enough, suggests that restrictionists had always regarded it as a first step in the direction of more comprehensive controls. On the other, Kyd's fears about what might happen if the Liberals were to get into power brings home the restrictionists' sense of the fragility of their achievements, their failure to make immigration into the kind of issue that Chinese labour had become for their opponents. Yet Kyd's hectoring did him no good. He lost to Samuel by 356 votes and was forced to try his luck elsewhere in 1909 and again in 1910, each time unsuccessfully.

The year 1907 was no better. In April, what remained of the East End anti-alien political base was substantially weakened by Evans-Gordon's resignation on account of ill-health. His seat was won by the Liberals in 1910, by which time Harry Lawson, who recaptured Mile End, was the sole remaining Unionist MP in East London. However, despite his forced retirement, Evans-Gordon continued to air his views, and, as we will see, as late as February 1911 – in the aftermath of the Sidney Street siege – he was still publishing on the alien question.[6] It was Evans-Gordon who was the first to articulate the newly emerging orthodoxy within the anti-alien camp after the Liberal victory. In a trenchant essay in Maxse's *National Review* in November 1906, he denounced what he saw as 'The Attack on the Aliens Act', arguing that the 'lengthy and uphill fight against ignorance, prejudice and apathy' by its supporters had been waged in vain.[7] The choice of publication and continuing involvement with the *Review* was significant: it indicated that the Act was passing into the mythology of the Radical Right as a key moment in its grand narrative of national betrayal. It was this mood of political unease, with its rhetoric of affronted patriotism, that provided a counterpoint to the struggle by the Liberal government to administer a law they had never sought.

Evans-Gordon argued that the new law was being emasculated by an abuse of the incoming Home Secretary's discretionary powers. In the first place, Herbert Gladstone had altered the legal definition of an immigrant ship by increasing the number of alien passengers that could be carried in steerage without being liable to inspection. Originally the Act had fixed this number at twenty, but Akers-Douglas, Gladstone's predecessor, had further reduced the figure to twelve in order to sharpen the Act's teeth.[8] This revision placed additional pressure on 'the machinery at the port', as Akers-Douglas liked to refer to the proposed Immigration Officers and Immigration Boards during the parliamentary debates, and Gladstone had restored the threshold to twenty. If this was not bad enough, Gladstone had loosened the clauses dealing with asylum. Having been informed by his permanent undersecretary of the brutal conditions in Russia following the 1905 Revolution, Gladstone instructed the Immigration Boards to give those immigrants seeking asylum on religious or political grounds 'the benefit of the doubt'.[9] In Evans-Gordon's eyes, this move destroyed the whole point of the safeguards that the law placed upon the granting of asylum because it effectively removed the burden of proof from the putative refugee. Under this new permissive interpretation, Evans-Gordon believed that anyone could claim to be a victim of religious or political persecution without fear of being challenged – and would undoubtedly do so.

Of course, aliens could not be trusted: according to Evans-Gordon, 'the want of veracity' among Russian and Polish Jews was 'notorious.' But in any case, those who had been excluded could always turn to 'money-lenders' to subsidise their return 'a few days' later as 'first-class passengers' – a practice he alleged was rife among Jewish migrants (464, 466). 'The Attack on the Aliens Act' therefore passed seamlessly from a discussion of 'the inrush of aliens' to identifying 'the true solution of the Jewish problem' (471). Evans-Gordon's preferred answer had some similarities to that which appeared in the margins of Violet Guttenberg's revision of *Daniel Deronda*, namely to outsource the 'problem' by settling

East European Jews somewhere else. However, unlike Guttenberg in *A Modern Exodus*, he did not look immediately to Palestine as their best destination, suggesting, somewhat obliquely, that Palestine was not yet 'ready for them'. In 1906, the programme that seemed to offer restrictionists 'a prudent, practical, statesman-like solution' was Israel Zangwill's highly contested scheme of 'founding a free colony' for the Jews, ideally under the auspices of the British Empire, a scheme known as 'territorialism' – 'Mr. Zangwill's great project', as Evans-Gordon dubbed it (471). He was far from being the only restrictionist to canvass this sort of panacea, nor was he the first. At a noisy, well-attended election meeting in Whitechapel in January, David Hope Kyd had also praised Zangwill's scheme as 'a statesman-like proposal'. If the electors were to return him to Parliament, he promised that 'he would vote for such a tract of land being granted' so that 'the influx of destitute aliens would be diverted ... and allowed to settle in Africa'.[10]

'JEWGANDA'

Kyd's promise – like Evans-Gordon's 'solution' – referred to what had become known as the 'East African Scheme' or the 'Uganda Offer' and it raises an immediate question.[11] What made this notion of 'a free colony' seem so plausible to both anti-alien lobbyists and Jewish activists like Zangwill in 1906? To find an answer, we must return to the ideas advanced by Theodor Herzl that were discussed in Chapter 1 and also to his evidence before the Royal Commission on Alien Immigration in July 1902. In his cross-examination of Herzl during the Commission hearings, Evans-Gordon asked the Zionist leader for his views on attempts to alleviate Jewish poverty by creating settlements in those parts of the world judged to be ripe for development, particularly by the Jewish Colonisation Society which had been founded by the businessman Baron Maurice de Hirsch in 1891. Herzl argued that philanthropic ventures like that in Argentina had been a failure 'because when you want a great settlement, you must have a flag and an idea' – in other words, moral resources were necessary rather than merely 'a large bag of money'.[12] These schemes did not entirely disappear in the early 1900s: for example, the manufacturer John De Kay planned to organise Jewish colonies in Mexico in 1909.[13] But the creation of a new Zionist movement under Herzl's leadership radically changed the terms in which these communal projects were imagined. No longer were they envisaged as small private enclaves; now they were increasingly conceived along nationalist lines. When Herzl sought to bring together the disparate proto-Zionist strands in the First Zionist Congress at Basle in August 1897, the movement's charter declared that its goal was 'the creation of a home for the Jewish people in Palestine to be secured by public law', the word 'public' underscoring a crucial shift of emphasis. The Basle Programme was inevitably somewhat vague as to how this 'home' was to become a reality, but it did note the political importance of working towards 'obtaining such governmental consent as will be necessary to the achievements of the aims of Zionism'.[14]

But what if diplomatic manoeuvres failed and the dream of a return to Palestine were to be forestalled, blocked, or delayed? This was the situation in which Herzl soon found himself, as Zionist overtures to Abdulhamid II, the ruler of the Ottoman Empire, under whose sway Palestine then fell, were unenthusiastically received. By the late 1890s, Herzl was beginning to consider other expedients. In *Der Judenstaat* (1896), his classic statement of the case for a Jewish homeland, Herzl had already cited Argentina as 'a vast area' with 'a sparse population and a mild climate' and paired it with Palestine as possible alternatives ('We shall take what is given us, and what is selected by Jewish public opinion.'); a few years later, he turned his mind to British possessions like Cyprus and South Africa.[15] At his most bullish, Herzl saw an island like Cyprus as a Mediterranean springboard into the Near East. In a diary entry from January 1901, Herzl fantasised that his people 'would rally on Cyprus and one day go over to Eretz Israel and take it by force, as it was taken from us long ago'.[16] Over the next twelve months, Cyprus – and also other British territories in Sinai and El Arish – was to assume increasing prominence in Herzl's plans. The suggestion that Britain might assist in finding a home for the Jewish people provided a potent undercurrent to the push towards an Aliens Bill, emerging into the wider public arena only when rumours gathered and questions began to be asked.

The idea of a Jewish settlement in East Africa was first mooted abruptly and provocatively by Lord Rothschild at a meeting with Herzl on July 5, 1902, while the latter was in London to testify before the Royal Commission on Alien Immigration. When Rothschild had blurted out "Take Uganda!", Herzl had demurred because he had his sights set on British land closer to Palestine. But in October, Herzl met with Joseph Chamberlain, the Colonial Secretary, who expressed general sympathy with plans for a 'self-governing Jewish colony', but explained that the Greek and Turkish population in Cyprus would oppose the idea and that the two other territories (Sinai and El Arish) were under the control of the Foreign Office.[17] Passed on to the far less sympathetic Lord Cromer,

Herzl struggled to make headway and turned to Chamberlain for help once more, only to find that he had left on a long African visit and would be away for four or five months. During his visit to the British East Africa Protectorate, Chamberlain had written a memo to himself noting that 'If Dr. Herzl were at all inclined to transfer his efforts to East Africa there would be no difficulty in finding land suitable for Jewish settlers'.[18] Sceptical that Herzl would accept a territory so distant from Palestine, Chamberlain nevertheless put this idea to him when they saw each other again on 24 April 1903.

Chamberlain's hunch was correct: Herzl continued to insist on 'a base in or near Palestine', and it took some weeks for him to accept that East Africa was worth considering.[19] At the meeting Chamberlain had mentioned that 'popular pressure' might lead to 'the necessity of passing an Alien Bill against the Jews', at which Herzl had cried 'Drain them elsewhere, but don't make an Alien Bill.'[20] Herzl's spontaneous response was partly a reflection of his deep-seated Anglophilia – he believed the Bill would be a stain on what he thought of as 'England's glory' as a free country – and partly it flowed from the views he had expressed the previous year before the Royal Commission when, in one exchange, he had affirmed that he wished there to be 'no restriction' on the movement of the Jews into Britain.[21] But Herzl's reaction also contained the seeds of a new argument. When Israel Zangwill spoke at a farewell meeting in Mile End for the British delegates to the Sixth Zionist Congress in August 1903, he attacked the recently published recommendations of the Royal Commission as 'tyrannical and un-English' and hinted knowledgeably that England would be likely to go out of its way 'to help them to solve the Jewish problem elsewhere', not least if they were seen to be making 'a serious effort to solve their own problems'. Whatever happened, 'they could not wait for another Kishineff, which was the turning point in their history. The whole of the Jewish energies of the world must be focused in some one spot, which might be at the same time a land of refuge and a place of preparation for Palestine, if it were not Palestine to start with'.[22] This was the predicament that the Sixth Congress would be seeking to resolve. Success would render the proposed alien immigration laws completely redundant; but, as Zangwill's choice of words suggests, success would also mean displacing or relocating the right of asylum.

The 'East African Scheme' split the Zionist Congress, but Herzl was able to convince enough delegates to support an inquiry into the feasibility of Guas Ngishu Plateau as place of settlement. Paradoxically, as many of Herzl's opponents were well aware, it was 'the representatives of the very East European Jews' for whom this land of refuge had been earmarked 'who so decisively rejected Herzl's Uganda ploy'.[23] For cultural Zionists like Chaim Weizmann, the scheme was a dangerously self-defeating deviation from the movement's true Palestinian goal. Outside the Jewish community, there were other, equally implacable opponents of the idea. In a scathing retrospective on the Congress in September 1903, Arnold White asked *Daily Express* readers with his usual pungency: "Is It to Be Jewganda?" and dismissed the whole enterprise as a nonsense. The Russian Jews had no wish to go there, and the harvesting of local resources like coffee and rubber was 'essentially a black man's task', 'unsuited for Europeans' in general and 'the finely drawn and intellectual inhabitants' of the ghetto in particular. White was adamant that the most vocal advocates of 'Jewganda' were those least likely to settle in Africa and he sardonically picked out Israel Zangwill as someone who 'cannot be spared from England' because 'his genius and the charm of his writing are already national possessions'.[24]

In fact, Zangwill was to spend much of the remainder of his life devoting 'his genius' to the search for 'some one spot' that could provide a safe haven for migrant East European Jews; and he certainly believed that their resettlement in East Africa would show that this was 'a white man's country' – indeed, in one flight of suburban lyricism he described it as a sub-equatorial equivalent to 'our own Surrey Hills', free from any taint of the East End slums with their sweating and overcrowding.[25] At the Seventh Zionist Congress in July/August 1905 – the first to take place in the shadow of Herzl's untimely death the previous year – Zangwill argued that the movement should accept the British offer. But, in the light of the unpropitious evidence from their own inquiry, he insisted on the crucial proviso that Congress should continue to press the government for land that offered better prospects. Unable to persuade the Congress even to vote on this proposition, Zangwill and some thirty delegates angrily walked out of the meeting and, two weeks later, he founded the Jewish Territorial Organization (the ITO).

Zangwill did not embrace a Palestinian solution again until 1914 and in the interim Territorialism was often linked to British discussions of East European immigration as an alternative future for the Jews. Signs of this concern are evident in what was to be Zangwill's last book of fiction, *Ghetto Comedies*, a collection of short stories published in 1907 in which Britain is a place where Jews will never quite belong. In 'Anglicization', a piece whose origins can be traced back to 1901, Simon Cohn, the English-

born son of two Polish Jews, shocks and disappoints his parents by volunteering to fight in the Boer War, throwing into question their assiduously
cultivated sense of having made themselves into very *English* Jews.[26] Yet
slowly they adapt and, once Simon's letters from South Africa start to
arrive, his determination and his bravery become a further source of their
pride in being English, particularly when Simon saves the life of a fellow
soldier named Winstay and is promoted. On his return, 'bronzed and
a man', Simon falls in love with Winstay's sister Lucy, only to discover
that her father thinks that 'the Jews were responsible for the war' and has
joined the 'League of Londoners for the suppression of the immigrant
alien' (72; 79–80). Although Simon and Lucy begin a secret courtship,
she finally refuses to marry him because he is a Jew, and the story ends
with Simon and his mother turning to each other for comfort, 'their love
the one thing saved from Anglicization' (86). Anglicisation has finally
become a source of shame.

Zangwill simultaneously invokes both the most secure and the least
stable elements of social identity here, and much of the power of the story
derives from his exploration of the phantasmatic movement between
them. Simon's father, who embodies a different kind of brutality than
Lucy's father, moves from abusive dismissal of his son's desire to serve
his country to espousing the same jingoistic denigration of the Boers
that is made by Simon in his letters. But at the moment that this identification occurs, Mrs. Cohn suddenly sees what the transfer of emotion
masks: when Simon's father is describing the Boers as 'ignorant of the
outside world' and obsessed with their own little community, 'awaiting
some vague future of glory that never came', he is unconsciously speaking of himself (69). Nevertheless, patriotic sentiment provides the indispensable medium in which such realisations occur. When Mrs. Cohn
visits St Paul's Cathedral for the farewell service for the new recruits, she
becomes aware for the first time of 'a world of alien things' in the talk of
the people around her, a world that she has never quite understood. By the
ceremony's close, she is caught up in 'the roaring crowd, with a fantastic
dream-sense of a night sky and a great stone building, dark with age and
solemnity, and unreal figures perched on railings and points of vantage'
and is thinking of herself as 'the mother of a hero' (64, 66). In another
register, it is patriotism that will destroy Simon's dream of romantic love,
for when Lucy writes in one of her wilfully blind notes to him that 'it is
only natural – isn't it? – that after shedding our blood and treasure for the
Empire we should not be in a mood to see our country overrun by dirty
aliens', we know that the writing is on the wall (82).

Utterly despondent, Simon woundingly takes up and comes close to fully identifying with the position expressed in Lucy's note, responding to his mother's anger at his rejection with the retort 'Why are you Jews surprised? … You've held yourself aloof from the others long enough, God knows. Yet you wonder they've got their prejudices, too' – a cry, at once, of disavowal and blame that he is unable to sustain (85). And not just for his mother's sake, but also for his own, because the accusatory interpellation 'you Jews', invoking a prejudice that believes it has its reasons, is the common currency of anti-alien invective. Zangwill's allusion to the Londoners' League was highly topical – his letters show that he had started writing this story *before* the League had been formed in the summer of 1901 and must therefore have added this reference later. By the time it was republished in 1907, 'Anglicization' had acquired a new and equally inflammatory topicality since one of the arguments against allowing Russian and Polish Jewish immigrants to enter Britain was that many of these men were fleeing from military service in the Far East and therefore were hardly likely to want to fight in defence of their adopted country. With this calumny in mind, Herbert Samuel had felt it necessary to remind the House during the Second Reading of the 1905 Aliens Bill that in the Anglo-Boer War, 'the Jewish population of England lost a larger proportion of their number in the field than the rest of the English nation'.[27]

Again and again in *Ghetto Comedies*, Zangwill worried away at the politics of emancipation and at the fraught, contested nature of what it meant to be Jewish. In 'The Jewish Trinity', another story with a failed marriage plot, the 'cosmopolitan artist' Leopold Barstein falls in love with Mabel Aaronsberg, the daughter of a prosperous manufacturer and former MP, and, although at first he thinks of her as 'merely a Jewess', he soon finds himself developing a Disraeli-like fascination with 'this mystery of race and blood' that draws them together (90, 92, 99). Before long Leopold begins to imagine a Zionist future with Mabel, but when he finally reveals to her his dream of their settling in Palestine after their marriage, she is horrified. 'One couldn't breathe', she tells him. To live 'entirely among Jews' would be to live in a 'great Ghetto!' (104). Sir Asher, Mabel's father, is just as dismissive, calling Zionism nothing more than a 'narrow tribalism' which he thinks would 'undermine all the rights we have so painfully won in the West' (113). Furious at the unravelling of his political and erotic future, Leopold charges Sir Asher with being the embodiment of a 'Jewish trinity' in which 'the Jew's a patriot everywhere, and a Jew everywhere and an anti-Semite everywhere': 'three-in-one and one-in-three' (115).

Zangwill's acerbic take on Anglo-Jewry was hardly calculated to win friends in high places, but it was within the Zionist movement that he faced the harshest criticism. Chaim Weizmann, then a rising figure in the Zionist arena (and subsequently the leader of the Zionist movement after the First World War), thought that Zangwill was 'acquainted neither with Judaism nor the Jews' and told him to his face that he was nothing but 'a photographer of the Ghetto' who had little understanding of the people's soul. At that time, this objection was a standard aesthetic critique of the superficiality of some forms of realism. But Weizmann also thought that a similar failing could be detected in Herzl's political approach to Zionism.[28] In his estimation, Herzl could not be considered a true nationalist because he was too fixated upon short-term considerations and too willing to compromise, improvising one desperate project after another, rather than concentrating upon the long march towards Palestine.[29] However, Zangwill was much, much worse: a cheap demagogue, a man in love with his own rhetorically produced image of himself as a leader, all the while appealing to the basest instincts of his followers. Weizmann was always prone to invoke the spectre of the *canaille* when contemplating his political opponents. In correspondence with Martin Buber about the supporters of the 'Uganda Offer' in October 1903, for example, he described the 'East End Jews (a mob and rabble)' as 'seized by an African fever complicated by a Herzl mania.'[30] Similarly, in a letter to the American Rabbi Judah Leon Magnes nearly two years later, Weizmann described the formation of branches of Zangwill's ITO in English cities as a process in which 'all the accumulated dirt on the lowest levels of Zionism's undertow is rising to the surface, only ... to disappear before long'. Zangwill was to be pitied.[31]

Perhaps surprisingly, Weizmann had initially been sympathetic to the East African initiative, but he came to feel that it would fatally weaken the Basle Programme. He was particularly worried by the argument that support for the East African scheme offered a substitute for immigration control and, on moving to England, he was keen to uncouple the East African option from the question of the Aliens Bill. On learning that the first Aliens Bill had been withdrawn in July 1904, Weizmann feared that the Bill to replace it would be 'much worse' for he believed that 'immigration and the Jewish question have become altogether much more acute' and felt certain that 'Uganda has also contributed a great deal to this'.[32] In his view, it was necessary for the whole of British Jewry to unite in opposition to anti-alien legislation, but at the same time he insisted that relieving the predicament of Jewish migrants should be clearly distinguished from the higher ideals of Zionism. Weizmann was therefore intensely critical of organisations like the English Zionist Federation which were reluctant to abandon East Africa, no matter what the results of the inquiry might show; and when he was elected to the EZF executive in January 1906, Weizmann helped to defeat a motion which would have supported the participation of Zangwill's ITO in the next Zionist Congress. Moreover, he used every opportunity to brief British politicians on the folly of pursuing the 'Uganda Offer', presenting arguments to Evans-Gordon – unsuccessfully, as it turned out – to show why it was to be resisted, while later explaining to Balfour that for Jews it was an outright impossibility.[33] But by January 1906, when this latter conversation took place, the Conservatives were as good as out of office.

In 1906, Balfour was already making favourable noises about 'the attainment of Palestine', foreseeing 'only economic difficulties', even though in fact, and despite Weizmann's eloquence, he remained sympathetic to Zangwill's territorialist programme (as of course did Evans-Gordon).[34] However, the incoming Liberal administration seemed to Weizmann to offer little hope on either the domestic or the international front – and there were certainly prominent Liberals like Herbert Gladstone and Winston Churchill who had also expressed support for Zangwill's programme. In February 1906, Weizmann, then living and working in Manchester, told his fiancée that a 'rather active propaganda campaign' against the Aliens Act had begun and the following month he was elected on to the protest committee. However, Weizmann was not at all sanguine: 'I have a feeling that the Liberal government will not be making any concessions either. They had promised a great deal before the elections. But the election promises, particularly those given to Jews, are reduced to 0'.[35]

This was not entirely accurate, at least so far as the Aliens Act was concerned. As we have seen, before the year was out, Evans-Gordon was complaining in the *National Review* that the new law was already being watered down in what amounted to an unconstitutional betrayal of its main intentions. Nevertheless, some leading sections of the Jewish community were dismayed that the Liberals made no effort to repeal the Act. And in Manchester, for example, disappointment at the failure to prevent the Act being passed led a number of local Jews to turn to territorialism as an alternative – much to Chaim Weizmann's chagrin.

The fact that the 1905 Aliens Act had passed into Liberal hands satisfied no one. The new status quo actually forced opposing political tendencies into more uncompromising positions, with convinced restrictionists still yearning for the tougher legislation that they felt had been denied them, while those who had resisted the Bill were deeply disappointed that the law remained on the statute book. For the incoming Liberal government, the Act presented an insoluble problem, the legacy of a failed parliamentary counteroffensive which had little hope of being overturned because of the strength of Tory opposition in the Lords. If Liberal hostility in 1904 and 1905 had helped to win Jewish votes, for example, the Act's implementation after the 1906 became an irritant that had the potential to become a vote loser.

Winston Churchill's brief career in Manchester politics is a good example of how victory could turn into defeat. In 1904, Churchill had crossed the floor of the House of Commons to become a Liberal and in the general election he stood successfully against Balfour in Manchester North-West, a seat in which the Jewish vote was crucial. But despite securing a clear majority, Churchill's campaign was dogged by political divisions among the territorialists in the constituency. Knowing that Churchill was set to be the next Under-Secretary of State for the Colonies, a member of the local ITO branch executive contacted Zangwill and suggested that this would be an extremely opportune moment for the territorialist leader to extract a promise from the Liberal candidate to assist their cause if elected. Churchill obliged by affirming his support for the ITO's aims, despite the Colonial Office's avowed hostility to its plans, and published his encouraging reply to Zangwill in the Jewish press. However, Conservative members of the Manchester ITO were incensed and encouraged the Tory candidate, William Joynson-Hicks, to retaliate by declaring that he too was behind Zangwill's movement and asking Zangwill to make this clear to Jewish voters. Zangwill's embarrassed attempt to extricate himself from this conflict outraged Churchill and led to strained relations between them. Nevertheless, the Jewish vote held up.

In the next bye-election in April 1908, Churchill defended his Manchester North-West seat, but on this occasion Joynson-Hicks emerged as the victor by just a few hundred votes, roughly one-third of the majority that his opponent had won in the previous contest two years earlier. At the time, Churchill believed that he had lost the seat because Catholic priests, fearing for the future of their denominational schools under the

Liberals, had encouraged their congregations to vote Conservative.[36] But Churchill's Jewish support was also much weaker, because the 'Ugandan Offer' had not been renewed and territorialist initiatives had stalled. Meanwhile, the Aliens Act had been in operation for nearly two and a half years and looked unlikely to disappear. Churchill did his best and was cheered by his audience in Manchester when he rather disingenuously proclaimed that the Liberals had 'practically smashed the Act', but there were enough critical voices in the community to suggest that some disgruntled Jewish voters either switched their vote or abstained.[37] On the other hand, the rather rash ideas that Churchill floated in his speeches, like changing the composition of Immigration Boards or lowering naturalisation fees, were cautiously and even coolly received within the Home Office. How then was the current state of the 1905 Act under the Liberals to be judged, and what were its prospects for the foreseeable future?

Churchill and Evans-Gordon at least agreed that the 1905 Act was not what it was or what it was meant to be, but the conclusions that they drew could scarcely be more different. We know from the latter's complaints in 'The Attack on the Aliens Act' that, in the early months of 1906, the new Liberal Home Secretary relaxed the rules covering entry into Britain, first by raising the number of alien steerage passengers that could legally be carried before a ship became liable to inspection, and then by advising the Immigration Boards that those arriving from Russia in the grim wake of the 1905 Revolution should normally have their claims to refugee status accepted. Both measures were anathema to advocates of strict immigration control, but in reality their effects were far from being a restrictionist's worst nightmare. The numbers of migrants in all categories tended to rise to a peak around 1906 and 1907, but they subsequently fell to a much lower level, despite some occasional fluctuations. In 1906, according to the Annual Report of the Inspector of Aliens (William Haldane Porter), the total number of aliens entering on immigrant ships stood at 27,639, or 71.7 per cent of all alien arrivals. By 1907, this figure had dropped to 17,982 but it still accounted for 65 per cent of all alien migrants coming into Britain (stabilizing at slightly more or slightly less than 60 per cent for the remainder of this period). The picture did change significantly in 1913, immediately before the outbreak of the Great War, when the numbers arriving in Britain reached a new high, particularly those coming from European and Mediterranean ports. Even so, the numbers of aliens carried by immigrant ships showed little variation during these years: in

1908, they had fallen to 13,050, or 59.9 per cent of all aliens, whereas in 1913, the corresponding figures were 13,466, or 59 per cent.[38]

Within the Jewish community there was considerable scepticism as to whether Gladstone's March 1906 memorandum urging a more generous approach to asylum claims by Russian and Polish refugees had made much difference. A year after Gladstone's directive was issued, the Jewish Board of Deputies wrote complaining that his instructions were being widely ignored. But these criticisms had little impact. Looking back over the first five years of the Act, M.J. Landa, a reporter for the *Jewish Chronicle*, pointed out that the number of individuals recognised as refugees was extremely small.[39] The government's own statistics showed that he was correct. The Annual Reports prepared by the Inspector under the Act revealed that, although 505 persons had been admitted as refugees in 1906, this figure had dropped sharply to 43 the following year, and continued to fall. In 1910, a mere five refugees were admitted.[40] Gladstone's call for leniency had only the briefest of shelf lives. In February 1911, Winston Churchill, the new Liberal Home Secretary, told members of the House that, although the instruction had not been revoked, 'the conditions prevailing when it was issued have altered.'[41] Churchill was admittedly speaking under the pressure of events, following the armed confrontation with 'criminal aliens' in the Siege of Sidney Street; but his remarks indicated that what had turned out to be a very limited window of opportunity was now firmly closed.

Despite Gladstone's modest attempts to reduce the severity of the Act, the period from 1906 to 1910 saw a concerted effort on the part of the traditional leaders of Anglo-Jewry to ensure that Jewish migrants seeking entry received just and equitable treatment. To this end, the Jewish Board of Deputies' Alien Immigration Committee, which had been working behind the scenes to amend the 1905 Aliens Bill, now turned its attention to monitoring how the Act worked in practice.[42] At the centre of its investigations were the rulings made by the Immigration Boards in response to appeals against the refusal by Immigration Officers to allow immigrants to land. Under the terms of the 1905 Act, an Immigration Board's decision was final, although in difficult cases matters of legal interpretation could be referred to the Home Secretary for adjudication. For in setting up 'the machinery' of immigration control, the Conservatives had always intended that these Boards should operate outside the judicial process, falling directly under the authority of the Home Secretary rather than being subject to review by the courts. It was for precisely this reason that critics of the Act like the liberal jurist A.V. Dicey believed that these administrative provisions violated the rule of law, offering the individual no protection against the designs of the state. The aim of the Boards was to deal with appeals swiftly and summarily, without becoming embrangled in lengthy legal argument. Swift they certainly were. Once notice of an appeal had been given, the Board's clerk had no more than twenty-four hours to convene a meeting, which often made it impossible for migrants to call supporting witnesses or someone who could help them to make their case. Moreover, witnesses could only be heard at the discretion of the Board, in sharp contrast to the appellant and the immigration officer who were legally entitled to speak at the hearing. By lobbying for additional amendments to the Act, the Alien Immigration Committee hoped to convince the Liberals to make this system less arbitrary.[43]

Under Gladstone, the work of the Immigration Boards did become more transparent than it might otherwise have been, at least in the sense that details of their proceedings became public knowledge, for among the measures introduced by the Home Secretary in March 1906 was a directive allowing journalists to attend the appeals tribunals. In making this provision, Gladstone hoped to dispel any rumours or false impressions that might circulate when appeals were held *in camera*. As a result, Immigration Board hearings were regularly reported in the *Jewish Chronicle* and this permitted comparison of their procedures and results. Predictably, the balance of decisions made by the different Boards varied considerably. For example, Grimsby and Hull were cheek by jowl and in both ports immigrants arriving there were typically Russian Jews en route to major urban centres like Manchester and Leeds. Yet in 1910, Hull's Immigration Board dismissed every single appeal against refused entry that it heard, whereas in neighbouring Grimsby 40 per cent of the appellants were successful. The proportion of immigrants appealing against a decision to exclude them because they lacked the means to support themselves and their dependents also varied significantly between Boards. At Dover, to take another example, a mere 5 per cent appealed exclusion on these grounds, as compared to London where no less than 90 per cent of immigrants refused entry lodged an appeal.[44] Local factors were undoubtedly important here: the men who sat on individual Immigration Boards mattered enormously, and migrants seeking to disembark in London would have benefited from their proximity to a large and well-organised Jewish community, which Dover lacked.

Reports of the hearings suggest that in the early years they would often be adversarial in character, with the immigration officer acting as a kind of public prosecutor against migrants whose grasp of what was happening was severely impeded by their having to rely on an interpreter.[45] Indeed, the power of immigration officers was actually increased after June 1906 when the Home Office ruled that more weight should be given to the officer's estimate of an immigrant's job prospects in reaching a decision as to whether or not an immigrant should be permitted to stay. Previously, the sum of £5 had been automatically taken as proof that an immigrant possessed (to quote the Act) 'the means of decently supporting himself', but over-reliance on this yardstick was felt to be open to abuse.[46] This shift of emphasis was not widely appreciated at first. When a prosperous Jewish butcher and his family travelling from Russia were refused entry at Grimsby in February 1908, despite the head of household having more than £40 on him, the *Grimsby News* reported the case as a sudden 'tightening of the cords'. An appeal was made to the local Board, but the officer justified his decision on the grounds that the man was old, could not speak English, and therefore would be unable to pursue his trade. The case was brought to the attention of the Jewish Board of Deputies by the President of the Grimsby Hebrew Immigration Society who insisted that the family were only visiting relatives in the United Kingdom, and the matter was subsequently raised in the House of Commons by a sympathetic MP.[47] In reply, Gladstone's under-secretary Herbert Samuel was unmoved by the plight of his co-religionist. He insisted that there was no corroborating evidence that the family were just visitors and backed the immigration officer's original decision.[48]

The Jewish Board of Deputies continued to complain about particular injustices, but its broader campaign to modify the Act met with very limited success. Although Gladstone had mixed feelings about a law that his party had actively opposed, he was perfectly clear that he was obliged to uphold it, even if to do so was, as he confessed to the House, 'no easy matter'.[49] Gladstone's reply to the Tower Hamlets MP Stuart Samuel, his under-secretary's more outspoken brother, in December 1906, shows how reluctant he was to depart from the spirit of the Act. Samuel had brought up a series of points that demonstrated how far the procedures of the Immigration Boards fell short of accepted legal standards: the absence of any requirement to give evidence on oath, the lack of legal representation, and the heavy reliance on the unexamined and 'uncorroborated testimony' of the immigration officer. But Gladstone dismissed these considerations as irrelevant. 'An immigration board is not a court', he said bluntly, and it was therefore inappropriate to expect 'a body which has not the powers of a court' to administer an oath, appoint legal counsel, and the like.[50]

Gladstone's riposte effectively brought to an end the Jewish Board of Deputies' cherished hope of winning the right to make a final appeal to a higher court such as the King's Bench Division, and so bringing immigration decisions under the rule of law. As prestigious and well-connected as the JBD was, it could make little headway against a government that was not prepared to take a stand on this issue. The JBD also suffered from its own compromised position on alien immigration. Its Alien Immigration Committee expressed worries about a variety of undesirables gaining entry on non-immigrant ships (i.e. those carrying twenty or fewer passengers in steerage), including the sick, political radicals, prostitutes, and those turned away by other countries. Indeed, on several occasions the Committee discussed seeking to extend the law in order to deal with the traffic carried on what were typically smaller ships – a move that would have gladdened Akers Douglas's heart.[51] The JDB's perspective partly reflected the limited constituency from which it drew its support and 'from which' – as David Feldman has noted – 'immigrant bodies were excluded'.[52] The desire to be seen to act responsibly undoubtedly curbed the JBD's sense of the possible. A plan in December 1907 to press the Prime Minister to repeal the 1905 Act quickly collapsed in the face of Lord Rothschild's advice that such a move would merely rally the anti-alien lobby which would immediately demand more severe legislation. In fact, as noted at the beginning of this chapter, anti-alien forces both in and outside parliament had suffered a major setback as a result of the Liberal landslide in 1906. At the grass-roots level, organisations that had initially seemed impressive, particularly the British Brothers' League, had been unable to capitalise on the local enthusiasm they had sparked and, once their parliamentary allies had been swept aside, their activities dwindled. Even though its name laid claim to a national voice, the BBL had hardly any influence outside East London and even on its home turf the League failed to organise a single open meeting after January 1904.[53]

ANARCHISM'S FATAL RETURN

From the restrictionist's standpoint, how the Act was managed was a function not only of the complexion of the political class, but, perhaps more importantly, of which individual occupied the post of Home Secretary. Leo Maxse's *National Review*, the periodical that came closest to serving as the house journal of the Radical Right, moved from one sceptical position to another on the question of anti-alien legislation, able to trust neither its own party nor the Liberals. Having initially viewed the Conservatives' plan to introduce an Aliens Bill as 'a mere placard which will disappear on the first convenient pretext', the *Review* consistently maintained a pose of thoroughgoing disbelief, telling its readers right up until June 1905 that, given the government's dismal record of dishonoured promises, it suspected that 'the present measure will be shelved' before too much longer.[54] When the Bill had finally received the Royal assent, Maxse claimed that it had been passed 'in such a form as to seriously impair its value, its future success being almost entirely dependent on the spirit in which it is administered'. By November 1906, that 'spirit' was no longer in doubt: 'Mr. Herbert Gladstone' had emerged as 'the friend of the alien'.[55]

The *National Review's* intransigence is best captured by its response to the news that Sir Charles Dilke and other leading Liberals intended to make the right of asylum the centrepiece of their opposition to the Bill when it was first introduced in March 1904. If protecting the British people from 'the evils exposed in the Report of the Royal Commission' was what mattered above all, then the Tories had an excellent reason to 'sacrifice the so-called right of asylum', for it did nothing but make England 'the happy hunting-ground of foreign anarchists and assassins'.[56] Yet, despite sharp disagreement in parliament about whether any such right of asylum actually existed in law, this 'so-called right' was not jettisoned and thus came to be regarded by the Act's critics as one of its chief defects, precisely because it was thought to encourage the entry of a new and more deadly type of criminal. Anarchism was, of course, hardly new; moreover, its most terrifying manifestations, the audacious *attentats* whose aim was to demonstrate the vulnerability of those in power, can be traced back to the late 1870s. The notion of 'propaganda by the deed' informed a series of failed attempts to assassinate Kaiser Wilhelm I in 1878 and also the dramatic wave of bombings in France and Spain that began in 1892 and culminated in the murder of the French president Sadi Carnot by an Italian anarchist on 24 June 1894. To these outrages we should add the attacks by Irish nationalists in Britain in the mid-1880s and the violent tactics used by a variety of kinds of revolutionaries in Russia dating from the 1860s, which led, after several near misses, to the assassination of Tsar Alexander II in March 1881, which had an enormous impact right across Europe.

Bombing and assassination were never the sole prerogative of anarchists per se, and such violent methods were deplored by significant sections of the movement. Indeed, by the beginning of the twentieth century, this mode of terrorism was increasingly being employed by radical nationalists. But, tellingly, the anarchist label stuck and was often used inaccurately or imprecisely. British newspaper reports of "anarchist" malfeasance peaked in the first half of the 1890s and then died down, only to be punctually revived when stories of some new horror fanned the embers. In the early 1900s, "anarchism" was routinely invoked in connection with immigrants and foreign refugees, usually in accounts of criminal cases or notoriously bloodthirsty acts, particularly in reports from the conservative press.[57] At a time when the rates of recorded crime in Britain were falling and some criminologists were even arguing that high levels of criminality belonged to the past, anarchism continued to represent the cutting edge of human depravity.[58]

In March 1906, an unsuccessful attempt on the life of King Alfonso XIII of Spain and his new bride as they were making their way through Madrid killed or injured many within or close to the royal wedding procession. The bombing was widely reported in the British press, including a sensational on-the-spot scoop by Edgar Wallace, the *Daily Mail*'s special correspondent, who later turned his experiences to good account in his 1908 sequel to *The Four Just Men*.[59] The 'outrage at Madrid' was especially shocking to British readers because Queen Victoria Eugenie was Edward VII's niece. This 'savage' episode 'unpleasantly recalls to our mind the living horror of anarchy', observed *Blackwood's Magazine*, noting that 'the purposeless and cowardly crime' had been condemned 'with a unanimity which the exploits of anarchists do not always inspire'. But the bulk of the article was less an attack on 'the degenerates who deal in explosives' than on the 'smug and sentimental satisfaction' that England took 'in protecting those who have outraged the law of their own land'. Once again, Herbert Gladstone was denounced for having declared that 'anarchists and other political offenders are "desirable aliens"' and giving them 'easy sanctuary'. Anarchists had only to 'declare that they have suffered for an opinion' and 'their word is accepted as the word of truth'. England might not 'breed anarchists' but it did offer them 'a willing shelter', and in so doing, 'our Government puts an open affront upon friendly nations' and offends those who should be our allies.

The column closed with a peculiarly apposite scene in which the policeman and the anarchist reach a stalemate 'in that curious game called law', or rather one specific, albeit unidentified, law – the 1905 Aliens Act. By the terms of this legislation, the anarchist 'pursues his avocation in Soho without let or hindrance', while the police officer, who knows full well the anarchist's murderous designs and suspects 'that he even has a bomb in his pocket, hesitates to arrest him, because he deems it against the rules of the sport in which they are both engaged'.[60] The sporting contest conjured up by *Blackwood's* columnist prefigures one of the most enduring evocations of the terrorist in modern fiction, the Professor in Joseph Conrad's *The Secret Agent* – 'the perfect anarchist', a man who regards 'revolution' and 'legality' as 'counter moves in the same game' and disdains to play.[61] On encountering Chief Inspector Heat in the street, the Professor mocks his claim to authority by exclaiming, 'Ah! The game!', to which Heat responds 'You may be sure our side will win in the end. ... Then that will be the game' (70). Heat is a betting man who puts 'unbounded faith' in the racing tips in the 'optimistic, rosy' sheets of the evening paper (151, 154). Against such racing certainties, the 'sudden holes in space and time' that open up 'in the close-woven stuff of relations between conspirator and police' are moments in which confidence in the orderliness of the contest dissolves into metaphysical doubt (63). The Professor has no susceptibility to anxieties of this sort, but he too needs time to bring his credo of total destruction to the point where the world can be thoroughly negated. His fellow anarchist, Comrade Ossipon, complains that the Professor's implacable dream of oblivion would produce nothing more than 'a damned hole' in time, and thus be the antithesis of any last shred of radical hope rather than 'the only way of progress' (222–223).

Conrad evidently started writing the novel in early February 1906, the month immediately after the 1905 Aliens Act had come into force, and by October the first instalment of a shorter version began serialization in the American weekly *Ridgway's*, billed as 'A Tale of Diplomatic Intrigue and Anarchist Treachery'.[62] The book does obliquely bear the imprint of the political moment out of which it grew, but it also invokes a number of other temporal referents. According to the material evidence of the text, the date on Winnie Verloc's wedding ring, combined with the length of her marriage to the novel's 'secret agent', indicates that these events are unfolding precisely in 1886. However, the central incident in this 'simple tale,' in which Winnie's simple-minded brother Stevie is the sole casualty, alludes to an abortive bomb attack on the Royal Observatory in Greenwich in 1894 by the French anarchist Martial Bourdain who died in the attempt. There are also intimations of slightly later dates: the International Anti-Anarchist Conference mentioned by the embassy official Mr Vladimir was held in Rome in 1898 (transposed in the book to Milan), and meetings and resolutions continued into the twentieth century. On 14 March 1904, delegates from ten countries met in St Petersburg and agreed on a secret protocol that dealt with the expulsion of political offenders, the creation of a network of anti-anarchist police bureaus in each state, and the sharing of police information between them. Two decades later, these initiatives led to the setting up of the organisation that subsequently became known as Interpol.[63]

Britain's attitude to these developments was equivocal. Having at first actively resisted calls for international meetings to combat anarchism, it did send representatives to the month-long conference in Rome, but then chose not to sign either the 1898 protocol or its 1904 successor. Nevertheless, the British government did support extradition in cases of assassination and argued that the notion that these were political crimes should not be accepted as a valid defence. At the fifth plenary in December 1898, the British Ambassador Sir Philip Currie also promised the Conference that the law on explosives would be amended in order to make it easier to prosecute cases of possession and to bring conspiracies to cause explosions in other countries within its remit. Sir Philip's pledges were no idle boasts, and draft legislation was apparently prepared, anticipating the political extradition laws floated by the imaginary Sir Philip Ramon in Wallace's *The Four Just Men*. But if these measures were considered highly desirable in some quarters, by 1902 there was little hope of fitting them into the Commons' busy schedule. More seriously, the British government had several fundamental reservations about how far the law could be changed. Writing in response to renewed efforts by Russia and Germany to clamp down on anarchists, the Marquess of Lansdowne, the British Foreign Secretary, insisted that Parliament would never allow 'the expulsion of aliens on the ground that they are believed to hold Anarchist opinions' and that there was no need to restrict the freedom of the press because the laws governing incitement to criminal behaviour were already more than adequate. It was 'the punishment of actual crime' that was at issue, not belief.[64]

Conrad was not privy to such highly confidential memoranda, but *The Secret Agent* is nonetheless written into the space between Continental indignation and British phlegm. In his Cabinet paper, Lansdowne had observed that, according to police records, 'no less than 97 per cent' of the anarchists living in Britain 'are of foreign nationality' – a distribution that figures as a basic datum in Conrad's novel.[65] What Mr Vladimir wishes to do is to stir the British government from its dogmatic slumbers, to jump-start its patient surveillance into active prosecution, to close the gap between the "Milan" Conference and the House of Commons. To this end he instructs his double agent Adolf Verloc to carry out an attack on one of its most revered scientific institutions, the Royal Observatory, symbolic home to the Greenwich meridian that had recently been adopted as the basis for the new international system of time zones. An atrocity of this magnitude, with 'all the shocking senselessness of gratuitous blasphemy', would demonstrate to Britain that the anarchists really are aiming 'to make a clean sweep of the whole of creation' (24–25). Mr Vladimir's wildly eloquent ventriloquism echoes the uncompromising sentiments of the Professor, and Verloc is utterly appalled.

Verloc fails miserably. His reluctant venture results not only in the accidental death of the gullible Stevie, but also in his own, once his wife has discovered what happened and dispensed summary justice. Mr Vladimir, the scheming First Secretary, is a failure of another kind, for the trail leads directly to his embassy and places him at the centre of the plot. His sentence, pronounced by the head of 'the so-called Special Crimes Department', the unnamed Assistant Commissioner who tracks him down, is a kind of expulsion, banishing him from the sanctuary of British high society in which he thrives (86). After the Assistant Commissioner has finally confronted Mr Vladimir outside the 'extremely exclusive club' of which the latter is an honorary member, his last words to the man he refers to as 'the inciter' of the outrage are: 'You're not going in here' (167). What might have been a polite inquiry is a flat statement of fact, an interdiction.

As Con Coroneos has observed, Mr Vladimir's punishment can be read as 'a form of poetic justice' the aptness of which seems to be proof against 'the hard, disabusing ironies of the novel', or at least to disclose a radically different order of irony.[66] It offers a moment of reckoning in which the duplicity of the First Secretary is exposed and checked and he is given his just deserts by being denied entry to a world that embraces the likes of a convicted criminal like Michaelis. Yet, as Coroneos also pointedly notes, what troubles this reading is its approximation to the sort of crowd-pleasing gesture that Conrad typically disdains, a xenophobic and near-sentimental satisfaction at the come-uppance of a devious foreign interloper unfit to bask in the warmth of British hospitality, a man no better – and, perhaps, worse – than the squalid conspirators whose vain schemes he means to squash once and for all. What needs to be added, however, is that poetic justice is necessarily couched in the language of restrictionism: denial of entry, expulsion, conspiracy, a sense of the closeness of the enemy within. To restrict immigration is to seek to realign a nation's concept of its own jurisdiction, to pursue the rank outsider to what the Assistant Commissioner calls 'the limits of our territory', in this case the doors to the foreign embassy, those non-places that represent 'abroad only by a fiction' – that is, purely 'theoretically' (167). By extension, the patriot might be said to be someone who sees through such artificial conventions and can therefore claim to know the truth of a nation.

But if poetic justice might be said to assume a populist hue, its instrument looks like little more than an elaborate social slight, a carefully calculated gesture that courts the charge of triviality. And this caveat is enough to raise doubts as to whether a populist tribunal would be satisfied that the punishment befits Mr Vladimir's crime. From a restrictionist view, the fact that the anarchist community remains untouched and the Professor still at large adds weight to the kinds of criticisms voiced in *Blackwood's Magazine*. But it also strengthens the unceasing relay of ironies mobilized by the novel.

The barring of Mr Vladimir from his London club is not the only case of poetic justice in *The Secret Agent*. The brutally instinctive retribution meted out by Winnie on behalf of her brother's dismembered body and her subsequent suicide also raises difficult questions of deserts and proportionality. If what Conrad depicts as Winnie's primitivism connects the cave dweller's 'simple ferocity' to the 'unbalanced nervous fury' of modernity's discontents, at once 'maternal and violent', her fearful anger is projected outwards and returns as a fantasy of what she knows to be 'men's justice', imagined as an assembly of 'strange gentlemen in silk hats who were calmly proceeding about the business of hanging her by the neck' (193, 196). At the level of individual fantasy, Conrad constantly muddies the line between the public and the private, and the ironic contrast between unspoken motives and social conventions can sometimes seem like labyrinthine digressions whose full impact has been deliberately delayed in order to heighten their effect. So, while the Assistant Commissioner is officially seeking to preserve the national interest, his mission is secretly driven by a desire to preserve his wife (and ipso facto himself) from the acute embarrassment that would ensue should he be forced to implicate the anarchist Michaelis – currently the darling of the capital's upper-class drawing rooms – in the Greenwich plot. In a further irony, the energy that the Assistant Commissioner brings to his investigation is fired by the opportunity the case gives him to enact a late metropolitan simulacrum of his earlier adventures 'in a tropical colony' where he had earned a considerable reputation for 'tracking and breaking up certain nefarious secret societies amongst the natives' (74). His London club – the same institution from which Mr Vladimir will be barred – is, naturally enough, 'the Explorers'. It is, *in nuce*, the empire writ small, a cosy respite from colonial striving.

This diminution is also discernible in other aspects of the Assistant Commissioner's quest and is underscored by his appearance in the field as 'a cool, reflective Don Quixote, with the sunken eyes of a dark enthusiast and a very deliberate manner'. As the heart of the empire, London is the least English metropolis imaginable, and to pass unnoticed through the streets of Charing Cross and Soho, this domesticated knight errant has to assume the character of 'one more of the queer foreign fish' that inhabit those parts (108). But foreignness is also quite other than it seems. The Assistant Commissioner's evening meal, preparatory to his visit to Verloc's seedy shop, is taken in a local Italian restaurant, which is, paradoxically, 'a peculiarly British institution' that is variously described as 'baited', 'immoral', and 'mocking', a snare for the unwary (109). Victorians tended to look down on Italian cuisine; in the first edition of her best-selling *Household Management*, published in 1861, the year in which Italy was unified into a nation-state, Mrs Beeton told her readers that, with the sole exception of macaroni, this was a country without any 'specially characteristic article of food'.[67] In *The Secret Agent*, however, the malaise of 'Italian' cooking is far more treacherous than a writer like Mrs Beeton could ever imagine, because not only does the Italian restaurant debase the culinary arts, but it sustains 'an atmosphere' that is wholly 'fraudulent', a hall of mirrors that quickly becomes a vortex of misrecognition and deception.

To a degree, the Assistant Commissioner escapes being lured into this curious force field in which the contemplative gaze of one habitué is likely to be met by the unseeing stare of another. Although he seems 'to lose some more of his identity', he does at least begin to register 'his foreign appearance' and then deliberately tries to intensify the effect by raising his jacket collar and twisting 'the ends of his black moustache'. His purposiveness gives him a clearer perspective on this remarkably insubstantial venue:

On going out the Assistant Commissioner made to himself the observation that the patrons of the place had lost in the frequentation of fraudulent cookery all their national and private characteristics ... these people were as denationalised as the dishes set before them with every circumstance of unstamped respectability. Neither was their personality stamped in any way, professionally, socially or racially. They seemed created for the Italian restaurant, unless the Italian restaurant had been perchance created for them.

But that last hypothesis was unthinkable, since one could not place them anywhere outside those special establishments. One never met these enigmatical persons elsewhere. It was impossible to form a precise idea what occupations they followed by day and where they went to bed at night. And he himself had become unplaced. It would have been impossible for anybody to guess his occupation. As to going to bed, there was doubt even in his own mind. (109)

In this extraordinary passage, what makes this institution 'peculiarly British' is its uncanny powers of absorption whereby the identities of those who find themselves dining there are almost entirely effaced, at once unknowable and – in the most literal sense of the word 'unplaced' – lost. To 'denationalize' in its original nineteenth-century usage meant to actively remove or eradicate a person or an institution's national character – hence, in George Eliot's *Impressions of Theophrastus Such* (1879), the Jews of the Diaspora are described as an 'expatriated, denationalized race'.[68] The Assistant Commissioner seems for a moment to stand above this abyss of selfhood, buoyed up by a 'pleasurable feeling of independence', yet his own sense of satisfaction ensures that he remains oblivious to the 'imperfect baffled thud' as 'the glass doors swing to behind his back' and is thus unable fully to recognise the vacuity that Britain is coming to represent (110). Immersed in a world that is neither one thing nor the other, he cannot quite draw the sobering conclusion that is staring him in the face: that, ultimately, there is nothing here for a man like him to defend. In a novel that takes great pains to leave Britain as it was, defended against outside interference but with the right to freedom of opinion intact, there can be no greater irony.

Preserving a distance from the genre is an essential part of Conrad's cool flirtation with the spy thriller, and so the desire for popular justice cannot finally be satisfied; or rather, to assuage that desire, one must search elsewhere in the genre that Conrad is reluctant to endorse. There is no need to look far: in the autumn of 1908, in his sequel to *The Four Just Men*, Edgar Wallace returned to the question of anarchism and the demand for justice and again placed political toleration at the centre of his novel. However, *The Council of Justice* represented a substantial retreat from the bold political scenario Wallace had outlined in the earlier book. Instead of pitting his anarchist heroes against an obdurate and misguided politician, the new enemy they are now obliged to confront is a kind of mirror image of themselves: an organisation of violent revolutionaries bent on the overthrow of the existing social order. By switching adversaries, Wallace complicated the conflicted relationship between the police and his own 'just men', deliberately making it far more difficult to sustain the notion that Manfred and his co-conspirators were 'foreign anarchists' dedicated to safeguarding the position of political refugees and thus saving England from its own illiberal excesses. Because England was now imagined to be in the grip of anarchist terror, a threat that had been treated sympathetically in the original novel, this reversal in direction and tone required some justification. Before the story properly commences, Wallace laid out an impassioned defence of what it is that the 'just men' stood for, stressing 'their wonderful intellects' and approvingly citing the French liberal philosopher Victor Cousin's dictum that 'the universal and absolute law is that natural justice which cannot be written down', a law that always stands above the legal code of any given nation-state.[69] In this apologia, Wallace described his own divided loyalties as though he were responding to real events. Torn between the recognition that his heroes' killings are acts of murder, including that of the Foreign Secretary in *The Four Just Men*, he confessed that all his sympathies were with them and suggested that many of his readers, 'the thousands of people who have written to me', took much the same view (10). By referring to his 'just men' as a 'council', the book's more official-sounding title was intended to indicate a new departure, initiating a break with the past.

In fact, however fanciful and melodramatic, Wallace's novel was very much rooted in the present. It took its inspiration from three main, if somewhat disparate, sources. Firstly, and most conspicuously, Wallace drew on the sense of alarm associated with anarchism, regarded as the most volatile and disruptive of all contemporary political forces. Anarchism had been a generalised name for lawlessness, rebellion, and violence against the state since the 1880s, and while it had been relatively weak in Britain, by the turn of the century it was increasingly being identified as an oppositional political tendency that was sweeping across the globe. After the wave of political assassinations in France, Spain, Austria, Italy, and the United States between 1894 and 1901, the fear of anarchism intensified and plots and rumours of plots multiplied. For example, in 1907, when *The Council of Justice* was in gestation, *The Times* featured anarchist stories from Denmark, Sweden, France, and Spain, ranging from cases of murder to a bomb attack on a railway station, not to mention accounts of arrests, injuries, and suicide.[70]

Secondly, Wallace's portrayal of the anarchists as an international body meeting in London, a scene with which *The Council of Justice* begins, can be traced to a number of leftist political conferences that had been held in the capital, including an international anarchist congress that had met there in 1881. However, its immediate source was in all probability a politically very different occasion. Early in May 1907, the British press began to report on preparations for the Fifth Russian Social Democratic Workers' Party Congress (RSDLP) which was due to take place behind closed doors in a church hall on the eastern edge of Islington. Under the headline 'Revolutionaries Arrive. Socialist Invasion Begins', the *Daily Mail* noted that these 'young men ... of undeniably foreign appearance' were evidently well funded for, having 'travelled first class they escaped the attentions of alien immigration officers on landing'.[71] While obviously *not* anarchists – although there were some early misunderstandings on this point – allusions to revolutionary violence and terrorism indicated that these Bolsheviks and Mensheviks were going to be discussed in very similar terms.

In comparison to Wallace's fevered imagination, the Russian Fifth Congress was small, with only around 330 delegates, barely a tenth of the numbers conjured up in his novel, but nevertheless the parallels with the press coverage are striking. The emphasis on obsessive secrecy, the use of passwords, the interest in the Congress taken by Scotland Yard were all faithfully reproduced in *The Council of Justice*. But the most vivid details in the newspaper reports concerned the presence of young female revolutionaries among the 'very un-English ... crowd of Russians, Poles, Letts, Finns, and Jews', women who were depicted as dedicated and fanatical and certainly deadlier than the male. Every day, according to the *Daily Mirror*, they would practice drawing their revolvers in front of the mirror, and were also rousing and pugnacious speakers.[72] On 16 May, in a story headlined 'Girl Nihilists', the *Mirror* reported that during one session of 'London's Secret Duma': 'The meeting was roused to fury by the half-hour eloquent speech of one of the young girl delegates, who called for "war at any price". ... This firebrand spoke of barricades and bombs much as the average English girl will chatter about bridge and lawn tennis. "Free Russia can only evolve out of a stream of blood," she'd declared'.[73]

In this memorable scene, one can surely discern the origins of the anarchist leader in *The Council of Justice*, the diminutive, passionate, and utterly ruthless young waif Maria, chiefly known as 'the Woman of Gratz'. Whether this figure should be taken for a melodramatic version of 'Dr Rosa Luxembourg', identified by *The Times* as arguing for unity among Menshevik and the Bolshevik Congress members (just as the Woman of Gratz attempts to unify the diverse anarchist factions), remains to be seen.[74]

If Wallace's gendering of the anarchist leadership performs a curious transformation of left-wing allegiances, the third and final ingredient reveals a still more cavalier approach to political history. From the opposite end of the extremist spectrum the 'Red Hundreds', the name given to the anarchist organisation in *The Council of Justice*, calls to mind the ferocious reputation of the infamous 'Black Hundreds', the ruthless counter-revolutionary and anti-Semitic groups operating in Russia that were particularly active between 1906 and 1914. During the month that the Fifth RSDLP Congress was in session, for example, reports of atrocities committed by the 'Black Hundreds', notably against Jews in Odessa, appeared in the British press.[75] A small change of nomenclature produced a generalised signifier of socialism, foreignness, and violence in the novel, inverting the political meaning of its likely source.

The 'first great congress of recognized Anarchism' described by Wallace is an international gathering in which French, German, English, and Yiddish are spoken; but it is also pointedly associated with a particular locale and its inhabitants. The Red Hundred meets in Middlesex Street in London's East End, in a hall specially built 'by an enthusiastic Christian gentleman with a weakness for the conversion of Jews to the new Presbyterian Church', a decidedly less than successful venture (20). Filled to capacity and with its windows and ventilation blocked off for reasons of security, the 'unclean' meeting-room reeks of poverty: its air is stiflingly 'unhealthy – the scent of an early morning doss-house' (22). And until the Red Hundred's leader Maria – the Woman of Gratz – takes the platform, the atmosphere is torpid, the 'guttural chatter' that can be heard sounding like a bored background noise (23). What is so electric about the oratory of this 'slim and fragile' young woman is her delivery. The phrases and ideology of 'the unwritten text of Anarchism' that she speaks have already degenerated into cliché: 'the right of the oppressed to overthrow the oppressor; the divinity of violence; the sacredness of sacrifice and martyrdom in the cause of enlightenment' (27). Yet Maria is the one person capable of bringing these tired slogans to life, of leading the struggle against the ruling class to victory.

However, Anarchism has been debased by more than a repetitive association with stale phrases. Paradoxically, given the almost Orwellian equation of poverty with smell, the Red Hundred has become 'handsomely profitable', attracting career criminals looking for a quick return, in addition to cultivating the use of violence as a perverse good in and of itself (85). Like the notions of Jewish conspiracy whose structure it mimics, Wallace's version of anarchism oscillates between pauperism and plutocracy, with the persona of the Woman of Gratz doubling as the small-town stray she was born to be and the regal 'Countess Slienvitch' she invents as a criminal masquerade. Similarly, the Red Hundred is openly cosmopolitan – its meetings are not some 'hole-and-corner gathering of hurried men speaking furtively' – while also somehow managing to be deeply clandestine and shrouded in mystery (13). The 'secret place in the metropolis' from which 'the Woman of Gratz reorganized her forces' after suffering a severe setback at the hands of the Council of Justice remains unknown; nevertheless, 'men and money' continue to pour in from 'every corner of Europe' (130). These resources are considerable, enabling the Red Hundred to mount a full-scale offensive that goes far beyond elaborately contrived acts of sabotage. Anticipating the Great War, 'the Reds' mount a Zeppelin attack on London that is only narrowly averted by the 'just men', stationed like air-raid wardens on the dome of St Paul's Cathedral (131).

Wallace was not the only writer to invent an assault on the capital and the details of his vision were hardly new. The projected aerial bombardment of London has its generic antecedents in E. Douglas Fawcett's 1893 scientific romance *Hartmann the Anarchist: or the Doom of the Great City*, a prime example of the much-noticed "dynamite novels" that flourished towards the end of the nineteenth century. But, unlike Fawcett's futuristic narrative, not only does London survive relatively unscathed, despite a long inventory of anarchist destruction; there is no new social system like Fawcett's model of socialism that can take its place. Politically, Wallace's anarchism stands for a false enlightenment that cannot supplant the status quo, however serious the latter's shortcomings may be. If *The Council of Justice* dramatises a struggle between two sets of world historical forces, 'both outside the pale of the law', reducing the police to powerless bystanders, the novel is compelled to push towards another, no less brutal kind of confrontation in which stark abstractions square off against each other (130). Sickened by the destruction and senseless killing that he has witnessed, Manfred tries to convince the Woman of Gratz that the two sides should agree a cease-fire, but his efforts to initiate a dialogue turn into a bitter argument. When she asks him what he is fighting for, Manfred quickly lists 'the happiness of my fellows, security for the weak, justice for the oppressed', only to have her dismiss his goals as 'canting platitudes' (162). Manfred can truthfully claim that he has staked his life on these principles and is wanted for murder by every nation in the civilised world as a result. But their opposing positions are deadlocked because each of these sworn enemies imagines their views are supported by the laws of history. 'There can be no truce' the Woman of Gratz insists, precisely because the anarchists 'have set ourselves to remove the obstacles in the path of struggling mankind – the accidental obstructions that old dead systems have bequeathed us'.

What obsesses Maria is the perpetuation of hereditary privilege that passes from father to son, that is, from those 'who some time ruled by might' to 'their haphazard progeny' (164). Manfred dismisses this patriarchal notion, telling her that good leaders need to learn how to lead and that a leaderless society is quite impossible: 'Another king will come – or the councillors, which is worse – or the dictator, who is worse than all'. What the anarchists cannot see is that they 'are fighting inevitable laws which decree that one man shall always have power over his fellows and rule them for the common good'. But Manfred does not have the last word. 'We're fighting ambition with terror', the Woman of Gratz tells him, 'we are imposing one natural law upon another – the fear of death upon the hunger for power. One by one they shall go, these rulers of yours' (165). And then she tries to kill him, but fails. Later in the book, when Manfred again attempts to argue for a truce, the Woman of Gratz destroys her own former comrades with the exultant cry, 'Long live anarchy!' (197).

In a sense, there had already been a truce, but it is a truce that has definitively been broken:

Great Britain had ever been immune from the active operations of the anarchist. It had been the sanctuary of the revolutionary for centuries, and Anarchism had hesitated to jeopardize the security of refugees by carrying on its propaganda on British soil. That the extremists of the movement had chafed under the restriction is well known, and when the Woman of Gratz openly declared war on England, she was acclaimed enthusiastically. (130)

A watershed has been reached and Britain has passed into a new political moment, driven by the recklessness of a female extremist. But the notion that the intrusion of an alien political culture was incompatible with social peace and that the country stood on the brink of disaster had long been part of anti-immigrant invective. As Evans-Gordon later observed, the idea that asylum could allow Britain to 'purchase immunity of a sort' was not only mistaken, but deeply 'un-English'.[76] Wallace's sensationalism lay in his graphic attempt to go beyond the wildest dreams of the anti-alien lobbies (even while pitting alien against alien, given that the 'Just Men' are still in the process of being domesticated for a mass readership). To give this nightmare substance, any thought of an accommodation between the rule of British law and these lawless phantasms had to be shown to be demonstrably false. The Woman of Gratz's open declaration of war on England is a tacit admission that the apparent quiescence of the anarchists was nothing but a sham.

The idea of a pact, of a liberal zone of tolerance within which the subversive activities of the revolutionary can be held in check, suspended, if not entirely neutralised, has played an important, if sometimes underacknowledged, role in articulating what is at stake in the principle of asylum. Where the refugee's plight has been associated with the use of force, the law of hospitality renders the violence of the Other unnecessary or gratuitous: for the justice of the asylum seeker's case has been recognised, her plea has been heard. But for those who feared that the political refugee will continue to harbour violent propensities, the notion of what one recent commentator has described as 'a covenant of security', or 'a kind of unspoken "gentlemen's agreement" that if the British authorities left them alone, they would not turn on the country that was nurturing them', was simply an illusion.[77] On this view, the granting of asylum is self-defeating, a dangerous indulgence, tantamount to the importation of a ticking bomb. So, in *The Council of Justice*, the offer of sanctuary to the revolutionary is always already absurd, a sign of the gullibility of democratic governments. As we saw earlier, the plot of *The Secret Agent* largely turns upon the dilemma of the potential threat posed by sheltering extremists, but in that text, political closure is resisted. The novel holds in tension two stark images of the anarchist in society: on the one hand, the figure of Michaelis, 'filling a privileged arm-chair' in a grand house, 'mild-voiced and quiet, with no more self-consciousness than a very small child, and with something of a child's charm – the appealing charm of trustfulness' (79); while on the other, there is 'the incorruptible Professor ... calling madness and despair to the regeneration of the world', silently moving through the city, 'unsuspected and deadly, like a pest in the street full of men' (227). Nevertheless, it is with the latter that the novel ends.

A few months after *The Council of Justice* was published, the first of two shockingly violent episodes occurred, events which again raised the question of whether a pact or 'a covenant of security' really existed. Once more aliens and anarchists were in the news, heavily featured on the front pages of *The Star* and the *Daily Graphic*. On 23 January 1909, a car carrying the week's wages was ambushed by two armed men who were waiting outside Schnurmann's rubber factory in Tottenham, North London. As the men were making their getaway, they fired shots at their pursuers, one of their bullets killing a ten-year-old boy who was close by, another causing the death of a policeman who tried to stop them, while a second officer was also seriously injured. There followed an extraordinary hue and cry, with members of the public on bicycles, horses, and in cars, some of them armed with shotguns, while the robbers tried to evade capture by hijacking in rapid succession a tram, a milk float, and a horse and cart, wounding drivers, passengers, and pursuers alike. After 'a five-mile flight through streets and over fields', the two men were finally cornered at a bridge over the River Lea, where one of them held the crowd at bay before turning his revolver on himself.[78] The other escaped, but was quickly tracked down in a coalman's cottage where he was shot in the head by an armed policeman. In addition to the two deaths, some sixteen people were wounded, including three policemen. Six days later, the two victims were given what was essentially a state funeral, with 2,500 soldiers and policemen walking behind the hearse; the Commissioner of the Metropolitan Police and Herbert Samuel, then under-secretary at the Home Office, were also in attendance.

Although there was considerable uncertainty surrounding the identities of the two men – *The Star* had initially described them as 'Italians', before labelling them 'Russian Anarchists from Riga' – there was no doubt that 'the Tottenham Outrage', as it quickly became known, restored the question of immigration control to the national political agenda. At the inquest into these deaths, the jury specifically instructed the coroner 'to draw the attention of the Home Secretary to the present peril which this country is subjected to under the existing Aliens Act', forcing Herbert Gladstone to make a detailed speech defending the government's record.[79] Among the newspapers, the *Daily Mail* was particularly vocal, describing the crimes as the work of 'Russian Terrorists' and depicting Tottenham Hale as an area 'so filled with Russians and Poles that it is locally known as "Aliens' Island"'.[80] In an editorial tendentiously headlined 'Our Alien Criminals', the *Mail* accused the Liberal administration of having 'nullified the Act' when it had issued instructions 'that anyone who states that he is a political refugee shall be admitted without question', orders which were said to be directly responsible for allowing the two East European gunmen into the country with such ease that one of them had been passed by immigration officers 'more than once'.[81] This became the standard argument against the Aliens Act. Less than a week after Gladstone's careful defence, the 'open door for the political refugee' again came under attack when an Old Bailey Judge and former Unionist MP James Rentoul delivered a savage speech at East London's Bishopsgate Institute, in which he inveighed against the policy that, in only the last few days, had brought before his court 'the Russian burglar, the Polish thief, the Italian stabber, and the German swindler', men who had no longer had a place in their countries of origin; 'in the matter of alien immigration,' he told a cheering audience, 'Empire should be placed above party advantage'.[82]

In vain Gladstone had sensibly tried to insist that 'the question relating to what were known as anarchists or revolutionaries was quite distinct from the general question of the regulation of foreign immigration'.[83] This distinction was given short shrift when history appeared to repeat itself the following year when the deaths of three more policemen set in train a chain of events that concluded with the dramatic 'Siege of Sidney Street' (also known as 'the Battle of Stepney' or 'the Battle of the East End') a few weeks later. On 16 December 1910, police were called to investigate suspicious noises late at night from inside a house in Houndsditch adjacent to a jeweller's shop and immediately came under fire from a gang of armed men. One sergeant was killed outright, a constable and another sergeant later died of their injuries, and two other policemen were wounded. Revolvers were issued to all members of the London police force, and across the capital a massive manhunt began. The discovery of the dead body of a Russian male was soon linked to the murders and two women who had apparently been looking after him were taken into custody. Further arrests of East European men and women quickly ensued. Then on 3 January 1911, Scotland Yard received a tip-off that brought them to a house in Sidney Street in the East End. The building was surrounded, the street cordoned off, and by daybreak the police found themselves under fire. In an extraordinary spectacle, more than 700 policemen (later reinforced by members of the Scots Guards) exchanged gunfire with what turned out to be two East Europeans with automatic pistols. An estimated 2,000 rounds of ammunition were fired before the building caught fire at around 1 PM, though sporadic shooting continued for some time before the Fire Brigade was able to intervene. Inside the gutted building the police discovered two bodies, one killed by a marksman's bullet, the other having died from suffocation. With the sole exception of a Russian woman who was imprisoned but given early release, everyone who had been arrested in connection with the crime and brought to trial was subsequently acquitted.

From the outset, the apparent similarities with the Tottenham murders became a primary focus for the press reports, epitomised by the *Daily Graphic*'s main headline 'CITY POLICEMEN MURDERED BY ALIEN BURGLARS', as did references to 'the Houndsditch Outrage', deliberately linking the crime to 'the Tottenham outrage of a little less than two years ago'.[84] As before, anarchism provided a rhetorical frame that gave the murders a minimal intelligibility: thus, in the pages of the *Graphic* these men were not just 'alien criminals,' but 'Anarchist-thieves', 'dangerous savages' so completely 'saturated by the virulent poison of Anarchist doctrines' that 'violence is their only faith'.[85] Its leader writer was convinced that no English criminal would use a gun as 'recklessly' as had happened in Tottenham and Houndsditch. The threat posed by anarchism had clearly been underestimated. In an interview with the *Graphic*, Sir Robert Anderson, former head of the Secret Service, argued that even daring to hold anarchist beliefs was a form of treason because, as he put it elsewhere, 'in treason the criminal intention is itself the crime'. The very idea that these revolutionaries could make 'inflammatory speeches' with impunity was a widespread misconception, and certainly there could be no 'implied understanding' between the police and 'criminals' like these.[86] By insisting on the reality of a 'covenant of security' as an explanation of what had gone wrong in Houndsditch, Anderson was again suggesting that asylum encouraged the most callous and implacable forms of violence. Yet, despite his elaborate legal assault on anarchist *ideas*, there was never any convincing evidence then or now that the murderers in Tottenham or Houndsditch were in fact anarchists.[87]

But it did matter that they were 'aliens' and it especially mattered that 'this part of Houndsditch' – and later Sidney Street – 'is the Jewish quarter'; or, to move from the *Graphic* to the more turbid language of the *Daily Mail*, this deadly terrain is 'the centre of a queer confusion of races', 'a labyrinth of evil lanes' that are 'meeting-places for some of the worst criminals in London', where 'practically every European tongue is spoken' and the 'newspaper posters are as often as not printed in Yiddish'.[88] What even the *Mail* could not quite bring itself to spell out openly appeared as doggerel in *The People* under the didactic title 'The Lessons of Houndsditch':

> But I think it's time to plead once more
>   to get rid of the cursed breed
> Of alien Jews who seem to have been the
>   authors of the deed.
> Remember Tottenham! Foreign Jews

> were the coward murderers there
> And it's pretty certain that aliens held
> the guns on the Houndsditch stair.
>
> What's the good of an Alien's Act, when
> we let the alien scum
> Swarm into England in droves and herd
> in every city slum.
> I would give them all – aye rich and
> poor – one day, not a moment more
> To clear out and hang them if they were
> found again on British shore.[89]

A week later, in response to the letters of protest it had received, *The People* was forced to deny that any slur had been 'intended' against 'the large number of aliens of the Jewish religion ... who are deservedly known for their loyal, industrious, and law-abiding character' – the perfectly idealised complement to the debased rich and poor constituting 'them all'.[90] Predictably, in its next issue, it returned to the fray, attacking the Liberals for making 'a dead letter of the Aliens Act' and demanding that 'suspected Anarchists, who cannot clear themselves', should be summarily deported.[91]

The drama of Sidney Street, with troops and heavy artillery ritualistically brought down from the Tower of London, proved to be a moment when the careful discriminations that Gladstone had sought to maintain in his adroit 1909 speech on the Tottenham murders seemed to flounder. As incoming Home Secretary, Churchill had been a high-profile and high-risk presence at the siege, but this bold gesture failed to bring him the popular acclaim for which he had doubtless hoped. His arrival on the scene was greeted by loud cries of 'Oo let 'em in?' and, as his own Private Secretary, Edward Marsh, noted at the time, this response was repeated on a 'nightly' basis when his appearance on local newsreels were 'received with unanimous boos and shouts of "shoot him"'.[92] In a letter to his close friend Lady Dorothy Gladstone (the wife of the former Home Secretary), Marsh wondered what it was that made these 'London music-hall audiences so uniformly and so bigotedly Tory'; but in the next paragraph he revealed that Churchill was, in effect, capitulating to the Tory press by producing a '"Criminal Aliens" Bill' which would give the Home Secretary the power to force the expulsion of a convicted alien in cases where the courts had been reluctant to exercise this option.[93] The Bill would also contain 'a provision for expelling aliens who are going to commit crimes before they commit them' – a measure that was, understandably, proving 'very difficult to draft'.[94]

Expulsion before the commission of an offence was the second of what Churchill roguishly referred to as 'two naughty principles' in a Home Office memo drafted the day after Marsh's letter to Lady Gladstone.[95] The first was to distinguish between the alien – particularly those who were unassimilated – and the British subject. In a letter to the king shortly after the siege, for example, Churchill floated the idea of barring aliens from owning firearms 'without a special license from the police authorities' or bringing in 'a special right of search for arms … in the case of aliens'.[96] He also wanted to give courts the power to require sureties for good behaviour for aliens alleged to be associating with known or suspected criminals and to imprison those who failed to find such sureties, pending deportation. Despite his assurances that his Bill would safeguard 'the great mass of non-naturalised alien population from the fear of being harshly used', Churchill's stance marked a new departure from the former Home Secretary's response to criticisms.[97] Herbert Gladstone had insisted that the Aliens Act – 'the policy of his predecessors' – had been designed 'to deal with aliens in bulk' and not criminal aliens per se, even citing detailed examples to show why 'the exclusion of the foreign criminal was *impossible* under the Aliens Act'.[98] By contrast, Churchill's aim was, as Marsh put it, 'to stiffen up the Aliens Act'.[99]

To this end, Churchill was even willing to give qualified support to a private member's bill that had been introduced by a Conservative backbencher, Edward Goulding, in February. This was the stuff that the *Mail* and *The People* had dreamed of. While overlapping with Churchill's own thinking, the general tenor of Goulding's draconian proposals can be judged from his plans to redefine an immigrant ship as one that carried even a single alien passenger and to introduce inspection in every British port. Churchill taunted Goulding that this clause would necessitate employing Immigration Officers in eighty additional ports and he took the precaution of bringing forward his own Aliens (Prevention of Crime) Bill just before Goulding's Aliens Bill had reached its Second Reading in April 1911 in the hope that the two schemes might be merged at the Committee stage (to the advantage of his own, more focussed Bill, of course). On Churchill's recommendation, Goulding's Bill was passed by a narrow majority of fifteen (chiefly Tory) votes, a sign of the Liberals' relative weakness after the general election of the previous year, but also of the widening cracks within the party on the alien question. Notwithstanding the Home Secretary's attempt to articulate what he plainly felt to be the popular mood, neither he nor Goulding was able to make any headway and their proposals dwindled in Committee. If immigration had always been a difficult issue for the Liberals, under Churchill's tenure as Home Secretary they were arguably more divided than at any previous period.

The demise of the two Aliens Bills in 1911 crowded out by more pressing matters at home and abroad seemed to confirm the bitter prognostications of the Edwardian Radical Right, indicating not only that immigration unchecked would lead to the breakdown of public order, but that the state would find itself unable to pass the measures necessary to prevent anything like the Sidney Street siege happening again. If the weaknesses in the existing legislation could not be corrected in the face of such shocking events, when would the restrictionist case make itself heard? Looking back at the impact of the 'popular ferment against the rush of Jewish immigrants into the East End' in his abrasive attempt to reopen the Jewish Question in 1922, Hilaire Belloc characterised the Edwardian era as a time of political 'hypocrisy', when racial problems could not be addressed frankly and decisively.[100] From this standpoint, the 1905 Aliens Act appeared as an irretrievable failure, a moment when the Conservatives lost the initiative rather than putting immigration control on a firm footing.

However, as the German anarchist Rudolf Rocker later recalled, amongst the migrant communities in the East End the Sidney Street episode was experienced as a 'nightmare period' in which 'anti-alien agitation' was again on the rise.[101] But the grass-roots response to Goulding's and Churchill's Bills produced some significant new developments. In the wake of the Sidney Street siege, the Jewish Protection Society was formed to mobilise the East End against anti-Semitic attacks and, although there was a split over strategy, a successor quickly emerged calling itself the Aliens Defence Committee. The ADC was chaired by Morris Myer who had arrived in London from Romania in 1902 and soon became a well-known, if sometimes captious, journalist for the Yiddish press who espoused social democratic politics. Under his leadership, the committee had an official voice that could credibly claim to speak on behalf of immigrants.[102] Even the committee's use of the highly charged term 'alien' in its name was a tactical innovation, for it seized hold of a legal concept that had been turned into a coded insult and showed that its content could be fought over and the conditions of those to whom it was applied could be improved. The ADC lobbied MPs and critiqued the Goulding Bill, created an alliance of between local organisations like trade union branches and friendly societies, and used community papers like *Der Yidisher Zhurnal* to promote its arguments.

The ADC enjoyed a brief career, flourishing and then faltering, in synch with the troubled fortunes of the 1911 Aliens Bills. But its strong East End base reflected a more militant mood, particularly amongst local workers. In 1912, Rocker and his group were able to organise support within the East End clothing industry for a strike by West End tailors, stopping the employers using them as strike-breakers against those on the other side of the city. This move precipitated a hard but ultimately successful strike in the East End involving both male and female garment workers, which in turn fed into solidarity with industrial action by dockers in the Port of London. In retrospect, these struggles, like the campaigns of the ADC and the formation of Workers' Circles or socialist mutual aid associations, were amongst the first signs of what was to be a growing wave of political and economic activism that continued up until the outbreak of the First World War. This was a phase in which anarcho-syndicalist currents thrived and for Rocker it represented 'the peak of our movement'.[103]

In spite of their clumsiness, Goulding's and Churchill's stillborn legislation represented a sign that attempts to envisage more effective forms of immigration control were already afoot. Christiane Reinecke has argued that the measures introduced in the wartime Aliens Restriction Act on 5 August 1914 had been in preparation by civil servants since 1910.[104] Non-British citizens were now required to register with the police and to carry identity cards, their movements were restricted, and there were new emergency powers of detention and expulsion without legal redress. The role of immigration officers was significantly strengthened, increasing their numbers and giving them the right to inspect any ship and to take into custody anyone attempting to enter or leave the country. The Act's main principles were carried forward into the inter-war period creating a stringent regime of passports, visas, and labour permits, together with a permanent National Aliens Register. In 1919, a revised and updated Aliens Restriction Act formally repealed the 1905 Aliens Act. The old Immigration Boards were discontinued and the decisions made by the Immigration Officer effectively became law.

Afterword

The year is 1924. The German armed forces are ready to invade the British Isles at any moment. The enemy navy has made preparations to move German troops across the North Sea and a network of supporters has been organised to help to ease the invaders' entry into Britain and to consolidate their grip on the country. Unless the British recognise the danger they are in, their future as an independent nation, let alone that of their Empire, looks bleak. But fortunately there are those, an embattled few, who do fully understand the nature of the threat Great Britain faces and who have begun to make the necessary legislative changes in parliament that will make it impossible for the Germans to succeed. Britain can still emerge victorious from its darkest hour.

This is not the 1924 of Ramsay MacDonald's Labour government, nor of the Conservative victory that followed it ten months later. Germany's Weimar Republic was not in the process of creating a new currency that would bring to an end the devastating hyperinflation that had wiped out the savings of its middle classes; French and Belgian troops were not still occupying the Ruhr after Germany had defaulted on its reparations payments agreed in the Treaty of Versailles; and Adolf Hitler was not in prison, busily writing *Mein Kampf.* The scenario outlined earlier forms part of the finale of an unusual, but not altogether untypical, early novel by a prolific, if relatively unknown, jobbing writer, which appeared in 1910.[1] James Blyth's *Ichabod* belongs, in part, to the mass of invasion scare stories that peaked towards the end of that decade. Anyone familiar with Erskine Childers' *The Riddle of the Sands* (1903) or William Le Queux's bestsellers *The Great War in England in 1897* (1894) and *The Invasion of 1910* (1906) – the latter sold more than a million copies – would know precisely where many of the main ingredients of Blyth's lurid plot had originated. Not to be outdone, *Ichabod* has two invasion scares: a clandestine German plan that is exposed and fatally undermined in 1909 by a plucky band of British patriots, amateurs with friends in high places, and an almost identical scheme that is cut short by a full-fledged pre-emptive military strike in the final chapter when Britain reveals its new and invincible secret weapon.

How does *Ichabod* differ from the run-of-the-mill invasion narrative? The Biblical allusion in the title gives the game away. In the First Book of Samuel (4: 21), after the ark of the covenant has been captured by the Philistines and thousands of Israelites have been killed, 'Ichabod' is the name given to her newborn son by the widow of one of the murdered priests. That name articulates a lament and denotes shame and loss: 'The glory has departed from Israel'. And in Blyth's novel, the name appears as a fantasised headline that the hero Noel Pettigrew would most like to see on the front page of the *Jewish Chronicle*; for it is his belief that the Jews are steadily destroying Britain. The Germans think that the Jews are their fifth column; in reality, however, it is the Jews who are manipulating the Germans and it is the Jews that Noel hates for having destroyed his family and his country. But, as in so many invasion stories of the period, there is a palpable sense of ambivalence here, a fear that it is the *patria* that is really failing and is continuing to fail, that the invocation of 'Ichabod' is a judgement on the British themselves.

Of course, anti-Semitism is hardly foreign territory for this genre. Several of Le Queux's most popular fictions have Jews at the centre of a conspiracy that threatens to bring down the country. The master spy Count Karl von Beilstein in *The Great War in England in 1897* (1894), for example, is 'a polished cosmopolitan' from 'the Jews' quarter in Frankfurt', a seasoned criminal who has escaped gaol by becoming 'a secret agent of the Tsar'.[2] And even in those novels that evince some sympathy for the Russian Jews, as in Le Queux's *Spies of the Kaiser* (1909), men like the 'thin-faced, shrivelled up old foreigner' Van Nierop are, as in *Ichabod*, part of a 'vast army' of German agents 'spread over our smiling land of England'.[3] What gives Blyth's novel its uniquely disagreeable flavour is the intensity with which it bears down upon the figure of the East End Jewish immigrant and its insistence that the danger these aliens represent is distinct from and far worse than that of German militarism. The language used to convey the horrors of Jewish settlement sustains an extraordinarily fervid sense of disgust and loathing, situating the life-world of the East-European racial body within the most critical pathological zone of public and political hygiene. By 1920, the omniscient narrator tells us, 'English folk' had not only been 'eliminated' to the 'east of Bishopsgate', but it was as though the Jewish East End had spread outwards into Hampstead and Gospel Oak, extending the reach of 'the Semitic blight': 'The area of their contamination was so vast, and the doctrine of *laissez faire* so popular with the authorities, that the ghettoes were scarcely policed at all, and the sanitary inspectors never thought of taking steps to remove the million nuisances which the filthy habits of the greeners committed'.[4]

In this epidemiology of race, 'filthy habits' are far from being an attribute of those newcomers condemned to live in cramped and squalid conditions, and still less are they to be regarded simply as a means by which disease is transmitted. The metaphor collapses into a noxious literalism: Jews thrive in such a 'pestilential atmosphere' because they represent the disease itself. It is 'the reek' of their 'putrid decay that made the air a poison', a diagnosis that is linked in the same sentence to the propensity of the 'alien Jew' to 'foul his own sleeping place as readily as a vulture' (208). Reading such passages, one is irresistibly reminded of the vicious medico-biological imagery of plagues, parasites, and foreign viruses deployed by the future German Chancellor in his all-too-real Landsberg Prison writings from 1924, the most infamous anti-Semitic text ever written.[5]

Blyth's conjuring of an imaginary future is clearly intended to create a distance from the late Edwardian present – the narrator actually claims to be looking back from the 1950s. But it is also a device that ascribes mythic status to what is depicted as *the* key historical event in the first half of the twentieth century: the passing of the 1905 Aliens Act. Britain's fate is effectively sealed once this law was given the Royal assent. To dramatise its consequences, *Ichabod* begins three years after the Act has come into operation. The family of John Pettigrew, who had formerly made a moderate living as a baker in Stepney, are now the victims of 'alien and Semitic competition, greed, dishonesty, and chicanery', and are crowded into 'the one sordid room' that they can afford (5). Exhausted by poverty and childbirth, John's wife Mary lies dying while an importunate Jewish creditor bangs on the door demanding the family's rent and John can do nothing but curse those who have allowed Jewish immigration to bring the country to its knees. Although this opening scene recalls early texts like Annie Field's short story 'Sturdy British Stock' (1891) or elements of John Steuart's *The Hebrew* (1903), the political specificity that marks John Pettigrew's suffering differs markedly from the broad-brush, loosely socio-logical portrait of racial conflict characteristic of these slum narratives.

John Pettigrew had pinned his faith on the 1903 Royal Commission on Alien Immigration, believing that its report would bring the British to their senses. To this end he 'had spent the last remnant of his money in procuring evidence in support of Major Evans-Gordon's contentions and in exposing certain nefarious trickeries of the pro-alien party' (5). But when he expectantly purchases a copy of the Act, he is shocked to read the clause exempting those fleeing religious or political persecution from the new criteria regulating entry (the narrator knowledgeably cites the relevant section and subsection by number). In this novel of national betrayal, Evans-Gordon belongs among a near-legendary pantheon of heroes, and it is no accident that, on what is grandiosely described as 'the first notable anti-Semitic adventure of the man who was to be the emperor of anti-Semites', the young Noel recites to himself a passage on the growth of anti-British feeling in the country from Arnold White's submission to the Royal Commission (again, adducing a specific numbered paragraph) in silent tribute to that 'able, chivalrous, and loyal gentleman' (37). Noel has a mentor, Colonel Manners, an upstanding retired army officer who lives in the East End, takes an interest in local affairs, especially where they raise questions of national security, and who is perhaps a sort of doppelgänger for Evans-Gordon himself; but it is Noel who is the former MP for Stepney's most worthy successor.

Noel's personal qualities are more than a match for what is depicted as the low cunning of his adversaries: he is courageous, clever, and, apart from a brief moment when he unwittingly falls in love with a beautiful rich Jewess, completely unswerving in his determination to rid England of these 'alien Semites' (85). Yet his victory over the Germans and their Jewish allies is ultimately brought about by the incredible scientific discovery to which he gives his name: 'Pettigrew's force'. This polymorphous source of energy is material – it is used to power a new, silent automobile that Noel has patented – while also operating on a psychic plane to tap into the unconscious and control the human mind, suggesting a bizarre amalgam of mesmerism, electromagnetic waves, and telepathy. Armed with such an extraordinary power, Noel is transformed into a kind of contra-Svengali, and much else besides.

England is now so hopelessly benighted that it takes a manifestation of 'Pettigrew's power' to initiate the rejuvenation of the body politic. In one of the strangest, yet strangely necessary, scenes in the novel, Noel orchestrates the passage of a new Aliens Act from a seat in the public gallery through 'a scintillating spark … from the top of a short metal wand' (291). The principal clauses of the Bill are as follows:

No alien to enter any part of the British Isles unless he could find two approved Englishmen to state – (1) That he was not of the Semitic race. (2) That he was a desirable immigrant, and unlikely to enter into competition with English working people …

Every alien, whether naturalised or not, whom certain persons specified had good reason to believe was a Jew, was to be deported, with his wife and family … (292–293)

Only by reaching down into the deepest recesses of the British *conscience collective* is it possible to begin to restore Britain to its former glory, to give voice to a demand that had long been repressed, and to heal the trauma represented by the suffering of those like the Pettigrews. For, in the eyes of patriots like Colonel Manners, the origins of this fantasised state of Jewish usurpation can ultimately be traced to a crisis of political leadership whose causes are psychological. It is 'a great disappointment to all of us that … the Government should have remained so infatuated or so terrified by Semitic threats and bombast as to leave the Act of 1905 as it was, and not only that, but actually to relax the workings of the Act', says the Colonel in an lengthy tirade that lays the blame for the Boer War at the door of 'the Semitic magnates of the Rand' (125). If Britain has been sleepwalking into a political catastrophe, it might well be because the political class has allowed itself to be mesmerised by its enemies. The seriousness of the crisis is shown by the fact that it transcends party lines.

The inclusively generalised address to 'all of us' (who really know) underscores the function of this text. Far from being simply what Blyth's publishers called an 'historical anticipation' of 'the next fifty years', a provocation that 'is sure to leave the reader, whatever his views may be, full of thoughts', *Ichabod* was designed to inaugurate a political myth. In a 1907 letter that became the introduction to his *Réflexions sur la violence*, the French syndicalist Georges Sorel defined such a myth as a picture or world-view whose purpose is not to describe or analyse, but express 'a determination to act'.[6] According to Sorel's Bergsonian schema, myth is the 'motive force' that inspires historical agents 'to break the bonds of habit which enclose us' (48); or again, myths articulate 'the convictions of a group', expressed 'in the language of movement', and thus they 'lead men to prepare themselves for a combat which will destroy the existing state of things' (50). The good of myth also lies in its capacity to replenish the social world by breathing a new sense of value into it: 'heroic myths' – in a phraseology that resonates powerfully with *Ichabod*'s own idiom – return the people to 'the belief in glory'.[7]

As later commentators on *Réflexions sur la violence* have noted, it matters little that Sorel's own world-making convictions lay firmly in the revolutionary socialist camp; as Sorel's sharpening of the language of social conflict might lead one to expect, 'there is no *theoretical* reason' within his work that could explain 'why the mythical reconstitution [of political life] should not move in the direction of fascism', an equally plausible extrapolation from Sorel's argument.[8] In fact, by 1912, one of his disciples, Édouard Berth, was already inscribing the 'awakening of Force and Blood against Gold' in the struggle against plutocracy in place of the myth of the proletarian general strike; and Sorel's work also proved an inspiration to figures on the Right like Charles Maurras and T.E. Hulme.[9] Blyth's *Ichabod* could certainly be re-read in this light, sketching out an emergent political myth for the Edwardian Radical Right. Like all myths of national glory, *Ichabod*'s narrative is imbued with the spirit of sacrifice. Noel must die in the battle to save England, and it is right and proper that he does so, having 'cleared our shores of the blight, the poisoning aphids, which sucked our blood' (315). He has founded the state anew and is condemned to be its vanishing mediator: 'had he lived, he would have been too powerful for a subject' (316).

In a similar vein, one could see the invasion theme as a major strand in a futurism of the Right that was committed to a violent clarification of the struggles ahead. Thus Le Queux's spy stories were devised not merely to entertain: they were also meant as a serious wake-up call, and Le Queux's penchant for self-promotion did not prevent an enthusiastic collaboration with the former commander-in-chief Lord Roberts in a campaign to bring in peacetime conscription under the auspices of the National Service League. Arthur Balfour was probably not far off the mark in claiming that 'a Le Queux novel was worth several thousand votes for the Conservative Party'.[10] It followed that this kind of 'prophetic fiction' was strongly anti-Socialist in a tradition that can be traced back to the 1890s in books like the journalist George Griffith's *The Angel of the Revolution: A Tale of the Coming Terror* (1893), a novel which also features a Jew pulling the strings of an international conspiracy known as 'The Brotherhood'. The year before *Ichabod* appeared, Blyth's publishers John Milne had brought out an anonymous novel entitled *Red England: A Tale of Socialist Terror* (1909), which purported to look back at England's history from a vantage point in the early 1970s to reveal how the country fell into the hands of revolutionary agitators and was forced to endure bureaucratic tyranny before the colonies and the British Navy came to the rescue. The *Dundee Advertiser* thought that 'it will reach many who would not look at sober history' and so 'may achieve much for the cause of Anti-Socialism'.[11] True to form, an influential ally of the Germans and the Jews in *Ichabod* is Bert Johns, an English labour leader who had misled the Royal Commission on Alien Immigration with 'a lot of nonsense about the brotherhood of mankind' (40).

As the most successful author of scientific romances, H.G. Wells was a particular bugbear for right-wing visionaries like Blyth – and, stylistically, T.E. Hulme hated 'more than anything the vague long pretentious words of Wells'.[12] *Ichabod* is scathingly dismissive of Wells's immensely popular fantasy, *The War in the Air* (1908), largely because it seemed to imply that sea power would no longer be decisive in the future. Such a suggestion was anathema to the Radical Right which set great store by campaigning to strengthen the British Navy through pressure groups like the Navy League (on whose executive Arnold White had served) and later the Imperial Maritime League (which numbered Rudyard Kipling among its supporters). However, in his 1909 novel *Tono-Bungay*, initially subtitled 'A Romance of Commerce', Wells had produced a diagnosis of the condition of England that had much in common with the presuppositions of Blyth's *Ichabod*, echoing its mood of loss and decline. After the entrepreneur Edward Ponderevo has purchased a splendid old house and estate, commensurate with his newly achieved position in the world, he elegiacally pronounces on its former greatness in a single word: 'Ichabod' – and, turning to his wife, he presciently adds 'We shall be like that, Susan, some day.'[13] In *Tono-Bungay* – named after a patent remedy that is a cure for nothing – 'men and nations, epochs and civilizations pass' and only the implacable reality of scientific truths endure (388). Edward Ponderevo is finally a casualty of the endless churn of Edwardian capitalism, 'a country hectic with a wasting aimless fever of trade and money-making and pleasure-seeking' (381).

In his attempt to make sense of this transient world, the narrator, Ponderevo's nephew George, figures English society as a series of theoretical models. Growing up in traditional rural society and living below stairs in a great country house (Bladesover), the son of a servant, George Ponderevo moves, via an apprenticeship in his uncle's chemist shop in a small Sussex town, to London. At first he mistakes the solidity of the country house for 'a little working model' of the entire social universe, but once he has experienced 'the fermenting chaos of London', he realises that its forms and functions are merely the redundant trappings of the past (13, 181). London is a place of strangers, of forces in motion, generating 'a vast impression of space and multitude and opportunity,' where people prosper and perish or sink into the city's 'grim underside' (95, 106). As if to epitomise the way in which this 'tumorous growth-process' is radically other, estranged from itself, the connecting thread that links the hollowing out of the old country house ideal to the disorder of the metropolis is the spectre of 'the Jews': 'an immigration of elements that have never understood and never will understand the great tradition, wedges of foreign settlement embedded in the heart of this yeasty English expansion' (102–103). In the East End, these elements coalesce into 'a shabbily bright foreign quarter' where 'a concourse of bright-eyed, eagle-nosed people' speaks 'some incomprehensible gibberish between the shops and the barrows' (103). At the other end of the social scale, the West End is a congeries of alien Bladesovers, populated by moneylenders, illicit traders in diamonds, and the like.

The countryside is no better. Since George left, Bladesover House has been rented by Sir Reuben and Lady Lichtenstein, parvenus who have supplanted the British gentry without the least grasp of the culture that sustained the previous occupants. The Lichtensteins' vulgarity is manifested in their cosmopolitan taste in books, 'English new books in gaudy catchpenny "artistic" covers, French and Italian novels in yellow, German art handbooks of almost incredible ugliness', and the description of their collection of china ornaments – 'all kinds of deliberately comic, highly glazed distortion' – might equally well be applied to the Lichtensteins themselves (65). What George at one moment disdains as a very limited sort of cleverness is quickly redefined as a 'more enterprising and intensely undignified variety of stupidity' (66). As in *Ichabod*, these Jews are represented as a pathological species, inimical to true Britishness, a 'phase' that accelerates 'the broad slow decay of the great social organism of England', a parasitic infestation that thrives on decomposing matter (66). According to Susan Ponderevo, 'plutocratic ladies' of the 'Oriental type', like Sir Reuben's wife, still have 'the old pawnshop in their blood' and are to be seen 'running their hands over other women's furs, scrutinizing their lace, even demanding to handle jewellery, appraising, envying, testing' (247). And although this observation is in fact the judgement of one set of parvenus upon another, it is seamlessly incorporated into George's sociological diagram of Edwardian England. For Wells, the Jews can provide little that is socially or culturally positive and their role seems to be to hasten the entropy and waste that are increasingly characteristic of a capitalist market economy.[14]

Blyth's anti-Semitism might seem to be more extreme than that of Wells: the "elimination" of 'English folk' is met by the "elimination" of the Jews and once Pettigrew's 'great Act' has been passed 'anti-Semite' ceases to be a 'term … of opprobrium' (308). But Blyth's narrator is at pains to interrupt this logic of extermination by excepting those 'good-hearted, even loyal' English Jews who have been in England 'for a century or more' and 'who hated the aliens as much as any Englishman could do' (185). This face-saving formula does not appear in any of George Ponderevo's working models. Yet the exception that proves the rule exists only to vivify the myth by sharpening the sense of social antagonism it invokes. In *When William Came* (1913), Saki's late excursion into the invasion scare genre, Britain has already been defeated by the Germans and the traveller Murrey Yeovil, through whose eyes the scale of the catastrophe is registered, comes home to find 'the alien standard floating over Buckingham Palace'.[15] What is really at stake in the conquest is brought out in a tense conversation between Murrey and his friend Doctor Holham while Murrey is recovering from the initial shock. In attempting to summarise the major changes afflicting Britain, particularly London, Holham draws attention to the increasing numbers of Jews in England since the invasion – an invasion within an invasion. The doctor frankly, defiantly admits to his own anti-Semitism – the exact same manoeuvre that is so prominent in *Ichabod* – and, despite praising those Jews who have embraced Britishness and remained loyal to their country at this critical historical moment, he has no hesitation in declaring that 'the Jew' has become so 'ubiquitous' that he 'may almost consider himself as of the dominant race' (72). The Jewish presence has symbolically transformed London into a *Mitteleuropäische* 'cosmopolitan city', a place of 'licence and social adaptability' that has lost its political stature and become the home of – that key word again – only a 'denationalized culture' (72). In the most fundamental sense, it is because of the entry of 'the Jew' that what is quintessentially British is falling into ruin.

The numbed defeatism, edged with a growing sense of outrage, is quite unlike the vicious deadpan wit of the dandies that populate Saki's short stories. There 'the Jew' is fair game as the target of the caustic insult or a convenient stage prop, stereotypically stylised, for the discomfiture of others. In 'The Almanack,' one of the Clovis stories (also published in 1913), Saki's urbane stalking-horse engineers a hunting accident for the overly cautious but utterly inept Joceyln Vanner by representing himself as a man too dangerous to be seen in company with because he is mixed up in a revolutionary plot in Rumania. The gullible Joceyln hangs on Clovis's every word and immediately follows his urgent instruction to slip away into the undergrowth where she is inadvertently killed by the hunt. The detail that is supposed to give his tall tale the seal of credibility is that the revolution is being financed in return for mineral concessions by a Rumanian Jew, his yacht conveniently anchored off the English coast.[16] It is as though by 1913, if not before, everyone took such proposed "facts" for granted. Saki's Rumanian Jew can be read as a displaced variant of another, slightly earlier seaborne 'Romanian Jew' – 'a naturalized Englishman' who is forever 'carping at things English' – the venal captain on the ill-starred West African voyage in search of a rare mineral in *Tono-Bungay*, a version of the inherently unpatriotic Jew in Arnold White's bestiary (321).

In Saki's writing, words are weapons and his characters' apparently casual barbs can kill. The distinctive *frisson* that gives his stories their force and suspense stems from the reader's difficulty in knowing how much damage his perfectly calculated phrases will actually inflict. Until the final phrase, we can never be sure, yet there is rarely any sense of anticlimax. In 'The Unrest-cure' (1911), one of his most disturbing tales, no one dies, but the threat of a 'massacre' hangs over a quiet country village.[17] Clovis overhears a conversation on a train in which 'a solid, sedate individual' named J.P. Huddle confesses to a friend that he has become very worried by his inability to tolerate sudden and unwonted change (127). When the unidentified friend tells Huddle that what he needs is the reverse of a Rest-cure, a bout of unfamiliar activity that will jolt him out of his rigid habits of mind, Clovis pricks up his ears: he knows the very thing. Noting down the address on Huddle's suitcase, Clovis sends him a telegram announcing that the local Bishop will be coming to stay and then turns up at the house, posing as the Bishop's secretary. The Bishop's impending visit is disconcerting enough, but when Clovis tells his host "The Bishop is out for blood, not tea" and plans "to massacre every Jew in the neighbourhood", Huddle is horrified but scarcely knows where to turn. Browbeaten by Clovis, terrified by the prospect of a scandal – Clovis insists that he has already "sent some photographs of you and your sister ... to the *Matin* and *Die Woche*" (131) – Huddle shouts vainly that he will inform the police, only to be told that Clovis's co-conspirators have already surrounded the house and that there can be no escape. Clovis slips away leaving the Huddle household to spend a sleepless night fantasising that a murder is being committed every time the slightest sound is heard.

Huddle is not being melodramatic when he blurts out "This thing will be a blot on the Twentieth Century!" – a remark that reminds the reader that Saki's narrative strategies rarely take any prisoners (131). Like *Ichabod*, Saki's "Unrest-cure" brings the pogrom into the heart of the English imagination. The local Jews are being innocently assembled – Sir Leon Birberry is perhaps a reincarnation of the plutocratic Mr Meyer from Kipling's *Puck of Pook's Hill* – and, just as the young Noel Pettigrew became an anti-Semitic adventurer, the local Boy-scouts have, so Clovis says, been drafted in to help with the killing. In one deft stroke, Saki connects the premodern religious persecution of the Jews with contemporary anti-Semitism, while daring his readers to think it could be anything other than a cruel joke.[18] At the story's close, 'the Twentieth Century was still unblotted' (133), but, at best, Saki's sadistic tale provided only a temporary respite, while indulging the most dangerously hostile fantasies. The history of the 1905 Aliens Act is a reminder of how pernicious those fantasies could be in a country that prided itself on its liberal heritage.

Notes

INTRODUCTION

1 5 Edw. VII, c.15.
2 33 Geo. III, c.4.
3 On the historical and cultural variability of borders, see Étienne Balibar's 1993 essay 'What Is a Border?' reprinted in *Politics and the Other Scene*, trans. Chris Turner (London: Verso, 2002) and also *Trés loin et tous près* (Paris: Bayard, 2007).
4 5 Edw. VII, c.15, 2 (1).
5 5 Edw. VII, c.15, 3 (1), (b).
6 5 Edw. VII, c.15, 8 (1) and (2).
7 Walter Nugent, *Crossings: The Great Transatlantic Migrations, 1870–1914* (Bloomington: Indiana University Press, 1992), pp. 31–32.
8 Quoted in 'Immigration Must Cease!', *The Evening News and Post*, 21 May 1891, 1.
9 See 'The Jewish Invasion. Some of the Outs and Ins of London Pauper Immigration', *The Evening News and Post*, 20 May 1891, 1.
10 Rudolf Rocker, *The London Years*, trans. Joseph Leftwich (London: Robert Anscombe, 1956), p. 156. Rocker had learned Yiddish in order to organise Jewish workers, but was not himself Jewish.
11 The description of Huguenot immigration as a 'friendly invasion' is taken from C.B. Shaw's essay, 'The Huguenot and Flemish invasion', in Arnold White, ed., *The Destitute Alien in Great Britain: A Series of Papers Dealing with the Subject of Foreign Pauper Immigration* (London: Swan Sonnenschein, 1892), p. 38.
12 Arnold White, *The Modern Jew* (London: Heinemann, 1899), pp. xii, 180–181. Reviewing an English translation of *The Protocols of the Elders of Zion*, which appeared 'from internal evidence to have been written by Jews for Jews', *The Times* noted that 'the goal relentlessly pursued through the centuries is the destruction of the Christian national states and the substitution of international Jewish domination.' 'The Jewish Peril', *The Times*, 8 May 1920, 15.
13 A.V. Dicey (writing as 'An Observer'), 'The Aliens Act', *The Nation*, 17 August 1905, 140–141. On the character of Dicey's liberalism, see Richard A. Cosgrove, *The Rule of Law: Albert Venn Dicey, Victorian Jurist*

(London: Macmillan, 1980) and David Sugarman, 'The Legal Boundaries of Liberty: Dicey, Liberalism and Legal Science', *The Modern Law Review* 46 (1983), 102–111.

14 A.V. Dicey, *The Law and Public Opinion* (London: Macmillan & Co., 1905), pp. 294, 297–298.

15 See Stefan Collini, *Liberalism and Sociology: L.T.Hobhouse and Political Argument in England 1880–1914* (Cambridge: Cambridge University Press, 1979), chapter 1.

16 R.C.K. Ensor, *England 1870–1914* (Oxford: Clarendon Press, 1936), p. 394.

17 Paul Foot, *Immigration and Race in British Politics* (Harmondsworth: Penguin, 1965).

18 John A. Garrard, *The English and Immigration 1880–1910* (London: Oxford University Press, 1971), p. vii.

19 See Chris Waters, '"Dark Strangers" in Our Midst: Discourses of Race and Nation in Britain, 1947–1963', *Journal of British Studies* 36 (1997), 207–238.

20 See John A. Garrard, 'Parallels of Protest: English Reactions to Jewish and Commonwealth Immigration,' *Race* 9 (1967), 47–66, 49 on which much of the first chapter of his book was based. The citation is Sheila Patterson, *Dark Strangers* (London: Tavistock, 1963).

21 Garrard, *The English and Immigration*, p. 205.

22 Bernard Gainer, *The Alien Invasion: The Origins of the Aliens Act of 1905* (London: Heinemann, 1972), p. 215.

23 *Ibid.*, p. 214.

24 For an excellent example, see David Feldman, *Englishmen and Jews: Social Relations and Political Culture 1840–1914* (New Haven: Yale University Press, 1994).

25 Robert Winder, *Bloody Foreigners: The Story of Immigration to Britain* (London: Little, Brown, 2004), pp. x, 3. Further references are given after quotations in the text.

26 Aristide R. Zolberg, 'Global Movements, Global Walls: Responses to Migration, 1885–1925,' in Wang Gungwu, ed., *Global History and Migrations* (Boulder: Westview Press, 1997), pp. 279–307, 279, 303. See also Eytan Meyers, 'The Causes of Convergence in Western Immigration Control', *Review of International Studies* 28 (2002), 123–141.

27 Dallal Stevens, *UK Asylum Law and Policy: Historical and Contemporary Perspectives* (London: Sweet & Maxwell, 2004), p. 42.

28 Tony Kushner and Katharine Knox, *Refugees in an Age of Genocide* (London: Frank Cass, 1999), p. 29.

29 Jeremy Harding, *The Uninvited: Refugees at the Rich Man's Gate* (London: Profile Books, 2000), p. 47.

30 Desmond King, 'Liberal and Illiberal Immigration Policy: A Comparison of Early British (1905) and US (1924) Legislation', *Totalitarian Movements and Political Religions* 1 (2000), 78–96. For King's general thesis, see his *In the Name of Liberalism: Illiberal Social Policy in the United States and Britain* (Oxford: Oxford University Press, 1999).

31 Randall Hansen and Desmond King, 'Illiberalism and the New Politics of Asylum: Liberalism's Dark Side', *The Political Quarterly* 71 (2000), 396–403, 398.

32 Sigmund Freud, 'Some Remarks on a Case of Obsessive-compulsive Neurosis [The 'Ratman'],' in Gillian Beer, ed., Louise Adey Huish trans., *The 'Wolfman' and Other Cases* (London: Penguin, 2002), pp. 153–154.

33 *Royal Commission on Alien Immigration*, 4 vols. (1903–1904), vol. II, Minutes of Evidence (Theodor Herzl, 7 July 1902), p. 212.

34 John Buchan, *The Thirty-Nine Steps* (1915; London: Pan, 1978), p. 11.

CHAPTER I MESSIANIC NEUTRALITY: GEORGE ELIOT AND
THE POLITICS OF NATIONAL IDENTITY

1 *The Complete Diaries of Theodor Herzl*, ed. Raphael Patai, trans. Harry Zohn, 5 vols. (New York: The Herzl Press/Thomas Yoseloff, 1960): 1, p. 273. Further references to this translation will appear in the text as parenthetical citations.

2 George Eliot, *Daniel Deronda*, ed. John Rignall (1876; London: J.M. Dent, 1999), p. 698. Further references to this edition will appear in the text as parenthetical citations.

3 Michael Ragussis, *Figures of Conversion: "The Jewish Question" and English National Identity* (Durham: Duke University Press, 1995), p. 263.

4 Israel Zangwill, 'The Return to Palestine', *The New Liberal Review* 2 (1901), 615–634, 616.

5 As quoted by Terence Cave in his introduction to the 2003 Penguin edition; see George Eliot, *Daniel Deronda* (London: Penguin, 2003), p. xiv.

6 Henry James, 'Daniel Deronda: A Conversation', reprinted in David Carroll ed., *George Eliot, The Critical Heritage* (London: Routledge and Kegan Paul, 1971), pp. 417–433.

7 Book IX of *Daniel Deronda* appeared in *Punch's Pocket Book for 1877*. For details, see John M. Picker, 'George Eliot and the Sequel Question', *New Literary History* 37 (2006), 361–388.

8 The *Nation*, 19 October 1876, reprinted in Carroll, *George Eliot*, pp. 399–404.

9 The *Gentleman's Magazine* (November 1876), reprinted in Carroll, *George Eliot*, pp. 406–416.

10 Catherine Gallagher, *The Body Economic: Life, Death, and Sensation in Political Economy and the Victorian Novel* (Princeton: Princeton University Press, 2006), p. 155.

11 Laurence Lerner, '*Daniel Deronda*: George Eliot's Struggle with Realism' in Alice Shalvi, ed., *Daniel Deronda: A Centenary Symposium* (Jerusalem: Jerusalem Academic Press, 1976), pp. 108–109.

12 Joseph Jacobs, Review of *Impressions of Theophrastus Such*, *The Athenaeum*, 7 June 1879, 720.

13 See J. Hillis Miller, *The Form of Victorian Fiction* (Notre Dame: University of Notre Dame Press, 1970), ch. 1.

14 Gershom Scholem, 'Towards an Understanding of the Messianic Idea in Judaism' in *The Messianic Idea in Judaism and Other Essays on Jewish Spirituality* (London: George Allen and Unwin, 1971), p. 1.

15 Amanda Anderson, *The Powers of Distance: Cosmopolitanism and the Cultivation of Detachment* (Princeton: Princeton University Press, 2001), pp. 123–124, 135.

16 *Ibid.*, pp. 143, 145.

17 Anson Rabinbach, *In the Shadow of Catastrophe: German Intellectuals between Apocalypse and Enlightenment* (Berkeley: University of California Press, 1997), p. 33.

18 Gershom Scholem, 'The Messianic Idea in Kabbalism' in Scholem, *The Messianic Idea*, p. 37.

19 Gershom Scholem, 'Toward an Understanding of the Messianic Idea in Judaism' in Scholem, *The Messianic Idea*, pp. 7–13.

20 Theodor Herzl, *The Jewish State*, revised trans. Jacob M. Alkow (Mineola: Dover, 1988), pp. 95–96.

21 E.H. Kossmann, *The Low Countries 1780–1940* (Oxford: Clarendon Press, 1978), p. 158.

22 Lode Wils, 'The Two Belgian Revolutions' in Kas Deprez and Louis Vos, eds., *Nationalism in Belgium: Shifting Identities, 1780–1995* (Basingstoke: Macmillan, 1998), p. 39.

23 Philippe Van Parijs, 'Must Europe be Belgian? On Democratic Citizenship in Multilingual Politics' in Catriona McKinnon and Iain Hampsher-Monk, eds., *The Demands of Citizenship* (London: Continuum, 2000), p. 238.

24 Herzl, *The Jewish State*, p. 146.

25 Theodor Herzl, trans. Paula Arnold, *Altneuland* (Haifa: Haifa Publishing Co., 1960), p. 109. On the initial criticisms of this novel, see Steven Beller, *Herzl* (London: Peter Halban, 2004), ch. 6.

26 *The Jewish Chronicle*, 21 July 1876, 251.

27 'The Rev. Dr. Hermann Adler on "Daniel Deronda"', *The Jewish Chronicle*, 15 December 1876, 586.

28 'Daniel Deronda', *The Jewish Chronicle*, 15 December 1876, 585.

29 Guedalla's Palestinian plans and his championing of Eliot's novel were received with some hostility in Eastern Europe in the 1870s. But with the rise of early Zionism and the Hebrew Renaissance in the mid-1880s, his ideas became more widely accepted. See Mikhal Dekel, '"Who Taught This Foreign Woman about the Ways and Lives of the Jews?" George Eliot and the Hebrew Renaissance', *ELH* 74 (2007), 783–798. Dekel argues that this new Zionist readership was largely male.

30 I am grateful to Eitan Bar-Yosef for providing this information.

31 Quoted in Shmuel Werses' seminal essay, 'The Jewish Reception of *Daniel Deronda*' in Shalvi ed., *Daniel Deronda: A Centenary Symposium*, p. 36, to whose work my account is much indebted.

32 Geoffrey Alderman, *Modern British Jewry* (Oxford: Clarendon Press, 1992), p. 231.

33 Aamir R. Mufti, *Enlightenment in the Colony: The Jewish Question and the Crisis of Postcolonial Culture* (Princeton: Princeton University Press, 2007), p. 109.

34 On Pinsker, see Shlomo Avineri, *The Making of Modern Zionism: The Intellectual Origins of the Jewish State* (London: Weidenfeld and Nicolson, 1981), ch. 7.

35 Leslie Stephen, *George Eliot* (London: Macmillan, 1902), p. 191; Dicey's 1876 review is reprinted in Carroll, *George Eliot*, p. 403.

36 Peter Brooks, *Realist Vision* (New Haven: Yale University Press, 2005), p. 111.

37 William Blackstone, *Commentaries on the Laws of England. A Facsimile of the First Edition of 1765–1769*, 4 vols. (Chicago: University of Chicago Press, 1979), I, pp. 354–361.

38 Frank Caestecker, *Alien Policy in Belgium, 1840–1940: The Creation of Guest Workers, Refugees and Illegal Aliens* (Oxford: Berghahn, 2000), p. 31.

39 See R.F. Foster, *Modern Ireland 1600–1972* (London: Penguin, 1989), pp. 366–367, 390–399.

40 *Ibid.*, pp. 345; see also pp. 348–362.

41 See the *Report of the Royal Commissioners for Inquiring into the Laws of Naturalization and Allegiance* (1869), Appendix 1, pp. 90–91. For a report of the Warren trial, see *The Times*, 4 November 1867, 10. Warren was one of the leaders of an armed group of men who sailed from Massachusetts to Sligo without papers or colours. Warren claimed alien status and unsuccessfully sought a jury half-composed of American citizens.

42 Michel Foucault, *Naissance de la biopolitique: Cours au Collège de France 1978–1979* (Paris: Seuil/Gallimard, 2004), p. 65, my translation.

43 Paul Hirst, *War and Power in the 21st Century* (Cambridge: Polity, 2001), pp. 63–64.

44 See Barry Hindess, 'Liberalism – What's in a Name?' in W. Larner and W. Walters, eds., *Global Governmentality: Governing Global International Spaces* (London: Routledge, 2004), pp. 23–39.

45 33 Vict. c. 14. The Naturalization Act, 1870. Section 3. Not all the Act's provisions were in the direction of greater liberality. Prior to 1870, British women who married foreign nationals remained British subjects; the new Naturalization Act removed this right. Had Daniel's mother married her Russian nobleman *after* 1870, she would no longer have been able to claim that she was 'English.'

46 *Ibid.*, Section 6.

47 Josephine McDonagh, *George Eliot* (Plymouth: Northcote House, 1997), p. 75.

48 *Ibid.*, p. 72. For a counterargument suggesting that in *Daniel Deronda* Eliot created a new mode of realism, one that approximates to the technology of Francis Galton's composite racial photography, see Daniel Novack, 'A Model Jew: "Literary Photographs" and the Jewish Body in *Daniel Deronda*', *Representations* 85 (2004), 58–97.

49 For useful case studies, see Andreas Fahrmeir, *Citizens and Aliens: Foreigners and the Law in Britain and the German States 1789–1870* (Oxford: Berghahn Books, 2000), chs. 2 and 3.

50 Aristide R. Zolberg, 'The Great Wall Against China: Responses to the First Immigration Crisis, 1885–1925' in Jan Lucassen and Leo Lucassen, eds., *Migration, Migration History, History: Old Paradigms and New Perspectives* (Bern: Peter Lang, 1997), p. 293.

51 *Ibid.*, p. 298; Adam McKeown, 'Global Migration, 1846–1940', *Journal of World History* 15 (2004), 156–160.

52 See Edward W. Said, 'Zionism from the Standpoint of Its Victims', *Social Text* 1 (1979), 18–19.

53 Hermann Adler, 'Can Jews Be Patriots?' *The Nineteenth Century* 7 (April 1878), 637–646, 646.

54 George Eliot, *Impressions of Theophrastus Such*, ed. Nancy Henry (1879; Iowa City: University of Iowa Press, 1994), p. 154. The title refers to the persecutors' cries in a run of anti-Jewish riots in Germany in 1819, though it may date back as far as the Crusades. Further references to this edition will appear in the text as parenthetical citations.

55 The calculations by Joseph Jacobs date from 1883 and are still generally accepted. See Alderman, *Modern British Jewry*, pp. 102–112.

56 *The Times*, 12 March 1877, 4.

57 'Daniel Deronda (Second and Concluding Article)', *Jewish Chronicle*, 22 December 1876, 601–602.

58 'Notes of the Week', *Jewish Chronicle*, 26 January 1877, 4. See also 'The Jews in Roumania', *The Times*, 27 January 1877, 6.

CHAPTER 2 PALACES AND SWEATSHOPS: EAST END
FICTIONS AND EAST END POLITICS

1 *Royal Commission on Alien Immigration* (1903–4), vol. II, Minutes of Evidence, p. 125.

2 Walter Besant, *All Sorts and Conditions of Men* (1882; Oxford University Press, 1997), pp. 84–5.

3 Margaret Harkness ("John Law"), *Captain Lobe: A Story of the Salvation Army* (1889; republished as *In Darkest London* in 1891; Cambridge: Black Apollo Press, 2003), p. 13. Further references to this edition will appear in the text as parenthetical citations. Harkness's ironic pseudonym "John Law" was a reference to an eighteenth-century Scottish political economist.

4 Arnold White ed., *The Destitute Alien in Great Britain: A Series of Papers Dealing with the Subject of Foreign Pauper Immigration* (London: Swan Sonnenschein, 1892), p. 3.

5 Rev. G.S. Reaney, 'The Moral Aspect,' in White, *The Destitute Alien*, pp. 82–84.

6 Simon Eliot, 'Sir Walter Besant,' *Oxford Dictionary of National Biography*, 61 vols. (2004), vol. 5 (Oxford: Oxford University Press, 2004), pp. 507–509.

7 J.W. von Archenholz cited in Roy Porter, *London: A Social History* (London: Penguin, 1996), pp. 141–142.

8 Besant, *All Sorts and Conditions of Men*, p. 28. Further references to this edition will appear in the text as parenthetical citations.

9 Walter Besant, *East London* (London: Chatto and Windus, 1901), chapter 1, 'What East London Is'.

10 Walter Besant, *Autobiography of Sir Walter Besant* (London: Hutchinson & Co., 1902), p. 244. The same phrase appears in *East London* where it is said that 'one cannot repeat it too often' (p. 115).

11 *Handbook and Guide to the People's Palace, Being an Account of Its Origin and Recreative Work* (1911), p. 34.

12 See *The Palace Journal*, vol. 7 (January 2–June 26), 1891.

13 *Ibid.*, pp. 13–14.

14 *Autobiography*, p. 246.

15 Besant, *East London*, p. 315.

16 *Autobiography*, p. 247.

17 *East London*, pp. 313–315.

18 'Sunday Opening of the People's Palace,' *Echo* 24 October 1887, *Cuttings: The People's Palace, Box C*, Tower Hamlets Local History Library and Archives.

19 M.S.R. James, 'The People's Palace and Its Library,' *The Library Journal*, October 1893, pp. 427–430.

20 Something very like the list of authors placed in the second tier in 1887 was later being read by the more literate workers in Edwardian Salford, for example. See Robert Roberts, *The Classic Slum* (Harmondsworth: Penguin, 1973), pp. 177–179.

21 Handbill, 11 May 1903. Benefit Concert for W.H. Wheeler. *Cuttings: The People's Palace, Box C*, Tower Hamlets Local History Library. On the hegemony implicit in middle-class patronage of the Palace, see William J. Fishman, *East End 1888: A year in a London borough among the labouring poor* (1988; London: Hanbury, 2001), pp. 314–316.

22 *East London*, p. 315.

23 *The Saturday Review*, 27 November 1886, *Cuttings: The People's Palace, Box C*, Tower Hamlets Local History Library.

24 'Alien Demonstration', *East London Observer*, 14 November 1903, 7

25 Helen Small, 'Introduction', *All Sorts and Conditions of Men*, p. x. See also Wim Neetens, 'Problems of a "Democratic Text": Walter Besant's Impossible Story', *Novel*, 23 (1990), 247–264.

26 See Rudyard Kipling, *Many Inventions* (1893; London: Macmillan, 1964), p. 231; and Somerset Maugham, *Liza of Lambeth* (1897; London: Pan Books, 1978), p. 99.

27 My thanks to Marcia Pointon and Jan Marsh for help in pinning down and confirming this source.

28 *Exodus* I: 13–14. In *All Sorts and Conditions of Man*'s own 'Israel in Egypt' scene, 'forced labour' is characterised as being 'told to make bricks without straw' (84).

29 *Art Journal*, May 1867, quoted by Patrick Conner, 'Wedding Archaeology to Art': Poynter's *Israel in Egypt*,' in Sarah Macready and F.H. Thompson, eds., *Influences in Victorian Art and Architecture* (London: The Society of Antiquaries, 1985), p. 112.

30 *Punch*, 15 June 1867, 246–247. For a recent account of Disraeli's role in the 1867 Reform Bill, see Paul Smith, *Disraeli: A Brief Life* (Cambridge: Cambridge University Press, 1996), pp. 140–147.

31 See E.T. Raymond, *Disraeli: the Alien Patriot* (London: Hodder and Stoughton, 1925). On the significance of the spelling 'D'Israeli', see Anthony S. Wohl, '"Dizzi-Ben-Dizzi": Disraeli as Alien,' *Journal of British Studies* 34 (July 1995), 381.

32 Israel Zangwill, *Dreamers of the Ghetto* (London: Heinemann, 1898).

33 Todd M. Endelman, *The Jews of Britain 1656–2000* (Berkeley: University of California Press, 2002), p. 81.

34 See David Feldman, *Englishmen and Jews: Social Relations and Political Culture 1840–1914* (New Haven: Yale University Press, 1994), pp. 167–168.

35 *East London*, p. 202.

36 Anon., Review of Sir Walter Besant, *East London*, 'Literature' (Supplement), *Illustrated London News*, 6 April 1901, iv.

37 L.F. Austin, 'Our Note Book,' *Illustrated London News*, 16 March 1901, 370.

38 Anon., Review of Arnold White, *Efficiency and Empire*, 'Literature' (Supplement), *Illustrated London News*, 25 May 1901, 756.

39 *East London*, p. 195.

40 *Cf.* also *In Darkest London*, p. 74.

41 Yvonne Kapp, *Eleanor Marx vol.2: The Crowded Years 1884–1898* (1976; London: Virago, 1979), pp. 220–221.

42 Extracts of reviews of Harkness's earlier novels opposite the title page of *In Darkest London. A New and Popular Edition of Captain Lobe: A Story of the Salvation Army*, with an Introduction by General Booth (London: William Reeves, 1891). For a pertinent reading of William Powell Frith's paintings, see Mary Cowling, *The Artist as Anthropologist: The Representation of Type and Character in Victorian Art* (Cambridge: Cambridge University Press, 1989).

43 Sally Ledger, *The New Woman: Fiction and feminism at the* fin de siècle (Manchester: Manchester University Press, 1997), p. 49.

44 Friedrich Engels, 'Letter to Margaret Harkness' (April 1888), reprinted in *Marxists on Literature: An Anthology*, ed. David Craig (Harmondsworth: Penguin, 1975), pp. 269–271.

45 Friedrich Engels, 'Letter to Edward Bernstein' (22 August 1889), quoted in Gareth Stedman Jones, *Outcast London: A Study in the Relationship between Classes in Victorian Society* (Oxford: Clarendon Press, 1971), p. 347.

46 Margaret Harkness, *Out of Work* (1888; London: Merlin, 1990), p. 2.

47 *Ibid.*, p. 200.

48 General Booth, *In Darkest England and the Way Out* (London: International Headquarters of the Salvation Army, 1890), pp. 11–12.

49 John Marriott, *The Other Empire: Metropolis, India and Progress in the Colonial Imagination* (Manchester: Manchester University Press, 2003), p. 172.

50 The *OED* dates the word 'slummer', meaning an inhabitant of the slums, from the late 1880s.

51 *Out of Work*, pp. 63–64, 165, 246.

52 *Ibid.*, pp. 232, 77.

53 Hannah Arendt, *The Origins of Totalitarianism* (New York, San Diego: Harcourt, Brace and Co., 1979), pp. 42–50.

54 Margaret Harkness, *A Manchester Shirtmaker: A Realistic Story of To-day* (London: Authors' Co-operative Publishing Co., 1890), p. 6. Further references to this edition will appear in the text as parenthetical citations.

55 N.N. Feltes, 'Misery or the production of misery: defining sweated labour in 1890,' *Social History*, 17 (1992), 441–452.

56 Beatrice Webb, *My Apprenticeship* (1926; Harmondsworth: Penguin, 1971), p. 339.

57 *Ibid.*, pp. 334–336.

58 Diary entry, 13 November 1889, quoted in John Goode, 'Margaret Harkness and the socialist novel,' in *The Socialist Novel in Britain: Towards the Recovery of a Tradition*, ed. H. Gustav Klaus (New York, St. Martin's Press, 1982), p. 52.

59 W.H. Wilkins, *The Alien Invasion* (London: Methuen, 1892), p. 69.

60 *Royal Commission on Alien Immigration*, vol. II, Minutes of Evidence, p. 126. As "Mr B" went on to explain, the Boot and Shoe Operatives Union's victory was short-lived; two years later, the employers brought in new machinery and began de-skilling and reducing wages throughout the trade.

61 For a detailed critique of this exceptionally tenacious assumption, see Marc Brodie, *The Politics of the Poor: The East End of London 1885–1914* (Oxford: Clarendon Press, 2004).

62 *Ibid.*, p. 198.

63 Israel Zangwill, *Children of the Ghetto: A Study of a Peculiar People*, ed. Meri-Jane Rochelson (1882; Detroit: Wayne State University Press, 1998), pp. 261, 265.

64 James Buzard, *Disorienting Fiction: The Autoethnographic Work of Nineteenth-Century British Novels* (Princeton: Princeton University Press, 2005), p.12.

65 Zangwill, *Dreamers of the Ghetto*, p. vii.

66 Roy Porter, *London: A Social History*, p. 268; William J. Fishman, *The Streets of East London* (London: Duckworth, 1979), p. 8.

67 See the *Jewish Chronicle* 25 May 1894, 7; 20 November 1896, 9; and 27 November 1896, 15–16.

CHAPTER 3 COUNTERPUBLICS OF ANTI-SEMITISM

1 Theodor Adorno, *Minima Moralia: Reflections from Damaged Life*, trans. E.F.N. Jephcott (London: Verso, 1974), p. 110.

2 Moshe Zimmermann, *Wilhelm Marr: The Patriarch of Anti-Semitism* (Oxford: Oxford University Press, 1986).

3 Peter Pulzer, *The Rise of Political Anti-Semitism in Germany and Austria* rev. ed. (London: Peter Halban, 1988), pp. 85, 90, 328.

4 'Jews' Free School', *The Times*, 29 June 1885, 11.

5 The phrase 'a Hebrew policy' comes from Edward A. Freeman's 1877 book, *The Ottoman Power in Europe; its Growth and Decline*, while Gladstone's 1976 letter appeared in a number of newspapers. See David Feldman, *Englishmen and Jews*, pp. 100–103.

6 See C.C. Aronsfeld, 'A German Antisemite in England: Adolf Stöcker's London Visit in 1883', *Jewish Social Studies*, XLIX (1987), 43–52 to which this paragraph is indebted. The newspaper quotations appear on pp. 47 and 48.

7 See Hermann Adler, 'Recent Phases of Judaeophobia', *The Nineteenth Century* 10 (December 1881), 813–829, 814; cf. Goldwin Smith, 'The Jewish Question', *The Nineteenth Century* 10 (October 1881), 494–515.

8 See 'The Deterioration of the Jewess', *Jewish World*, 22 February 1889, 5.

9 Both titles were written by Louis Martin. See Jean Guiffan, *Histoire de l'anglophobie en France: de Jeanne d'Arc à la vache folle* (Rennes: Terre de Brume Éditions, 2004), pp. 132–133. See also Robert Tombs, '"Lesser Breeds Without the Law": The British Establishment and the Dreyfus Affair, 1894–1899', *Historical Journal* 41 (1998), 495–510.

10 Arnold White, Letter to the Editor, *The Times*, 10 July 1894, 12.

11 Arnold White, *English Democracy; Its Promises and Perils* (London: Swan Sonnenschein, 1894), p. 151. All subsequent references will be noted in the text.

12 Geoff Eley, *Reshaping the German Right: Radical Nationalism and Political Change after Bismarck* (New Haven: Yale University Press, 1980), p. 358.

13 Michael Warner, *Publics and Counterpublics* (New York: Zone Books, 2002), pp. 56–57.

14 Peter Brooks, *The Melodramatic Imagination: Henry James, Melodrama, and the Mode of Excess* (1976; New York: Columbia University Press, 1984), p. 17.

15 Elaine Hadley, *Melodramatic Tactics: Theatricalized Dissent in the English Marketplace, 1800–1885* (Stanford: Stanford University Press, 1995).

16 Boucicault's play was an 'authorised adaptation' of Eugène Grange and Adolphe d'Ennery's dramatic hit *Les Bohémiens de Paris* from 1843. See Dion Boucicault, *After Dark: A Drama of London Life in 1868* (New York: Samuel French's Standard Drama No. 360, 1871). All subsequent references will be noted in the text as parenthetical citations.

17 See the poster for the performance at the Imperial Theatre, Bordesley, Birmingham on 6 August 1900, Birmingham Central Library, Local Studies and History Section.

18 In the penultimate scene, Tom is given a chance to redeem himself by saving Captain Chumley's life for a second time, when he pulls the unconscious Chumley away from the path of an oncoming train.

19 Slightly less elaborately, Gordon Chumley has moved between Australia, the Crimea, and London.

20 The material discussed later in the chapter is taken from the collection of posters, programmes, and other papers held by the Local Studies and History section of Birmingham Central Library.

21 See Nicholas Daly, *Literature, Technology, and Modernity, 1860–2000* (Cambridge: Cambridge University Press, 2004), p. 27.

22 See Nadia Valman, *The Jewess in Nineteenth-Century British Literary Culture* (Cambridge: Cambridge University Press, 2007).

23 'Princess's Theatre,' *The Times*, 27 November 1899, 10.

24 'The Election', *East London Advertiser*, 6 October 1900, 8.

25 'Princess's Theatre,' *The Times*, 27 November 1899, 10.

26 What Peter Bailey has styled 'the exultant cum skeptical double register of music hall patriotism'. See his 'Kipling's Bully Pulpit: Patriotism, Performance and Publicity in the Victorian Music Hall', *Kipling Journal* 85 (2011), 28–41.

27 *Trilby* was originally serialised in *Harper's New Monthly Magazine* between 1893 and 1894. The play had been performed outside London, as far afield as Glasgow, in September.

28 See Clement Scott's column, 'The Playhouses', *Illustrated London News*, 9 November 1895, 573.

29 George Taylor, 'Svengali: mesmerist and aesthete', in *British Theatre in the 1890s: Essays on Drama and the Stage*, ed. Richard Foulkes (Cambridge: Cambridge University Press, 1992), pp. 108–109.

30 George Du Maurier, *Trilby*, ed. Daniel Pick (1894; London: Penguin, 1994), p. 227.

31 See George Taylor's notes to Potter's adaptation in *Trilby and Other Plays*, ed. George Taylor (Oxford: Oxford University Press, 1996), p. 296.

32 Taylor, 'Svengali: mesmerist and aesthete', pp. 108–109.

33 *Trilby and Other Plays*, p. 266.

34 *Trilby*, p. 259. All subsequent references will be noted in the text.

35 Oscar Wilde, *The Picture of Dorian Gray*, ed. Robert Mighall (1891; London: Penguin, 2000), p. 49.

36 *Trilby and Other Plays*, p. 228. Cf. p. 222.

37 *Ibid.*, pp. 212–213.

38 Israel Zangwill to Edward Dicey, 25 May 1904, Central Zionist Archive, Jerusalem, Zangwill Papers, A120/617.

39 *Times Literary Supplement*, 19 June 1903, 193.

40 John A. Steuart, *The Hebrew: A Story of the Time* (London: Hodder and Stoughton, 1903), p. 476. All subsequent references will be noted in the text.

41 Jonathan Freedman, *The Temple of Culture: Assimilation and Anti-Semitism in Literary Anglo-America* (Oxford: Oxford University Press, 2000), chapter 2.

42 *Trilby and Other Plays*, p. 204.

43 *Ibid.*, p. 212.

44 Goldwin Smith, 'The Jewish Question', *The Nineteenth Century* 10 (October 1881), 494–515.

45 The attack on "Ikey Mo" is from a speech in June 1900, cited in Jonathan Schneer, *London 1900: The Imperial Metropolis* (New Haven: Yale University Press, 1999), p. 258.

46 G.F.B., "A Short History of the War", *The Speaker*, 8 February 1902, 529. These are the second and fourth stanzas from a total of four. The poem was also reprinted in local Liberal Association publications.

47 Compare 'Mr. T.R. Dewar at Wapping' (p. 2) with 'Mr. T.R. Dewar and the Jews' (p. 3) in the *Eastern Post and City Chronicle*, 3 October 1900. Thanks to an astute and well-respected Jewish president of the local Conservative Association, Dewar managed to secure a large Jewish vote (against a Jewish Liberal candidate), despite losing Lord Rothschild's earlier endorsement. See Niall Ferguson, *The World's Banker: The History of the House of Rothschild* (London: Weidenfeld and Nicolson, 1998), p. 799, and Marc Brodie, *The Politics of the Poor*, pp. 186–187.

48 Most importantly by G.R. Searle. See, for example, his essay 'The "Revolt from the Right" in Edwardian Britain', in *Nationalist and Racialist Movements in Britain and Germany Before 1914*, eds. Paul Kennedy and Anthony Nicholls (Basingstoke: Macmillan, 1981), pp. 21–39.

49 G.R. Searle, 'Critics of Edwardian Society: the Case of the Radical Right', in *The Edwardian Age: Conflict and Stability 1900–1914*, ed. Alan O'Day (London: Macmillan, 1979), p. 85. On Willoughby de Broke, see Gregory D. Phillips, 'Lord Willoughby de Broke and the Politics of Radical Toryism, 1909–1914', *Journal of British Studies* 20 (1980), 215: 'Most people want a new Party. They simply won't work for Balfour or Lansdowne again. I won't.'

50 G.R. Searle, *A New England? Peace and War 1886–1918* (Oxford: Clarendon Press, 2004), p. 512.

51 Andrew S. Thompson, 'Tariff Reform: An Imperial Strategy, 1903–1913', *Historical Journal*, 40 (1997), 1033–1054, 1057.

52 *The Leo Amery Diaries. Volume 1: 1896–1929*, eds. John Barnes and David Nicholson (London: Hutchinson, 1980), p. 48.

53 Alan Sykes, 'The Radical Right and the Crisis of Conservatism before the First World War', *Historical Journal*, 26 (1983), 670–676.

54 Leo Maxse, *National Review* 35, April 1900, 201–202.

55 Leo Maxse, *National Review* 45, April 1905, 214–215.

56 Speech to the Birmingham Liberal Unionist Association, 16 May 1902, quoted in L.S. Amery, *My Political Life. Vol. 1 England Before the Storm 1896–1914* (London: Hutchinson, 1953), pp. 231–232. See also Dilwyn Porter, 'Joseph Chamberlain and the Origins of the Tariff Reform Movement', *Moirae* III (1978), 1.

57 'Episodes of the Month: "Squalid Bonds"', *National Review* 41, August 1903, 894–895.

58 Amery, *My Political Life. Vol. 1*, p. 238.

59 Quoted in Michael Bentley, *Politics without Democracy 1815–1914: Perception and Preoccupation in British Government* (London: Fontana, 1984), p. 308.

60 Andrew S. Thompson, 'Tariff Reform', 1037.

61 Joseph Chamberlain, 'How the Policy Affects Working Men', in *Imperial Union and Tariff Reform: Speeches Delivered from May 15 to November 4, 1903* (London: The De La More Press, 2nd ed., 1910), p. 100.

62 Chamberlain, 'A Demand for Inquiry' (15 May 1903), in *Imperial Union and Tariff Reform*, p. 3.

63 'Trade Unions and Tariff Reform' (London, 17 May 1905), in *Mr. Chamberlain's Speeches Vol. II*, ed. Charles W. Boyd (London: Constable, 1914), p. 320.

64 See 'Tariff Reform, Trade Unionism, and Shipping' (Liverpool, 27 October 1903), in *Mr. Chamberlain's Speeches Vol. II*, p. 204. Chamberlain liked to mischievously quote the socialist Keir Hardie in support of these arguments.

65 *Alien Immigration*, Tariff Reform League Pamphlet No. 65, c. 1905.

66 David Faber, *Speaking for England: Leo, Julian and John Amery – The Tragedy of a Political Family* (London: The Free Press, 2005), p. 12.

67 *National Review* 38, January 1902, 691.

68 *National Review* (December 1897), quoted in John A. Hutcheson, Jr., *Leopold Maxse and the National Review, 1893–1914: Right-Wing Politics and Journalism in the Edwardian Era* (New York: Garland, 1989), p. 88.

69 Letter to Sir Edward Carson (4 September 1917), quoted in *The Leo Amery Diaries Vol. 1*, p. 170.

70 Amery, *My Political Life. Vol. I*, p. 388.

71 George Wyndham, *The Development of the State* (London: Constable, 1904), pp. 14, 32–33, 46. All subsequent references will be noted in the text.

72 The last two quoted phrases are taken from a letter to the Lord Bishop of Ossary (28 November 1904) in which Wyndham seeks to clarify this part of his Address. See *Letters of George Wyndham 1877–1913 Vol. II*, compiled by Guy Wyndham (Edinburgh, Privately Printed: T. and A. Constable, 1915), p. 110.

73 Letter to his Mother (25 January 1910) in *Letters of George Wyndham Vol. II*, p. 381.

74 Letter to Hilaire Belloc (29 January 1913) in *Letters*, pp. 520–522. There are seven verses in all.

75 Kipling quoted by Wyndham in a letter to Mrs. Mary Drew (October 1906), *Letters of George Wyndham Vol. II*, p. 203.

76 Kipling to James M. Conland (2 December 1900) in *The Letters of Rudyard Kipling Vol. III 1900–1910*, ed. Thomas Pinney (London: Macmillan, 1996), pp. 37–40.

77 Letter to Sir Charles P. Crewe (19 July 1907), *Letters Vol. III*, p. 254.

78 Letter to H.A. Gwynne (15 November 1907), *Letters Vol. III*, p. 279.

79 Amery, *My Political Life. Vol. I*, p. 135.

80 Rudyard Kipling, *Puck of Pook's Hill*, ed. Sarah Wintle (1906; London: Penguin, 1987), pp. 56–57. All subsequent references will be noted in the text as parenthetical citations.

81 Matthew Arnold, *Culture and Anarchy*, ed. Samuel Lipman (1869; New Haven: Yale University Press, 1994), p. 88.

82 Karl Marx, 'On the Jewish Question' (1843), in *Writings of the Young Marx on Philosophy and Society*, ed. and trans. Loyd D. Easton and Kurt H. Guddat (New York: Anchor Books, 1967), p. 243.

83 Arnold White, *The Modern Jew* (London: Heinemann, 1899), pp. ix, xii, 167. All subsequent references will appear in the text.

84 See Arnold White, 'The Unemployed', *Fortnightly Review* 54 New Series (October 1893), 454–463. The same point is made in *The Modern Jew*, pp. 190–191.

85 Edouard Drumont, 'The Jewish Question in France,' *National Review* 38, January 1902, 698. All subsequent references will be noted in the text.

86 'Aloofness' is White's chosen term. An entire chapter of *The Modern Jew* is devoted to it.

87 Arnold White, 'A Typical Alien Immigrant', *Contemporary Review* LXXIII (February 1898), 242. Cf. the almost identical formulation in *The Modern Jew*, p. 90.

88 *The Modern Jew*, p. 218.

89 *Ibid.*, p. 199.

90 *Ibid.*, p. 279.

91 In his evidence to the Royal Commission James W. Johnson, the new Chairman of the BBL, claimed to have over 45,000 signatories to the League's Manifesto. See *RCAI, Vol. II: Minutes of Evidence* (24 July 1902), p. 289.

92 Colin Holmes, *Anti-Semitism in British Society* (London: Edward Arnold, 1979), pp. 89–97.

93 'The Anti-Alien Crusade', *East London Observer*, 18 January 1902, 2.

94 *Ibid.*

95 'England for the English', *East London Advertiser*, 18 January 1902, 8.

96 'The Anti-Alien Crusade', 2.

97 *Ibid.*

98 A.T. Williams, *RCAI, Vol. II: Minutes of Evidence* (15 May 1902), pp. 102–3.

99 In a speech to the Jewish Whitechapel Costers Union, quoted in John A. Garrard, *The English and Immigration: A Comparative Study of the Jewish Influx 1880–1910* (London: Oxford University Press, 1971), p. 81.

100 See Garrard, *The English and Immigration*, p. 78.

101 Quoted in Daniel Keogh and Andrew McCarthy eds., *Limerick Boycott 1904: Anti-Semitism in Ireland* (Cork: Mercier Press, 2005), p. 65. Father John Creagh was a locally born priest whose inflammatory sermons attacked the Jews as the enemy of all Christians and also condemned their practice of usury.

102 William Stanley Shaw, *Alien Immigration. The Jews at Limerick*. Handbill (London, April 1904).

103 'Editorial', *Daily Express*, 1 April 1904, reprinted in Keogh and McCarthy, *Limerick Boycott 1904: Anti-Semitism in Ireland*, p. 92.

104 William Evans-Gordon, 'The Aliens Bill', *The Times*, 25 April 1904, 7.

105 'Mr. Balfour and the Aliens Bill', *The Times*, 11 May 1904, 7.

106 Israel Zangwill, 'Mr. Balfour on Anti-Semitism', *The Times*, 13 May 1904, 15.

107 Israel Zangwill to Prof. A.V. Dicey, 17 May 1904, Central Zionist Archive, A120/617.

108 Israel Zangwill to Mr. Goldstein, 25 April 1907, Central Zionist Archive, A120/369.

CHAPTER 4 WRITING THE 1905 ALIENS ACT

1 *The Evening News and Post*, 1 June 1891, 1, including the subheading "SEND THEM BACK!" The figure referred to was an estimate of 'the large number of the poorest class of Jewish emigrants' that would be carried on four steamships in the summer and autumn of that year before the Baltic shipping route closed for the winter.

2 Robert Louis Stevenson, *The Amateur Emigrant* (London: The Hogarth Press, 1984), p. 17.

3 *Royal Commission on Alien Immigration* (1903–1904), vol. II, Minutes of Evidence (Dr. Herbert Williams, 19 June 1902), p. 208. There were 272 horses, compared to 133 Russian adults and children.

4 *Royal Commission*, vol. II (W. L. Calkin, 21 May 1903), p. 855. Calkin did, however, insist that the company abided by the health regulations in force in the Port of London and had even dismissed captains who had not followed them; see para. 23359.

5 Major W. Evans-Gordon, *The Alien Immigrant* (London: Heinemann, 1903), p. 103.

6 *Royal Commission*, Vol. II, p. 451.

7 Evans-Gordon, *The Alien Immigrant*, p. 46.

8 *East London Observer*, 28 August 1886. See also *The Times*, 24 August 1886 and the *Jewish World*, 27 August 1886, Samuel Montagu's Cuttings books, AJ/1, Parkes Collection, University of Southampton.

9 *Royal Commission*, vol. II, (28 April 1902), p. 15.

10 See Felicity O'Mahony, 'Michael Davitt's Travels Abroad, 1884–1905' in *Treasures of the Library, Trinity College Dublin*, ed. Peter Fox (Dublin: Royal Irish Academy, 1986), pp. 205–214. Cf. Evans-Gordon, *The Alien Immigrant*, p. 52.

11 Trinity College Library, Dublin, MSS 9651/1, pp. 44–45 (Undated 48pp. typescript).

12 'England for Outcasts', *The Evening News and Post*, 15 June 1891, 1. Further instalments of these reports appeared on 17, 22, and 24 June 1891, each prominently displayed on the paper's front page.

13 Judith Walkowitz, 'The Indian Woman, the Flower Girl, and the Jew: Photojournalism in Edwardian London', *Victorian Studies* 42 (1998/1999), 3–46.

14 *Royal Commission*, vol. I, The Report, pp. 40, 42.

15 *Royal Commission*, vol. II, Minutes of Evidence (J. Axelrad, 24 July 1902), p. 293.

16 See Vital, *Zionism: The Formative Years* (Oxford: Clarendon Press, 1982), pp. 138–139.

17 'At the Zionist Congress To-day', *Westminster Gazette*, 13 August 1900, 6.

18 *Ibid.*

19 'The Home of the Alien. VIII', The *Standard*, 12 January 1905, 3.

20 See 'The Home of the Alien. V; VII; VIII; XII', The *Standard*, 10, 12, 13, 18 January 1905, 2, 3.

21 'The Home of the Alien. V', The *Standard*, 10 January 1905, 2.

22 'The "Standard" and the Aliens', *Jewish Chronicle*, 17 February 1905, 10.

23 'The Home of the Alien. X', The *Standard*, 16 January 1905, 2.

24 For a partial transcript of Chamberlain's speech, see 'Political Leaders on Alien Immigration', *Jewish Chronicle*, 23 December 1904, 13.

25 'The Home of the Alien. V', The *Standard*, 10 January 1905, 2.

26 Letter to J.B. Pinker (16 June 1901) in *The Collected Letters of Joseph Conrad, vol. 2 1898–1902*, eds. Frederick R. Karl and Laurence Davies (Cambridge: Cambridge University Press, 1986), p. 333.

27 Edward Said, *Reflections on Exile and Other Literary and Cultural Essays* (London: Granta, 2001), p. 555; Frederick R. Karl, *Joseph Conrad: The Three Lives* (New York: Farrar, Straus & Giroux, 1979), p. 734.

28 The *Times Literary Supplement*, 20 September 1907, 285. Conrad had become a naturalized British subject in August 1886.

29 This point forms the conclusion of Ranajit Guha, 'The Turn', *Critical Inquiry* 31 (2005), 425–430, a sensitive account of the shifts in Said's readings of 'Amy Foster' over a period of fourteen years.

30 For details of the changes made by Conrad both before and after initial publication, see Gail Fraser, 'Conrad's Revisions to "Amy Foster" ', *Conradiana* 20 (1988), 181–193.

31 See Colin Holmes, *Anti-Semitism in British Society 1876–1939* (London: Edward Arnold, 1979), pp. 89–90; Bernard Gainer, *The Alien Invasion: The Origins of the Aliens Act of 1905* (London: Heinemann, 1972), p. 182.

32 Joseph Conrad, 'Amy Foster' in *Typhoon and Other Tales*, ed. Cedric Watts (Oxford: Oxford University Press, 2002), p. 154. Subsequent references will appear in the text.

33 Letter to H.D. Davray (2 April 1902) in *Collected Letters, vol. 2*, pp. 398–399.

34 Fraser, 'Conrad's Revisions', 187.

35 See Evans-Gordon, *The Alien Immigrant*, p. 65.

36 Unsigned (Charles J.C.W. Hyne), 'Mr. Conrad's Way', *Academy* (19 May 1903), 463–464, reprinted in *Joseph Conrad. The Critical Heritage*, ed. Norman Sherry (London: Routledge, 1973), p. 154.

37 Giorgio Agamben, *Homo Sacer: Sovereign Power and Bare Life*, trans. Daniel Heller-Roazen (Stanford, CA: Stanford University Press, 1998), p. 4, my emphasis. 'Bare life' is Heller-Roazen's translation of the Italian 'la nuda vita', elsewhere rendered as 'naked life'.

38 Agamben, *Homo Sacer*, pp. 169–171.

39 Giorgio Agamben, *State of Exception*, trans. Kevin Attell (Chicago: University of Chicago Press, 2005), p. 1. For a pointed critique of Agamben's episodic history, see Peter Fitzpatrick, 'Bare Sovereignty: *Homo Sacer* and the Insistence of Law' in *Politics, Metaphysics, and Death: Essays on Giorgio Agamben's* Homo

Sacer ed. Andrew Norris (Durham NC: Duke University Press, 2005), pp. 49–73.

40 *Report of the Inter-Departmental Committee to Consider the Doubts and Difficulties which have arisen in connection with the Interpretation and Administration of the Acts relating to Naturalization* (London: HMSO, 1901), p. 15.

41 Letter to H.-D. Davray (2 April 1902), *Collected Letters, vol. 2*, pp. 398–399.

42 Sigmund Freud, *Civilization and Its Discontents*, trans. David McLintock (1930; London: Penguin, 2002), pp. 50–51. McLintock departs from the *Standard Edition* in rendering this phrase as 'the narcissism of small differences'. Freud adds that such 'hostility to outsiders' is 'a way of satisfying the tendency to aggression and facilitating solidarity within the community'.

43 See Walter H. Long, 'Alien Immigration', National Archives, Kew, CAB 37/67/79.

44 Gerald Balfour, 'Alien Immigration', National Archives, Kew, CAB 37/59/146, pp. 6–9.

45 See John Burns, *Parliamentary Debates*, 4th Series, 25 April 1904, vol. 133, cols. 1149–59; H. Lawson, *Parl. Deb.*, 4th Series, 2 May 1905, vol. 145, col. 735. Lawson's father, the proprietor of the *Daily Telegraph*, was Jewish and the full family name was Levy-Lawson. Lawson took over the *Telegraph* in 1903 and also served as Mayor of Stepney from 1907 to 1909 after losing his Mile End seat in the 1906 Liberal landslide.

46 Sir Charles Dilke, *Parl. Deb.*, 4th Series, 29 March 1904, vol. 132, col. 994; 25 April 1904, vol. 133, cols. 1074–1075.

47 Sir Henry Campbell-Bannerman, *Parl. Deb.*, 8 June 1904, vol. 135, col. 1092.

48 Herbert Samuel to Beatrice Samuel (22 February 1904), A/157/171–208. Herbert Samuel, *Diary*, 9 March 1904, A/22, Viscount Samuel Papers, House of Lords Record Office, London. The Labour Importation Ordinance had been approved by the Colonial Secretary Alfred Lyttelton on 10 February.

49 See The *Manchester Guardian*, 28 March 1904, 5; *The Times*, 28 March 1904, 7.

50 On the significance of this phase of Liberal populism, see Jon Lawrence, *Speaking for the People: Party, Language and Popular Politics in England, 1867–1914* (Cambridge: Cambridge University Press, 1998), chapter 8. Among the examples of Liberal propaganda Lawrence cites is a 1904 party leaflet which asked its readers: 'will you allow these Chinese to come as slaves and take the bread out of the mouth of the British workman?'

51 Dilke, *Parl. Deb.*, 29 March 1904, vol. 132, cols. 991–992.

52 Herbert Samuel, 'The Chinese Labour Question', The *Contemporary Review* LXXXV (1904), 458. Samuel argues that, although Chinese immigration may bring in 'Englishmen by hundreds' to perform skilled tasks in South Africa, it 'will exclude them by thousands' (464).

53 Dilke, *Parl. Deb.*, 29 March 1904, vol. 132, col. 995.

54 A.J. Balfour, *Parl. Deb.*, 2 May 1905, vol. 145, col. 796.

55 Evans-Gordon, *Parl. Deb.*, 2 May 1905, vol. 145, col. 721.

56 S. Forde Ridley, *Parl. Deb.*, 25 April 1904, vol. 133, cols. 1121–1122.

57 Saki (H.H. Munro), 'Reginald at the Theatre,' *Westminster Gazette*, 17 July 1902. Reprinted in Saki, *Reginald* (London: Methuen, 1904), p. 29.

58 See 'The Anti-Alien Crusade,' *East London Observer* (18 January 1902), 2.

59 Evans-Gordon, *Parl. Deb.*, 2 May 1905, vol. 145, col. 724.

60 Herbert Samuel, *Parl. Deb.*, 2 May 1905, vol. 145, col. 725.

61 *Ibid.*, col. 731.

62 A.J. Balfour, *Parl. Deb.*, 2 May 1905, vol. 145, cols. 795–796.

63 Balfour, *Parl. Deb.*, 20 July 1905, vol.149, cols. 1281–1283. Stuart Samuel was Herbert Samuel's older brother and Liberal MP for Whitechapel.

64 The poster is reproduced in *The Edwardian Era*, eds. Jane Beckett and Deborah Cherry (London: Phaidon Press and Barbican Art Gallery, 1987), p. 19. Herbert Samuel's friend Graham Wallas used the Chinese Labour campaign as key example of the manipulation of 'subconscious non-rational inference' in politics. See his *Human Nature in Politics* (London: Archibald Constable, 1908), pp. 107–108.

65 Violet Guttenberg, *A Modern Exodus* (London: Greening & Co., 1904), p. 17. All subsequent references will appear in the text.

66 This point is made by Eitan Bar-Yosef in *The Holy Land in English Culture 1799–1917* (Oxford: Clarendon Press, 2005), pp. 239–240, who also includes M.P. Shiel's *The Lord of the Sea* (1901) among the roster of 'novels written in Deronda's shadow'.

67 The grounds for this conviction are worth recording. Moore now thinks anti-Semitism is 'a savage and retrograde movement, incompatible both with our Christianity and our advanced state of civilisation.' Guttenberg, *A Modern Exodus*, p. 328.

68 See Gainer, *The Alien Invasion*, p. 196.

69 Edgar Wallace, *The Four Just Men* (New York: Dover Publications, 1984), pp. 57, 100. This edition reprints the text of the Tallis Press 1905 original together with an additional chapter explaining how the Foreign Secretary was murdered, which was added when the novel was republished in 1911. All further references will appear in the text as parenthetical citations.

CHAPTER 5 RESTRICTION AND ITS DISCONTENTS

1 Martin Pugh, *The Making of Modern British Politics 1867–1939* (Oxford: Blackwell, 1993), p. 139. These figures ignore twenty-nine seats won by Labour and eighty-three by the Irish Nationalists.

2 See A.K. Russell, *Liberal Landslide: The General Election of 1906* (Newton Abbot: David and Charles, 1973), pp. 65, 83.

3 John A. Garrard, *The English and Immigration: A Comparative Study of the Jewish Influx 1880–1910* (London: Oxford University Press, 1971), p. 138.

4 'Aliens and the East End', *Daily Mail*, 1 Jan. 1906; 'Whitechapel', *Daily Mail*, 16 January 1906. Clippings, David Hope Kyd Collection, British Library of Political and Economic Science.

5 Leaflets and handbills, Hope Kyd Collection, January 1906.

6 See Sir William Evans-Gordon, 'The Stranger Within Our Gates', *Nineteenth Century and After* LXIX (1911), 210–216.

7 Sir William Evans-Gordon, 'The Attack on the Aliens Act', *National Review* 48 (November 1906), 460. All subsequent references to this source appear as parenthetical citations.

8 On the definition of an 'immigrant ship' in the law that was signed on 11 August 1905, see 5 Edw. 7. c. 13 (Aliens Act, 1905), Section 8 (2), p. 27.

9 *Parliamentary Debates*, 4th Series, 12 March 1906, vol. 153, cols. 916–917.

10 *East London Advertiser*, 13 January 1906. Clipping, David Hope Kyd Collection.

11 As a number of commentators have noted, the association of the offer with Uganda is geographically misleading. However, the name did stick and will be used here.

12 *Royal Commission on Alien Immigration*, vol. II, Minutes of Evidence (Herzl, 7 July 1902), p. 217.

13 See 'The Future of the Jews – Mexico as a Land of Promise', *Daily Graphic*, 23 January 1909, 11.

14 The Basle Programme, as set out in David Vital, *Zionism: the Formative Years* (Oxford: Clarendon Press, 1982), p. 4, fn. 2.

15 Theodor Herzl, *The Jewish State*, trans. Jacob M. Alkow (Mineola: Dover, 1988), pp. 95–96.

16 *The Complete Diaries of Theodor Herzl* vol. III, ed. Raphael Patai, trans. Harry Zohn (New York: The Herzl Press/Thomas Yoseloff, 1960), p. 1023.

17 *Complete Diaries of Theodor Herzl* vol. IV (23 October 1902), p. 1364. In English in the original.

18 Joseph Chamberlain, 'Notes on Mombassa and East Africa Protectorate', quoted in Vital, *Zionism: The Formative Years*, p. 158.

19 *Complete Diaries of Theodor Herzl* vol. IV (24 April 1903), p. 1473.

20 *Ibid.*, p. 1475.

21 *Ibid.* See also Herzl's evidence before the *Royal Commission on Alien Immigration*, vol. II (7 July 1902), p. 220.

22 'The Jewish Question', *The Times*, 17 August 1903, 10.

23 Steven Beller, *Herzl* (1991; London: Peter Halban, 2004), p. 117.

24 Arnold White, 'Is It to Be Jewganda? Dark Outlook for Zionist Colonies in Eastern Africa', *Daily Express*, 4 September 1903, 4.

25 As he had told the Sixth Zionist Congress; see 'Sixth Zionist Congress. East Africa and Palestine', *Jewish World*, 11 September 1903, 485. For a fuller reading of this episode, see my essay, 'Imperial Zion: Israel Zangwill and the English Origins of Territorialism', in *Between the East End and East Africa: "The Jew" in Late Victorian and Edwardian Culture*, eds. Eitan Bar-Yosef and Nadia Valman (London: Palgrave Macmillan, 2008), pp. 131–143.

26 Israel Zangwill, *Ghetto Comedies* (London: William Heinemann, 1907). All subsequent references will appear in the text as parenthetical citations. According to a letter to David Eder (to whom the collection was

finally dedicated), Zangwill was writing this 'very topical' short story in early February 1901; see David Eder, *Memoirs of a Modern Pioneer*, ed. J.B.Hobman (London: Victor Gollancz, 1945), p. 52. The story first appeared in the American magazine *Cosmopolitan* vol. 32 (February 1902) under the title "S. Cohn & Son" and also in *Pall Mall Magazine* 26 (1902) as "S. Cohn & Son, or Anglicization". My thanks to Meri-Jane Rochelson for supplying these details of first publication.

27 Herbert Samuel, *Parliamentary Debates*, 4th Series, 2 May 1905, vol. 145, col. 731.

28 Letter to Menahem Ussishkin, and Others (Geneva, 20 October 1903) in *The Letters and Papers of Chaim Weizmann*, 23 vols. (1968–80), vol. III Series A. Letters, ed. Meyer W. Weisgal (London: Oxford University Press, 1972), p. 63.

29 On Weizmann's critique of Herzl in this period, see Gedalia Yogev's Introduction to *Letters and Papers of Chaim Weizmann*, vol. III, p. xxvi.

30 Letter to Martin Buber (London, 13 October 1903), *Letters and Papers of Chaim Weizmann*, vol. III, p. 50.

31 Letter to Judah Leon Magnes (Manchester, 10 September 1905) in *Letters and Papers of Chaim Weizmann*, vol. IV, eds. Camillo Dresner and Barnet Litvinoff (London: Oxford University Press, 1973), p. 148.

32 Letter to Ussishkin (London, 14 July 1904) in *Letters and Papers of Chaim Weizmann* vol. III, p. 285.

33 On Evans-Gordon, whom Weizmann had met in Russia in 1902 when he was investigating immigration while sitting on the Royal Commission, see Weizmann's letter to Vera Khatzman (London, 8 October 1903), in *Letters and Papers*, vol. III, p. 44.

34 On A.J. Balfour, see the letter to Vera Khatzman (9 January 1906) in *Letters and Papers*, vol. IV, p. 219. However, on 21 February, Balfour wrote to Zangwill indicating support for following up the territorialist programme, while at the same time noting its unacceptability to 'several leading members of the Jewish community, English and foreign'. Quoted in Michael J. Cohen, *Churchill and the Jews* (London: Frank Cass, Second, revised edn., 2003), pp. 27–28.

35 Letter to Vera Khatzman (Manchester, 26 February 1906) in *Letters and Papers*, vol. IV, pp. 250–251.

36 See Paul Addison, *Churchill on the Home Front 1900–1955* (London: Pimlico, 1993), p. 64.

37 Derby Hall, Manchester, 14 April 1908; quoted in Cohen, *Churchill and the Jews*, p. 36.

38 These figures are taken from Jill Pellew's table consolidating data from the Annual Reports between 1906–1913; see Jill Pellew, 'The Home Office and the Aliens Act, 1905', *Historical Journal*, 32 (1989), 383.

39 M.J. Landa, *The Alien Problem and Its Remedy* (London: P.S. King, 1911), p. 224.

40 As reproduced in David Feldman, *Englishmen and Jews: Social Relations and Political Culture 1840–1914* (New Haven: Yale University Press, 1994), p. 355.

41 Winston Churchill, *Parliamentary Debates*, 5th Series, 9 February 1911, vol. 21, col. 442.

42 Minutes of the Alien Immigration Committee, 25 February 1906, London Metropolitan Archives, Jewish Board of Deputies Papers (JBD), ACC 3121 C13/1/5.

43 See the Minutes of the joint meeting between the Alien Immigration Committee and the JBD's Law and Parliamentary Committee on 25 February 1906. JBD, ACC 3121 C13/1/5.

44 Christopher Vincenzi, 'The Aliens Act 1905', *New Community*, 12 (1985), 282.

45 'The Aliens Act and Its Administration', *Jewish Chronicle*, 11 October 1907, 14–15.

46 See 5 Edw. 7. c. 13 (Aliens Act, 1905) Section 3 (a), p.22. For an account of the vicissitudes of the five-pound test of entry including stories of five pounds sterling being passed from hand to hand, with interest charged on the loan, see Pellew, 'The Home Office and the Aliens Act, 1905', 376–377.

47 See JBD, ACC 3121/B/02/001/014 which contains a transcript of the article in the *Grimsby News*, 3 March 1908.

48 *Parliamentary Debates*, 4th Series, 17 March 1908, vol. 186, cols. 413–414.

49 Herbert Gladstone, *Parliamentary Debates*, 4th Series, 5 March 1906, vol. 153, col. 158.

50 Herbert Gladstone, *Parliamentary Debates*, 4th Series, 20 December 1906, vol. 167, cols. 1677–1678.

51 See, for example, the Minutes of the meetings on 20 January 1907, 10 March 1907, and 3 October 1907 and also those of the Special Vigilance Committee on 18 March 1907. JBD ACC 3121 C13/1/5.

52 Feldman, *Englishmen and Jews*, p. 358.

53 Colin Holmes, *Anti-Semitism in British Society* (London: Edward Arnold, 1979), p. 93.

54 See the 'Episodes of the Month' column in the *National Review* 43 (May 1904), 370; 45 (June 1905), 591.

55 'Episodes of the Month', *National Review* 46 (September 1905), 23; 48 (November 1906), 372.

56 'Episodes of the Month', *National Review* 43 (May 1904), 371–372.

57 See Haia Shpayer-Makov, 'Anarchism in British Public Opinion 1880–1914', *Victorian Studies* 31 (1988), 496.

58 On patterns of Victorian and Edwardian crime, see Jose Harris, *Private Lives, Public Spirit: Britain 1870–1914* (London: Penguin, 1994), pp. 208–215.

59 Margaret Lane, *Edgar Wallace: the Biography of a Phenomenon* (New York: Doubleday, Doran & Co., 1939), pp. 197–201. *The Council of Justice* features an attempted royal assassination in the Calle Mayor.

60 'Musings without Method,' *Blackwood's Magazine* CLXXX (July 1906), 128–131.

61 Joseph Conrad, *The Secret Agent* ed. John Lyon (1907; Oxford University Press, 2004), p. 52. All subsequent references will appear in the text as parenthetical citations.

62 See *The Collected Letters of Joseph Conrad* vol. 3, 1903–1907, ed. Frederick R. Karl and Laurence Davies (Cambridge: Cambridge University Press, 1988), pp. 316, 370–371.

63 See Richard Bach Jensen, 'The International Anti-Anarchist Conference of 1898 and the Origins of Interpol', *Journal of Contemporary History* 16 (1981), 323–347. The countries were Germany, Austria-Hungary, Denmark, Sweden, Norway, Russia, Rumania, Serbia, Bulgaria, and Turkey.

64 The Marquess of Lansdowne to Sir F. Lascelles and Sir C. Scott, 27 January 1902, circulated as a confidential Cabinet Paper, National Archives, Kew CAB 37/60/20, p. 3. The Russian and German initiative was in part a reaction to further outrages including the assassination of U.S. President McKinley in September 1901.

65 National Archives, CAB 37/60/20, p. 2.

66 Con Coroneos, 'Conrad, Kropotkin and Anarchist Geography', *The Conradian* 18 (1994), 17–18.

67 Quoted by Elizabeth David in the introduction to the Penguin edition of *Italian Food* (Harmondsworth: Penguin, 1963), p. 19.

68 George Eliot, *Impressions of Theophrastus Such* ed. Nancy Henry (1879; Iowa City: University of Iowa Press, 1994), p. 155. In the twentieth century, the verb to 'denationalize' took on a new meaning when it came to refer to the return of a publicly owned industry to private hands. See *The Compact Edition of the OED* vols. I, p. 685 and III, p. 193 (Oxford: Clarendon Press, 1987).

69 Edgar Wallace, *The Council of Justice* (London: Ward, Lock & Co., 1908), p. 11. All subsequent references will appear in the text as parenthetical citations.

70 See *The Times*, 19 March 1907, 8; 21 March, 3 and 22 May, 5; 8 July, 5; 9 October, 7; 14 November, 6.

71 *Daily Mail*, 9 May 1907, 5

72 'Revolutionists' Duma in London. Women's Revolver Practice', *Daily Mirror*, 11 May 1907, 5.

73 'Girl Nihilists. Young Delegate's Fiery Speech at Meeting of London's Secret Duma', *Daily Mirror*, 16 May 1907, 4.

74 For more sober reports of the Fifth RSDLP Congress, see *The Times*, 18 May 1907, 7 (for references to Rosa Luxembourg); 20 May, 4; and 22 May, 5. An official Party account can be found in L. Muravyova and I. Sivolap-Kaftanova, *Lenin in London* trans. Jane Sayer (Moscow: Progress Publishers, 1983), pp. 167–169. Another influence on the depiction of 'the Woman of Gratz' may have been the Russian anarchist 'Red' Emma Goldman who had spoken at an antiwar meeting in London in 1900.

75 *The Times*, 22 May 1907, 5.

76 Sir William Evans-Gordon, 'The Stranger within Our Gates', 215.

77 The phrase 'covenant of security' is taken from the political commentator Melanie Phillips; see *Londonistan: How Britain is Creating a Terror State Within* (London: Gibson Square, 2006), p. 92. Cf. Dominique Thomas, *Le Londonistan: Le djihad au Coeur de l'Europe* (Paris: Éditions Michalon, 2005).

78 'Terrorist Murders in London', *Daily Mail*, 25 January 1909, 7.

79 'Another Incident at Tottenham', *Daily Graphic*, 27 January 1909, 7.

80 'Terrorist Murders in London', *Daily Mail*, 25 January 1909, 7.

81 'Our Alien Criminals', *Daily Mail*, 27 January 1909, 6.

82 'Criminal Aliens', *Daily Telegraph*, 11 February 1909, 14. The title of Rentoul's speech was 'The British Empire; Its Greatness, Glory, and Freedom'.

83 'Political Speeches,' *The Times*, 5 February 1909, 10.

84 See the *Daily Graphic*, 19 December 1910, 1, 3, 9.

85 *Ibid.*, 3.

86 'Creed That Is Crime', *Daily Graphic*, 5 January 1911, 9. See also Sir Robert Anderson, 'The Problem of the Criminal Alien', *Nineteenth Century and After* LXIX (February 1911), 217–219.

87 For studies of these events, see Donald Rumbelow, *The Houndsditch Murders and the Siege of Sidney Street* (London: Macmillan, 1973) and Colin Rogers, *The Battle of Stepney. The Sidney Street Siege: Its Causes and Consequences* (London: Hale, 1981). See also Colin Holmes's detailed review of Rumbelow, 'In search of Sidney Street,' *Bulletin of the Society for the Study of Labour History* 29 (1974), 70–77.

88 'Our Defenceless Police', *Daily Mail*, 19 December 1910, 7.

89 The last two verses of 'The Lessons of Houndsditch' (by Madge St. Maury), *The People*, 18 December 1910, 12.

90 'The Lessons of Houndsditch', *The People*, 1 January 1911, 12.

91 'The Dangerous Alien', *The People*, 8 January 1911, 12.

92 See Peter de Mendelssohn, *The Age of Churchill: Heritage and Adventure 1874–1911* (London: Thames & Hudson, 1961), p. 507 and Christopher Hassall, *Edward Marsh. Patron of the Arts: A Biography* (London: Longmans, Green & Co., 1959), p. 171.

93 Hassall, *Edward Marsh*, p. 171. The letter was dated 18 January 1911.

94 *Ibid.*

95 The HO Memorandum (19 January 1911) is reproduced in Randolph S. Churchill, *Winston S. Churchill*. 5 vols. (1967–1982), vol. II. Companion Part 2. 1907–1911 (London: Heinemann, 1969), pp. 1244–1245.

96 WSC to the King (Home Office, 6 January 1911), *ibid.*, pp. 1239–1240.

97 Memorandum by WSC, *ibid.*, pp. 1244–1245.

98 'Political Speeches', *The Times*, 5 February 1909, 10, my emphasis.

99 Letter to Lady Gladstone (5 January 1911) quoted in Hassall, *op.cit*, pp. 170–171.

100 Hilaire Belloc, *The Jews* (London: Constable, 1922), p. 37.

101 Rudolf Rocker, *The London Years* trans. Joseph Leftwich (1956; Nottingham: Five Leaves Press, 2005), p. 127.

102 This brief account of the ADC is indebted to David Feldman's pioneering work in *Englishmen and Jews, op.cit*, pp. 364–366. For more on Myer's career, see William J. Fishman, *East End Jewish Radicals 1875–1914* (1975; Nottingham: Five Leaves Press, 2004), pp. 261, 274 and Sharman Kadish, *Bolsheviks and British Jews: the Anglo-Jewish Community, Britain*

and the Russian Revolution (London: Frank Cass, 1992), pp. 126–127, pp. 185–196.

103 Rocker, *The London Years*, p. 132.

104 Christiane Reinecke, 'Governing Aliens in Times of Upheaval: Immigration Control and Modern State Practice in Early Twentieth-Century Britain, Compared with Prussia', *International Review of Social History* 54 (2009), 39–65.

AFTERWORD

1 For a brief sketch of James Blyth's career, see the entry in Sandra Kemp, Charlotte Mitchell, and David Trotter, *Edwardian Fiction: An Oxford Companion* (Oxford: Oxford University Press, 1997), pp. 36–37.

2 William Le Queux, *The Great War in England in 1897* (London: Tower Publishing Co. Ltd., 1894), pp. 28–30. The story was first serialised in Lord Northcliffe's popular miscellany *Answers*.

3 William Le Queux, *Spies of the Kaiser: Plotting the Downfall of England* (London: Hurst and Blackett, 1909), pp. 39, 272.

4 James Blyth, *Ichabod* (London: John Milne, 1910), pp. 205–206. Subsequent page numbers will be presented in the text as parenthetical citations.

5 See Neil Gregor, *How to Read Hitler* (London: Granta, 2005), chapter 6.

6 George Sorel, 'Letter to Daniel Halévy', in *Reflections on Violence*, trans. T.E. Hulme and J. Roth (New York: Collier Books, 1961), p. 50. Subsequent page numbers appear in the text as parenthetical citations.

7 Sorel, p. 49. Instructively, Sorel is citing Ernest Renan's *Histoire du peuple d'Israël* here.

8 Ernesto Laclau and Chantal Mouffe, *Hegemony and Socialist Strategy: Towards a Radical Democratic Politics*, trans. Winston Moore and Paul Cammack (London: Verso, 1985), p. 41.

9 Édouard Berth, quoted in Laclau and Mouffe, *ibid.*

10 David Stafford, *The Silent Game: The Real World of Imaginary Spies* (Toronto: Lester and Orpen Dennys Ltd., 1988), p. 27.

11 See 'A List of New Books, Autumn 1909' p. 8, appended by the publishers to the text of *Ichabod*.

12 T.E. Hulme, 'Cinders' (1906–1907) in *Selected Writings* ed. Patrick McGuiness (Manchester: Carcanet, 1998), p. 27.

13 H.G. Wells, *Tono-Bungay* ed. Patrick Parrinder and Edward Mendelson (London: Penguin Classics, 2005), p. 250. Subsequent page numbers are shown in the text as parenthetical citations.

14 For an astute reading of *Tono-Bungay* as a 'parable' of capitalist entropy, see 'Archive and Entropy' in Thomas Richards, *The Imperial Archive: Knowledge and the Fantasy of Empire* (London: Verso, 1993), chapter 3. *Tono-Bungay* can also usefully be read as a riposte to the more temperate account of the 'condition of England' in Ford Madox Ford's *England and the English* trilogy (1905–1907); see Andrzej Gasiorek, 'Ford Among the Aliens' in Dennis Brown and

Jenny Plastow eds., *Ford Madox Ford and Englishness* (Amsterdam: Rodopi, 2006), pp. 63–82.

15 Saki, *When William Came*, intro. I.F. Clarke (with George Chesney's *The Battle of Dorking*, Oxford: Oxford University Press, 1997), p. 169. Subsequent page numbers appear in the text as parenthetical citations.

16 'The Almanack', *Morning Post*, 17 June 1913, reprinted in A.J. Langguth, *Saki: A Life of Hector Hugh Munro* (Oxford: Oxford University Press, 1982), pp. 293–298.

17 Saki (H.H. Munro), *The Complete Short Stories* (London: Penguin Classics, 2000), pp. 127–133. Subsequent page numbers are shown in the text as parenthetical citations.

18 For an excellent account of the interpretative dilemmas in reading Saki's story, see Christopher Lane, 'The Unrest Cure According to Lawrence, Saki, and Lewis,' *Modernism/modernity* 11 (2004), 769–796.

Index

Lightning Source UK Ltd.
Milton Keynes UK
UKOW04n1814090815

256644UK00001B/10/P